CELTICS LEGENDS

CELTICS LEGENDS

Pivotal Moments, Players & Personalities

Lew Freedman

INDIANAPOLIS, INDIANA

Published by Blue River Press
Indianapolis, Indiana
www.brpressbooks.com

Distributed by Cardinal Publishers Group
A Tom Doherty Company, Inc.
www.cardinalpub.com

ISBN: 978-1-68157-178-2

LCCN: 2022940697

Cover Illustration: Keith Lowe
Book Design: Rick Korab, Korab Company Design
Editor: Dani McCormick, Tessa Schmitt

Printed in the United States of America

10 9 8 7 6 5 4 3 2 1   23 24 25 26 27 28 29 30

TABLE OF CONTENTS

ABOUT THE AUTHOR

Lew Freedman is an award-winning journalist who has worked for the Philadelphia Inquirer, Chicago Tribune, Anchorage Daily News, and currently writes for the Seymour Tribune in Indiana. The winner of more than 300 awards and the author of more than 100 books, Freedman is a member of the U.S. Basketball Writers Hall of Fame.

A native of Boston, Massachusetts, Freedman has followed the Boston Celtics his whole life and has written stories about the team for various publications. He, his wife Debra, and dog Boston, live in Indiana.

INTRODUCTION

The Boston Celtics are the gold standard of professional basketball. Other teams periodically catch up and surpass the Celtics in given National Basketball Association seasons, but gazing through binoculars at the lens of history, the Celtics, more so than any team in the sport and equally as much as the finest teams in any American professional sport, represent a special higher level of excellence.

Present at the conception of the league, the Celtics have won seventeen world championships, the equal most of any team. They drafted the first African-American player and helped break the league's color line in 1950. The team anointed the first African-American coach in pro basketball history and one of the first in American sports history.

Bob Cousy is credited with inventing the modern point-guard role, Bill Russell is credited with virtually inventing defense, and coach Red Auerbach, the first recognized "genius" to run a pro basketball franchise, showed the world what could be accomplished by relying on the fast break. Boston pioneered the sixth-man role – currently celebrated with an official NBA award recognizing the key contributions of the best player off the bench.

Between 1957 and 1969, the Celtics put together a championship run, the likes of which may not be seen again in any professional sport, winning eleven titles in thirteen years.

Many of the greatest players who ever lived wore Celtics green on the court, sometimes for entire careers, sometimes as late-in-career acquisitions. The Celtics, through Auerbach's eye for talent, were able to fill in roster holes with players who had been All-Stars elsewhere and keep their championship train chugging along despite always having the last pick in the college draft.

During one stretch, the Celtics were so good, and had such depth, that their second-string backcourt was elected to the Hall of Fame some years after the first-string Hall-of-Famers retired.

For decades, the Celtics played in the picturesque, yet often denigrated Boston Garden. Opponents despised the "Gahden," but if you played for the home team, it was like having an extra friend on your side.

There was a time when seats near the rooftop in a building with a capacity of 13,909 sold for just two dollars. The cigarette smoke rose to the sky, too, sometimes obscuring views. Anyone who sat in the cheap seats could identify with legendary broadcaster Johnny Most, whose nightly game introduction included the phrase, "High above courtside at the Boston Garden." The smoke did not get in Johnny's eyes, but opponents say he was blinded nonetheless by the disease of homer-ism.

I grew up at a fortunate time in Boston and was an eye-witness of many of the Celtics teams' greatest achievements when they were winning all of those titles in a row (eight at one point). The men who did so played like gods of the game, but were not so far removed from their fans.

Over time – as a young teen attending public appearances obtaining autographs, as an attendee of "Jungle Jim" Loscutoff's basketball camps, and finally, as a sportswriter – I got to meet and talk with many of the Celtic players who made that 1950s–1960s championship era so great. Later I was able to meet and interview other Celtics of future eras.

My favorite personal Celtics story goes like this: When I was about twelve years old, I wrote to Bob Cousy – care of the Celtics' offices – requesting an autographed picture. I received one and still have it, although the signature is fading. About 10 years ago, after I wrote a book about the Celtics of that early dynasty, I got a thank-you letter of praise from Cousy.

That seemed to be a full-circle moment in my life.

During the course of researching this book, I came across the occasional anecdote I had never heard, which made me laugh. Of course, center Bill Russell was the linchpin of the Celtics Dynasty era from 1957 to 1969, literally the man in the middle of a team that almost miraculously brought those eleven world titles home to Boston in thirteen years.

Many years ago in the mid-1970s, after Russell and a much lesser-known Celtics teammate named Ron Watts made television commercials about staying in touch via long distance, the comparatively unknown Watts became a phenomenon with a much higher profile than he had as a two-year bench-warmer in the NBA.

Referring to the last three years of Russell's career when he was player-coach of the Celtics and the club won its last two championships of that era, Watts says, "It can now be revealed. I was the real coach of the Celtics. Bill Russell only masqueraded as coach."

Everyone watching recognized Russell, but no one recognized Watts. Thousands of people reached out to Bell Telephone company and the Celtics offices seeking the answer to "Who's he?" One reporter quoted Celtics public relations man Howie McHugh, who fielded the inquiries, as saying, "I got letters from as far away as Norman, Oklahoma." (As if that was the equivalent of Thailand.) "I didn't even know those people knew what a basketball looked like."

The commercial was intended to be light-hearted, and presumably, most viewers got the joke. K.C. Jones, another Celtics great, said everywhere he went, people were asking him who that guy was on TV with Russell.

Watts, who appeared in just twenty-eight regular-season games total during his NBA career, with a 1.4 points per game scoring average, maintained his sense of humor. When he heard of Jones's comment, Watts said, "That's strange, because all of my friends stop me on the street and say, 'Ron, who's that tall, black fellow I see you talking with on TV? He looks vaguely familiar.'"

Watts was a six-foot-six All-American at Wake Forest and the Celtics made him a No. 2 draft pick in 1965. The only problems were knee injuries that prevented him from developing in the pros. Watts even had a sense of humor about that situation, if only later. "Injuries cut short what promised to be a bleak career," Watts told a Philadelphia sportswriter.

America can be a strange place. A man who played professional basketball became better-known across the country for appearing anonymously in a television commercial. Watts did enjoy his supernova attention, another brief spurt of name recognition. "All this fanfare," he said. "It's like I stepped through the looking glass into Wonderland."

Think of basketball fans who did not come of age until the 1970s growing up watching the NBA and learning that one team, the Boston Celtics, so dominated the sport for so long they won eleven championships in thirteen years. That realization was so unlikely it must have seemed like Wonderland.

—Lew Freedman
August, 2022

Celtic Mystique

he phrase does not explain a tangible idea. Celtic Mystique represents the aura of the Boston Celtics, the feeling surrounding the team and the organization stemming from the days of the Dynasty, between 1957 and 1969, when the franchise experienced continual wins.

As good as the Celtics were at the time, this mood or atmosphere insinuated its way into their accomplishments as well. It did not necessarily create fear in opponents, but background dread that if something unusual needed to occur for the Celtics to prevail, it would. Call it luck, timing, or an odd way of tipping the balance, but something almost ethereal was in the air supporting the Celtics in the clutch. At least subconsciously and frustratingly to other NBA players, the Celtics became viewed as invincible.

Certainly, the team was blessed with the type of players who could make special moments happen on the floor to turn a game, but there was something else, something vaguer, that seemed to be instilled in a player once he pulled on the green and white uniform.

Bob Cousy, the Celtics' first superstar, collaborated on a book with long-time newspaperman Bob Ryan once which attempted to define Celtic Mystique. The title is Cousy on The Celtic Mystique.

One thing noted in this volume was tradition. Tradition is built over time. The contention was made (and this was in 1988) that the Celtics may not have been world champions at the exact moment, but they were America's Team, sometimes for good or bad. "No basketball team in the world stirs up passions the way the Boston Celtics do," Cousy said.

That may not be true currently, but anyone with a sense of basketball history, or who looks back and reads the empirical record, cannot help but be astonished by what the Celtics achieved when they won so many championships in such a condensed time. Ryan and Cousy made the case that there were two things ingrained in any visual sighting from a game played in Boston. First, if a TV viewer is just flipping channels and his eyes alight on the parquet floor, he knows instantly this basketball game is being played in Boston. There is no other court like it. Second, look up. The championship banners hang from the rafters as an acknowledgment and a record of the past. Now every professional team, and many college teams, display banners of any championship earned. But the Celtics were the first to do so. A third thing, in tribute to the past, commingled with the championship banners, are the same type of banners honoring retired numbers. The Celtics have a passel of retired numbers.

The Celtics under Red Auerbach stressed defense more than offense, did not care what individual scored the most points on the team, introduced the concept of a sixth-man to stir things up, and never talked about player stats, only wins and losses. They played without jealousies and it helped that Auerbach did not make decisions based on race, but rather on skill. In the midst of the Civil Rights struggle, the Celtics were exemplars, playing whites and blacks together in the starting lineup all the time. Forward Paul Silas was a veteran when he came to Boston for the 1972–73 season. He had heard the phrase "Celtic Mystique," but said he was a skeptic. After the

Celtics won a championship, he said, "Now I know what Celtic Mystique is." The ingredients added up to a recipe that led to a title.

Even thirty-plus years ago, Cousy predicted that the Celtics would be the last true dynasty in the NBA. Now there are more cities, more players, more equalizing factors.

"No team will dominate the NBA for long periods again," Cousy said. "The true impact of the Celtic Mystique is that people are attempting to imitate, or perhaps even improve on, the things Red Auerbach was preaching from the day I met him thirty-eight years ago."

Walter Brown

He was the man who made it all happen. When things were at low ebb, when things got tough, owner Walter A. Brown sacrificed. He put up rather than shut down. And he lived long enough, (although not truly long enough) to see his Boston Celtics become the best basketball team in the world.

Brown was the founder and owner of the Celtics when the National Basketball Association got going. He also owned the Boston Bruins hockey team; the Boston Garden, where both professional franchises played their home games; and the Ice Capades, the winter ice skating show that was more popular than both teams for many years.

Being the owner of a National Hockey League team and an NBA team might be a license to print money nowadays in the hands of a savvy boss, but Brown went through the growing-pains era. There was a time in the 1950s when financial stress led him to mortgage his home rather than sell off the Celtics. He kept his support strong. He was a man with commitment and style and one of those people for whom a handshake was a gentleman's agreement.

"Walter Brown was a gentleman in the old-fashioned sense of the word," Red Auerbach said of Brown. "He always tipped his hat to ladies [and] held the door for people, whether it was the queen of England or the janitor in the building where our offices were. He was polite, never talked down to people. In fact, if he had a weakness as an owner, he was too generous."

Born in 1905 in Hopkinton, Massachusetts – where the starting line of the 26.2-mile Boston Marathon is located – Brown also served as the president of the Boston Athletic Association, the governing body of the venerable foot race. Brown was ultimately elected to the Hockey Hall of Fame and the Naismith Memorial Basketball Hall of Fame for his leadership.

While the road was long (Brown lost $500,000 in his first four years running the team), Brown's faith in the Celtics – and notably in Auerbach, his long-time coach and chief personnel executive – paid off with a run of eleven championships in thirteen years, not all of which he lived to see. To reach that point, Brown verged on personal bankruptcy. At one low point, Brown even vented on-air at the sight of only a few thousand fans in the Garden, commenting to broadcaster Curt Gowdy, "I'm going to go broke."

In one of his finest moments, in 1950, Brown made forward Chuck Cooper, of Duquesne University in Pittsburgh, Boston's second-round draft pick. Cooper became the first African-American selected in the NBA draft. Other owners questioned whether Brown knew what he was doing, essentially assuming Brown did not know Cooper was a black man. Brown knew exactly what he was doing and, in a famous retort, told his fellow league bosses that he didn't care if a player was purple or his skin tone was polka dotted, if Brown thought he could play, then he could play for the Boston Celtics.

That was Brown putting his mouth – and his money – where his beliefs were. Auerbach considered Brown a mentor and friend as well as boss, saying he learned much from Brown. Auerbach said one of those things was, "'Take a man for what he is and what he does, and forget everything else you've heard about him.' Walter really believed that. He never gave a damn about a person's color, religion, nationality, or anything else. He simply cared about the man."

In 1950, the Celtics were still struggling to catch on in Boston.

Auerbach was an insider and understood the challenges. He was worried Brown might give up and fold the team. In his autobiography, Auerbach recalled the times:

> *"Everyone had tried to warn him that basketball just wouldn't catch on in Boston. It was a baseball town in the summer and a hockey town in the winter. There was so little interest in basketball that the city's high schools didn't even include the sport in their varsity programs."*

Not many people saw Walter Brown without his business suit on in public, but the unlucky ones occasionally caught him when his temper was interrupting. Although he might try to influence Auerbach's thinking in favor of a certain player – most notably Bob Cousy – when the Celtics had a chance to obtain him, Brown let Auerbach make the personnel moves that built the team into a champion. He had the power to be a meddling owner, but chose instead to support the judgment of the men he hired to do a job.

Cousy, who had made a name for himself in Boston during his days with Holy Cross College in nearby Worcester, became available to the Celtics in a dispersal draft of failed NBA teams. Brown knew Cousy would be a hit in Boston. Auerbach though, did not lust for Cousy's presence on his roster. However, the six-foot-one point guard later became the foundation of Boston success and the two became close friends.

Just as he did when talking about the team with Gowdy, Brown's tendency to lose his temper when his team lost, or could not muster enough of a run to take over first place got him into trouble sometimes. He once bad-mouthed Cousy, then apologized. "Maybe I ought to fire myself," Brown said. "I'm so eager to have a winner that I'm more of a fan than an executive. I get upset when I lose games. I'm going to keep my mouth shut."

Yet Brown often stood up for the players. He paid them

more than other teams and supported the idea of a players union when it was created in the 1950s. There was no doubt at times he was overextended. Brown's wife Marjorie once said the couple had just paid off their home when the Celtics began bleeding money and Brown took out a new mortgage. He also sold some of his stock in the Ice Capades to keep the basketball team going.

"Almost everything we owned was locked up in the Celtics," Marjorie Brown said. "All I could think of was, 'What will happen to us if it's all lost?' I was worried. But Walter loved that team." Others said Brown was simply stubborn and did not wish to admit he failed. But, she said, "The Celtics were Walter's idea from the beginning, and he just never stopped believing in them."

In 1957, the Celtics broke through and won their first NBA title. They won again in 1959, 1960, 1961, 1962, 1963, and 1964 with Brown beaming and in charge. The organization was dealt a severe blow, though, when Brown passed away from a heart attack on September 7, 1964. He was at his vacation home on Cape Cod and was just fifty-nine years old.

Opening night of the 1964–65 season was scheduled just six weeks after Brown died. That night the Celtics retired the team's No. 1 in Brown's memory. The Celtics were determined to win that season's championship to honor Brown – and they did. They also kept right on winning more titles. There is no doubt that Walter Brown would say that winning was the best way of all to preserve his memory and his contributions to the franchise.

Boston Celtics Owners

The founder of the Boston Celtics and the single most outstanding owner in team history was Walter A. Brown. Looking at the rafters at the TD Garden, fans at every game can see the No. 1 among the retired numbers.

That was not a number retired to honor any individual player who starred for the club, but for Brown, who put his money on the line to support the Celtics during their leanest years in the early days of the National Basketball Association

Brown owned the Boston Garden, the Ice Capades and the Boston Bruins hockey team, during his career in the limelight in Boston. Much earlier, he coached the United States to its first world hockey championship in 1933. From 1951 until 1964, Brown oversaw the Boston Athletic Association, which supervises the running of the Boston Marathon.

He presided over the franchise long enough to see the Celtics attain glory and kick off their run of eight straight championships. However, Brown, the only Celtics owner in the Hall of Fame, died suddenly at age fifty-nine in 1964.

A key minority owner of the Celtics alongside Brown was Lou Pieri, also a significant sports figure in New England. After Walter Brown passed away, Pieri was co-owner of the Celtics with Brown's widow Marjorie.

Over the decades the following additional groups and individuals served as owners or co-owners of the Celtics:

- Boston Basketball Partners
- Boston Garden-Arena Corporation
- John Y. Brown
- Alan Cohen
- Woody Erdman
- Don Gaston
- H. Irving Grousbeck
- Wyc Grousbeck
- Glenn Hutchins
- Marvin Kratter
- Irv Levin
- Harry Mangurian Jr.
- Stephen Pagliuca
- Robert Schmertz
- Trans-National Communications

Besides Walter Brown, who remains revered in Celtics history, few of the others are remembered as standouts by the fan base. The Grousbecks are currently in charge and are basically respected as a management team.

John Y. Brown Jr., who was no relation to the founding Brown family, is often singled out as being perhaps the worst owner in Celtics history during his tenure in the 1970s. Although Brown helped build Kentucky Fried Chicken into a monster company and served as governor of Kentucky, while operating the Celtics he nearly performed the unthinkable: driving Red Auerbach, the Celtics icon, into the hands of the hated New York Knicks.

Auerbach, team president and general manager at the time, saw Brown conduct poor trades without even consulting him. Brown eventually sold out to his partner Harry Mangurian. Auerbach stuck around.

Boston Celtics Hall-of-Famers

he Naismith Memorial Basketball Hall of Fame is located in Springfield, Massachusetts, approximately ninety miles west of Boston the home of the Celtics. It is named after James Naismith, who invented the game of basketball in 1891 at the Springfield YMCA.

Naismith, who was originally from Canada, was born in 1861 and died in 1939. He wrote the original rules of the game and created the basketball team at Kansas University, one of the most distinguished of college programs.

The Hall of Fame opened in 1959 and is now part of a sophisticated museum complex. Numerous enshrinees played or coached for the Celtics. Others were selected in the contributor category, some of them spending the entirety of their careers with the club. Still others merely passed through Boston for a season or a few years at various stages of their careers.

LIST OF HALL OF FAME ENSHRINEES IN ORDER OF INDUCTION

Ed Macauley	player	1960
Andy Phillip	player (college)	1961
John "Honey" Russell	player	1964
Walter Brown	contributor	1965
Bill Mokray	contributor	1965
Alvin "Doggie" Julian	coach	1967
Arnold "Red" Auerbach	coach	1968
Bob Cousy	player	1970
Bill Russell	player	1974
Bill Sharman	player	1975
Frank Ramsey	player	1981
John Havlicek	player	1983
Sam Jones	player	1983
Tom Heinsohn	player	1985–86
Bob Houbregs	player	1986–87
Pete Maravich	player	1986–87
Clyde Lovellette	player	1987–88
K.C. Jones	player	1988–89
Dave Bing	player	1989–90
Nate "Tiny" Archibald	player	1990–91
Dave Cowens	player	1990–91
Bill Walton	player	1992–93
Bailey Howell	player	1996–97
Larry Bird	player	1997–98
Arnie Risen	player	1997–98
Kevin McHale	player	1998–99
John Thompson	coach	1998–99
Wayne Embry	contributor	1998–99
Robert Parish	player	2002–2003
Dominique Wilkins	player	2005–2006
Dave Gavitt	contributor	2005–2006
Dennis Johnson	player	2009–2010
Tom "Satch" Sanders	contributor	2010–2011
Jo Jo White	player	2015

Top Five Players

 isting the top five players in Boston Celtics history is a gargantuan task given how many of them were chosen for inclusion in the Naismith Memorial Basketball Hall of Fame and how the franchise put together the greatest championship run in National Basketball Association history.

So many made major contributions, many all at the same time, that any ranking is sure to be controversial. This list ranks five players in order of importance, if not outright individual skills.

1. **Bill Russell**, center, 1956–1969, eleven-time world champion, twelve-time All-Star, five-time Most Valuable Player, one of the two best rebounders ever.

2. **Bob Cousy**, guard, 1950–1963, six-time world champion, thirteen-time All-Star, face of the franchise during its growing years in the 1950s, virtual inventor of the point-guard position.

3. **Larry Bird**, forward, 1979–1992, three-time world champion, twelve-time All Star, key player in the renewal of a championship club during the 1980s.

4. **John Havlicek**, guard-forward, 1962–1978, eight-time world champion, thirteen-time All-Star, the player who bridged the original Dynasty to the resurrected championship club of the 1970s and the franchise's all-time leading scorer.

5. **Sam Jones**, guard, 1957–1969, 10-time world champion, five-time All-Star.

Honorable Mentions: Tom Heinsohn, forward, 1956–1965, eight-time world champion, six-time All-Star, rookie of the year; and **Bill Sharman**, guard, 1951–1961, four-time world champion, eight-time All-Star. Forward **Paul Pierce** was a 10-time All-Star and a key figure on the 2008 championship team, who played most of his 19-year NBA career with the Celtics.

Red Auerbach

he cigar. There never has been a sports coach whose image was so entangled with an iconic item the way Red Auerbach was with his victory cigars. He only lit up in the closing minutes of a Celtics game when he was convinced the result was sealed. Opponents despised this symbol of Boston superiority, called Auerbach arrogant for flaunting the cigar in their faces, and he loved every minute of their discomfort.

Arnold "Red" Auerbach was a singular figure in National Basketball Association history. He was a builder, coach, and personnel wizard; the man was responsible for constructing and leading the Boston Celtics Dynasty. From its earliest days, Auerbach was a critical component of the franchise, and for decades thereafter.

Auerbach was born in 1917 in Brooklyn, New York; played ball in a much less sophisticated age than the modern NBA; graduated from George Washington University in 1940; and began his coaching career the next year at a high school. He coached during his US navy service, too. Once beyond high school, Auerbach's world was centered in the nation's capital. That's where his wife Dorothy and his children lived. Even during his decades affiliated with the Celtics, Auerbach kept his home in Washington, DC, living in less-permanent quarters in Boston during the season. He was known for his long-standing devotion to Chinese takeout in the hotels he stayed at.

Almost forgotten due to his legendary connection to the Celtics, Auerbach first coached in the NBA for the Washington Capitols from 1946 to 1949. Briefly, Auerbach was an assistant coach for the Duke college team, but swiftly returned to the pros for the 1949–50 season with the Tri-Cities Blackhawks. He came to Boston for the 1950–51 season. Auerbach was the right-hand man to Walter Brown – the Celtics' first owner – at a time when Brown really didn't have a left-hand man because the front office was so small and money was so tight.

In twenty NBA coaching seasons, Auerbach had just one losing mark, 28–29, with Tri-Cities. He guided the Celtics bench for sixteen years, through the 1965–66 season, winning nine world championships. His teams won 66.2 percent of their regular-season games and when he became a full-time executive, Auerbach left behind a legacy that included a then-NBA record of 938 wins.

"I took my lumps those first few years," Auerbach said. "People forget that. They think we came out of the chute winning championships and just kept on winning. I wish that were true, but it wasn't the case."

Auerbach was on the payroll even when Brown had difficulty meeting the payroll. He constructed a winning Celtics team with shrewd drafts and trades, but recognized the one missing piece between good and great was a dominating center. He finagled the moves that allowed Boston to obtain Bill Russell.

He was wise enough to step back from the bench when it became clear the workload had changed and his team needed a full-time general manager (and later president) and a full-time coach. And at a time of testy race relations across the United States, he had no worries about promoting an outspoken black man, Russell, to become the new coach.

"We're like a family," Auerbach explained when he

announced Russell's hire as his successor. "It wouldn't be easy bringing in someone from outside and making him a part of the family. Russ can do the job."

Nor was there any time when others counted how many white and black players started that Auerbach ever worried about the color of a player's skin. The Celtics under Auerbach became the first NBA team to ever start five African-Americans in a game in 1964.

"I think what he did was treat the black guys as human beings," said forward Tom Heinsohn, who was white and was president of the players union for years during this period of Celtics dominance. "And they respected that. He went to bat for them over a lot of things. A lot of other players did not treat the black players nicely."

Heinsohn, who passed away at eighty-six years old in November of 2020 spent longer with the Celtics in multiple capacities than any other individual, including Auerbach, and became the sage wise man of the organization.

Russell, the most outspoken African-American on the team by far and one of the best-known most-strongly publicly opinionated black athletes in the country, may not have wanted to practice hard, but Auerbach recognized how much he gave the team, so he only rarely upbraided him. Russell accepted Auerbach's criticisms when they came because he respected his authority, his manner, and knew the coach always had his back. Decades later, Russell, who always claimed Auerbach was the greatest pro coach ever, wrote a book about their friendship.

It is curious how Auerbach began his habit of lighting what became called by others his victory cigar. He had smoked cigars for years but never during a game. One day he began thinking how much the late-game behavior of certain coaches irritated him. Even when a game was clearly decided, it irked him to watch them yell and scream and posture, draw attention to themselves.

Auerbach said he tried to find a way to signal that he

knew a game was over and he wasn't trying to run up the score besides clearing the bench. He wanted to demonstrate he was relaxed. He had never considered smoking but noted that then-New York Knicks coach Joe Lapchick smoked on the bench.

"So I decided if we had a game comfortably in hand, I'd smoke, too," Auerbach said. "I'd light a cigar and just sit back. Then it became a big thing. I never did it on the road – never. That would have been rubbing it in."

In one of the great taunting responses of all time, management of the Cincinnati Royals gave out five thousand cigars to fans at a home game and told them to light up when the Royals beat the Celtics. When Auerbach realized this, he told his players he would kill them if they did not win that game. Then, as usual, at least most of the time, the Celtics won in the clutch.

In fact, for the most part, whether Auerbach was puffing on cigars or not, he was winning games. Under his bench guidance, the Celtics won the NBA crown in 1957, 1959, 1960, 1961, 1962, 1963, 1964, 1965, and 1966. Auerbach announced his intention of stepping down as coach prior to the 1965–66 season, saying he did so in order to give the other teams in the league one last crack at him.

Many players shared in many of the championships, but at the time of the 1961 victory, a 4–1 Finals romp over the St. Louis Hawks, Auerbach declared, "This is the greatest team ever assembled."

In 1964, the year after Bob Cousy retired, the Celtics won again anyway. Auerbach relished the contributions of sixth-man John Havlicek, basically vindicating his own strategy through his use of the player.

"Havlicek led the team in scoring, yet never started a game," Auerbach said.

Auerbach was short and balding, with great faith in his knowledge of basketball. He wrote books about the game and traveled to Europe to give coaching clinics long before the

1992 US Olympic Dream Team spread the gospel of the sport.

After he stopped coaching, Auerbach went right on building, drafting, trading, and acquiring players for future teams. He drafted people such as second-generation stars as Dave Cowens, Jo Jo White, Larry Bird, Kevin McHale, and so many more.

Auerbach was feisty. He was Depression era-raised and he learned early that those who hustle survive and thrive. He was a coach always looking for an edge. That might mean yelling at referees to influence the next call, showing indifference to critics, standing up for his guys, or playing psychological games. Visiting players always swore their locker room at the Boston Garden was always too hot on hot-weather days, too cold on cold-weather days, and the water in the showers was always chilly. All of it was Auerbach's conspiratorial doings, they claimed. Mostly, Auerbach just laughed at these accusations.

The coach urged his players to act in that manner, to seek that edge, as well. If they had to fake an injury to get the whistle blown, then so be it. Trash talk the other guys from the bench? No problem. And on the court, too, by having players remind their foes that they were in constant danger of fouling out of the game.

"What's dirty?" Auerbach said. "What's tricky? Hell, winning basketball? If it's legal, and it helps you win, you do it."

Auerbach had always been a watchdog of owner Walter Brown's money, but as time passed and pro basketball expanded and became a richer sport, Auerbach had to adapt. In one of his most clever moves, Auerbach took a risk on drafting college star Larry Bird early. Bird was eligible early because of his transfer between Indiana University and Indiana State, and everyone knew he was going to stay in school for another year. Still, the Celtics drafted Bird and had a year to sign him before the next draft. In a departure, Auerbach gave Bird a $650,000 salary as a rookie. Bird made it all worthwhile throughout the 1980s.

Between coaching and as acting as general manager – president, Auerbach was officially employed by the Celtics for twenty-nine years. In that time, the Celtics won sixteen championships. Auerbach won enough to be inducted into the Naismith Memorial Basketball Hall of Fame in 1969. The NBA's coach-of-the-year-award is called the Red Auerbach Trophy. He never wore a jersey number and owner Walter Brown was honored with No. 1 hanging in the rafters, so, to suitably honor Auerbach, the franchise symbolically retired No. 2.

Auerbach died at eighty-nine years old in 2006 from a heart attack. That was only one of many times during his career and in his retirement that many called him a basketball genius.

"He was relentless and produced the greatest basketball dynasty so far that this country has ever seen and certainly the NBA has ever seen," said Bob Cousy. Cousy was the only one outside of Auerbach's family who called him Arnold.

One way Boston basketball fans get to remember Red Auerbach whenever they attend a game at the TD Garden is to gaze down from the seats at a facsimile autograph emblazoned on the court. The imprint reads "Red Auerbach Parquet Floor," two enduring symbols of the Boston Celtics meshed together.

The History of Boston Celtics Draft Picks

All names in order of pick

1940s

[1947] Bulbs Ehlers, Purdue; Bob Alameida, California; Hank Biasatti, Long Island University; Johnny Ezersky, Rhode Island; George Felt, Northwestern; Jack Hewson, Temple; John Kelly, Notre Dame; George Petrovick, American Basketball League; Gene Stump, DePaul. **[1948]** George Hauptfuhrer, Harvard; Johnny Bach, Fordham; Norman Carey, Oregon State; Bob Curran, Holy Cross; Neil Dooley, Colgate; Jack Hauser, Denver; Marshall Hawkins, Tennessee; Tom Kelly, New York University; Murray Mitchell, Sam Houston State; Guinn Phillips, Texas Wesleyan; Ray Wehde, Iowa State. **[1949]** Tony Lavelli, Yale; George Kaftan, Holy Cross; Joe Mullaney, Holy Cross; Duane Klueh, Indiana State; Ed Little, Denver; Jim Simpson, Bates; Emerson Speicher, Bowling Green; Bill Tom, Rice; Bill Vandenburgh, Washington; Russ Washburn, Colby; Bill Weight, Brigham Young.

1950s

[1950] Chuck Share, Bowling Green; Chuck Cooper, Duquesne; Bob Donham, Ohio State; Ken Reeves, Louisville; Jack Shelton, Oklahoma State; Mo Mahoney, Brown University; Dale Barnstable, Kentucky; Frank Oftring, Holy Cross; Bob Cope, Montana; Matt Forman, Holy Cross. **[1951]** Ernie Barrett, Kansas State; Bill Garrett, Indiana; John Furlong, Pepperdine; Bob Barnett, Evansville; Rip

Gish, Western Kentucky; Jim Luisi, St. Francis; John Azary, Columbia; Hugo Kappler, North Carolina State. **[1952]** Bill Stauffer, Missouri; Jim Iverson, Kansas State; J. C.Maze, Southwest Texas State; Herm Hedderick, Canisius; Don Johnson, Oklahoma State; Jim Buchanan, Nebraska; Fred Eydt, Cornell; Gordon Mungier, Spring Hill College; Jim Dilling, Holy Cross; Gene Conley, Washington State. **[1953]** Frank Ramsey, Kentucky; Chet Noe, Oregon; Ciff Hagan, Kentucky; Earle Markey, Holy Cross; John Holup, George Washington; Vernon Stokes, St. Francis; Lou Tsiopoulos, Kentucky; Ted Lallier, Colby; Lewis Gilcrease, Southwest Texas State; Tom Lillis, St. Louis; Gil Reich, Kansas; Jim Dogerty, Whitworth. **[1954]** Togo Palazzi, Holy Cross; Morrison, Idaho; Henry Daubenschmidt, St. Francis; Ron Perry, Holy Cross; Troy Burris, West Texas A&M; Otto Krieghauser, Washington of St. Louis; Paul Estergaard, Bradley; Jim Young, Santa Clara; Tony Daukas, Boston College; Bill Johnson, Nebraska; **[1955]** Jim Loscutoff, Oregon; Dickie Hemric, Wake Forest; Buzzy Wilkinson, Virginia; Bart Leach, Pennsylvania; Bob Patterson, Tulsa; John Mahoney, William & Mary; John Moore, UCLA; Dean Parsons, Washington; Nick Romanoff, University of the Pacific; Jim Ahearn, Connecticut; Carl Hartman, Alderson Broaddus College; Mark Davis, Marietta; Henry Dooley, Wiley; Bob Scuddelari, Cooper Union. **[1956]** Tommy Heinsohn, Holy Cross; K.C., Jones, San Francisco; George Linn, Alabama; Dan Swartz, Morehead State; Bill Logan, Iowa; Don Boldebuck, Houston; O'Neal Weaver, Midwestern State; Vic Molodet, North Carolina State; Jim Houston, Brandeis; Theophileus Lloyd, Maryland. **[1957]** Sam Jones, North Carolina Central; Dick O'Neal, Texas Christian; Chuck Schramm, Western Illinois; Jim Ashmore, Mississippi State; Grady Wallace, South Carolina; Maury King, Kansas; Dick Brott, Denver; Bill Von Weyhe; Rhode Island; Joe Gibbon, Mississippi; Jack Butcher, Memphis; Dick Neal, Indiana. **[1958]** Bernie Swain, Texas Southern; Jimmy Smith, Franciscan University of Steubenville; Jim Cunningham, Fordham; Dom Flora, Washington & Lee; Gene Brown, San Francisco; Dave Keleher, Morehead State; Rudy Fenderson,

Brandeis. **[1959]** John Richter, North Carolina State; Gene Guarilia, George Washington; Ralph Crosswaite; Western Kentucky; Ed Kazakavich, Scranton; Roy Lange, William & Mary; Bob Cumings, Boston University.

1960s

[1960] Tom Sanders, New York University; Leroy Wright, University of the Pacific; Mike Graney, Notre Dame; Sid Cohen, Kentucky; Wayne Lawrence, Texas A&M; George Newman, Kentucky. **[1961]** Gary Phillips, Houston; Al Butler, Niagara; Bill Depp, Vanderbilt; Carl Cole, Eastern Kentucky; Bob DiStefano, North Carolina State; Ned Twyman, Duquesne; Mel Klein, Northern University. **[1962]** John Havlicek, Ohio State; Jack Foley, Holy Cross; Jim Hadnot, Providence; Roger Strickland, Jacksonville; Gary Daniels, The Citadel; Jim Hooley, Boston College; Clyde Arnold, Duquesne; Chuck Chevalier, Boston College; Mike Cingiser, Brown. **[1963]** Bill Green, Colorado State; Chuck Kriston, Valparaiso; Connie McGuire, Southeastern Oklahoma State; Red Stroud, Mississippi State; Vinnie Ernst, Providence; Herm Magee, Philadelphia University. **[1964]** Mel Counts, Oregon State; Ron Bonham, Cincinnati; John Thompson, Providence; Joe Strawder, Bradley; Nick Werkman, Seton Hall; Levern Tart, Bradley; Rich Falk, Northwestern; Jeff Blue, Butler; Charles Kelley, West Virginia University Institute of Technology. **[1965]** Ollie Johnson, San Francisco; Ron Watts, Wake Forest; Toby Kimball, Connecticut; Richie Tarrant, St. Michael's; Don Davidson, Davidson; Haskell Tison, Duke; George Deehan, Lenoir-Rhyne. **[1966]** Jim Barnett, Oregon; Leon Clark, Wyoming; Gary Turner, Texas Christian; John Austin, Boston College; Charlie Hunter, Oklahoma City; Jerry Ward, Maryland; Russ Gumina, San Francisco. **[1967]** Mal Graham, New York University; Nevil Shed, Texas at El Paso; Mike Redd, Kentucky Wesleyan; Ed Hummer, Princeton; Edgar Lacey, UCLA; Andrew Anderson, Canisius; Henry Brown, U. of Massachusetts-Lowell; Rick Weitzman, Northeastern. **[1968]** Don Chaney, Houston; Garfield Smith, Eastern Kentucky; Rich Johnson, Grambling; Thad Jaracz, Kentucky; Jerry

Newsom, Indiana State; Mike Lewis, Duke; Julius Keye, Alcorn State; Bill Butler, St. Bonaventure; Ivan Leschinsky, Long Island U.; Tom Neimeir, Evansville; Bill Langheld, Fordham; Art Stephenson, Rhode Island; Keith Hockstein, Holy Cross. **[1969]** Jo Jo White, Kansas; Julius Keye, Alcorn State; Steve Kuberski, Bradley; George Thompson, Marquette; Dolph Pulliam, Drake; Jim Johnson, Wisconsin; Bob Whitmore, Notre Dame; Gordon Smith, Cincinnati; Jim Picka, High Point University; Larry Frinston, Kenyon College; Rod Forbes, Boston State; Billy Evans, Boston College.

1970s
[1970] Dave Cowens, Florida State; Rex Morgan, Jacksonville;Willie Williams, Florida State; Jon McKinney, Norfolk State; Tom Carter, Paul Quinn College; Rod McIntyre, Jacksonville; Charlie Scott, North Carolina; Bobby Croft, Tennessee; Tom Little, Seattle; 10. Mike Maloy, Davidson. **[1971]** Clarence Glover, Western Kentucky; Jim Rose, Western Kentucky; Dave Robisch, Kansas; Randy Denton, Duke; Skip Young, Florida State; John Ribock, South Carolina; Ray Green, California U. of Pennsylvania; Dale Dover, Harvard; Reggie Brooks, Southern New Hampshire; John Dalton, Suffolk University; Leroy Chalk, Nebraska. **[1972]** Paul Westphal, Southern Cal; Dennis Wuycik, North Carolina; Wayne Grabiec, Michigan; Nate Stephens, Long Beach; Bryan Adrian, Davidson; Doug Holcomb, Memphis; Wally Wright, Widener; Stephen Previs, North Carolina; Sam McCarney, Oral Roberts; Marty Hunt, Kenyon; Mark Minor, Ohio State; Phil Stephens, South Carolina State. **[1973]** Steve Downing, Indiana; Phil Hankinson, Pennsylvania; Martinez Denmon, Iowa State; Richie Fuqua, Oral Roberts; Byron Jones, San Francisco; Mike Stewart, Santa Clara; Robert White, Sam Houston State; Corky Taylor, Minnesota; Steve Turner, Vanderbilt; Ed Hastings, Villanova; Bruce Winkler, Santa Clara; Scott Koelzer, Montana State; Rick Williams, Iowa; James Gilchrist, Florida Southern; Sam Barber, Bethune-Cookman; Lamont King, Long Beach; Peter Gavitt, Maine; Tom Austin, University of Massachusetts. **[1974]** Glenn McDonald, Long Beach;

Kevin Stacom, Providence; Roscoe Pondexter, Long Beach; Lerman Battle, Fairmont State; Ben Clyde, Florida State; Gene Harmon, Creighton; Ron Brown, Penn State; Richard Wallace, Georgia Southern; Al Skinner, University of Massachusetts; Phil Rogers, Fairfield. **[1975]** Tom Boswell, South Carolina; Jerome Anderson, West Virginia; Cyrus Mann, Illinois State; Darryl Brown, Fordham; Rick Coleman, Jacksonville; Al Boswell, Oral Roberts; Roger Morningstar, Kansas; Robert Rhodes, Albany State; Bill Endicott, University of Massachusetts. **[1976]** Norm Cook, Kansas; Jerry Fort, Nebraska; Lewis Linder, Kentucky State; Louis McKinney, St. Louis; Art Collins, St. Thomas; Ralph Drollinger, UCLA; John Clark, Northeastern; Bill Collins, Boston College; Otho Tucker, University of Illinois. **[1977]** Cedric Maxwell, University of North Carolina-Charlotte; Skip Brown, Wake Forest; Jeff Cummings, Tulane; Bill Langloh, Virginia; Roy Pace, Rutgers-Camden; Dave Klye, Cleveland State; Tom Harris, Bowling Green. **[1978]** Larry Bird, Indiana State; Freeman Williams, Portland State; Jeff Judkins, Utah; Dana Skinner, Merrimack; David Stergakos, Bloomfield College; Greg Tynes, Seton Hall; Dave Winey, Minnesota; Steve Balkun, Fairfield; Kim Fisher, Fairfield; Les Anderson, George Washington; Walter Harrigan, Brandeis. **[1979]** Wayne Kreklowm Drake; Malcolm, Briar Cliff; Nick Galis, Seton Hall; Jimmy Allen, New Haven; Marvin Delph, Arkansas; Steve Castellan, Virginia; Glenn Sudhop, North Carolina State; Kevin Sinnett, Navy; Alton Byrd, Columbia.

1980s
[1980] Kevin McHale, Minnesota; Arnette Hallman, Purdue; Ron Perry, Holy Cross; Don Newman, Idaho; Kevin Hamilton, Iona; Rufus Harris, Maine; Kenny Evans, Norfolk State; Les Hanson, Virginia Poly Tech Institute; Steve Wright, Boston University; Brian Jung, Northwestern; John Nolan, Providence. **[1981]** Charles Bradley, Wyoming; Tracy Jackson, Notre Dame; Danny Ainge, Brigham Young; John Johnson, Michigan; Stanley Williams, LaSalle; Glen Grunwald, Indiana; Steve Waite, Iowa; Tom Seaman, Holy

Cross; George Morrow, Creighton; Greg McCray, Virginia Commonwealth; Ken Matthews, North Carolina State. **[1982]** Darren Tillis, Cleveland State; Tony Guy, Kansas; Perry Moss, Northeastern; William Brown, St. Peter's College; John Schweitz, Richmond; Phil Collins, West Virginia; Ed Spriggs, Georgetown University; Panagiotis Giannakis, Greece; Landon Turner, Indiana. **[1983]** Greg Kite, Brigham Young; Winfred King, East Tennessee State; Craig Robinson, Virginia; Carlos Clark, Mississippi; Bob Reitz, Stonehill; Paul Atkins, Houston Baptist; Roy Jackson; Trent Johnson, Pittsburgh; John Rice, University of Massachusetts-Boston; Andy Kupec, Bentley. **[1984]** Michael Young, Houston; Ronnie Williams, Florida; Rick Carlisle, Virginia; Kevin Mullin, Princeton; Todd Orlando, Bentley; Steve Carfino, Iowa; Mark Van Valkenburg, Framingham State; Champ Godboldt, Holy Cross; Joe Dixon, Merrimack; Dan Trant, Clark. **[1985]** Sam Vincent, Michigan State; Andre Battle, Loyola of Chicago; Cliff Weber, Liberty; Albert Butts, LaSalle; Ralph Lewis, LaSalle; Chris Remly, Rutgers. **[1986]** Len Bias, Maryland; Tony Benford, Texas Tech; 5. Dave Colbert, Dayton; Greg Wendt, Detroit Mercy; Tom Ivey, Boston University. **[1987]** Reggie Lewis, Northeastern; Brad Lohaus, Iowa; Tom Sheehey, Virginia; Darryl Kennedy, Oklahoma; Dave Butler, California; Tim Naegeli, Wisconsin Stevens-Point; Jerry Corcoran, Northeastern. **[1988]** Brian Shaw, Santa Barbara; Gerald Paddio, UNLV. **[1989]** Michael Smith, Brigham Young; Dino Radja, Yugoslavia.

1990s
[1990] Dee Brown, Jacksonville. **[1991]** Rick Fox, North Carolina. **[1992]** Jon Barry, Georgia Tech; Darren Morningstar, Pittsburgh. **[1993]** Acie Earl, Iowa. **[1994]** Eric Montross, North Carolina; Andrei Fetisov, Spain. **[1995]** Eric Williams, Providence; Junior Burrough, Virginia. **[1996]** Antoine Walker, Kentucky; Steve Hamer, Tennessee. **[1997]** Ron Mercer, Kentucky; Ben Pepper, Australia. **[1998]** Paul Pierce, Kansas. **[1999]** Kris Clack, Texas.

2000s

[2000] Jerome Moiso, UCLA. [2001] Joe Johnson, Arkansas; Kedrick Brown, Okaloosa-Walton Community College; Joe Forte, North Carolina. [2002] Darius Songaila, Wake Forest. [2003] Troy Bell, Boston College; Dahntay Jones, Duke; Brandon Hunter, Ohio University. [2004] Al Jefferson, Prentiss; Delonte West, St. Joseph's; Tony Allen, Oklahoma State; Justin Reed, Mississippi. [2005] Gerald Green, Gulf Shores Academy; Ryan Gomes, Providence; Orien Greene, Louisiana-Lafayette. [2006] Randy Foye, Villanova. [2007] Jeff Green, Georgetown; Gabe Pruitt, USC. 2008] J. R. Giddens, New Mexico; Semih Erden, Turkey. [2009] Lester Hudson, Tennessee-Martin. [2010] Avery Bradley, Texas; Luke Harangody, Notre Dame. [2011] MarShon Brooks, Providence; E'Twaun Moore, Purdue. [2012] Fab Melo, Syracuse; Kris Joseph, Syracuse. [2013] Lucas Nogueira, Spain; (only pick). [2014] Marcus Smart, Oklahoma State; James Young, Kentucky. [2015] Terry Rozier, Louisville; R.J. Hunter, Georgia State; Jordan Mickey, Louisiana State; Marcus Thornton, William & Mary. [2016] Jaylen Brown, California; Guerschon Yabusele, France; Ante Ziric, Croatia; Deyonte Davis, Michigan State; Rade Zagorac, Serbia; Demetrius Jackson, Notre Dame; Ben Bentil, Providence; Abdel Nader, Iowa State. [2017] Jayson Tatum, Duke; Semi Ojeleye, Southern Methodist; Kadeem Allen, Arizona; Jabari Bird, California. [2018] Robert Williams, Texas A&M. [2019] Romeo Langford, Indiana; Matisse Thybulle, Washington; Grant Williams, Tennessee; Tremont Waters, Louisiana State. [2020] Aaron Nesmith, Vanderbilt; Payton Pritchard, Oregon; Desmond Bane, Texas Christian (traded to Memphis Grizzlies). 2021: Juhann Begarin.

Celtics Draft Picks

**T**he first National Basketball Association draft of college players took place in 1947. In the earliest days of the draft, the teams chose many more players than they do in the modern era. Often, ten players were selected, sometimes even more.

Gradually, over time, the NBA reduced the rounds of its draft until it bottomed out at two picks in 1989. This was based on the fact that a team going into the season with a twelve-player roster did not have the need for twenty players in training camp.

In the early days of the draft, many players were selected sight-unseen. There were no college basketball games on television. Players could not put together personal highlight tapes. Sometimes, pro coaches did see players in their areas play live. Other times they relied on word-of-mouth scouting from friends, or other coaches they trusted.

As is the case now, teams could also acquire additional draft picks in trades. Up until 1966, the NBA allowed teams to have first dibs on what were called territorial draft picks. This meant a team could take a player who was a star at a local or regional college and sacrifice its numbered pick for that person. The theory behind this was to help teams build fan bases with familiar names. The Celtics exercised this provision in 1956 when they made forward Tommy Heinsohn of Holy Cross a territorial No. 1 pick. Holy Cross is located in Worcester, Massachusetts, thirty-five miles from Boston.

The first draft, when the Celtics were still in the Basketball Association of America before it merged with the National Basketball League, took place on July 1, 1947. The first player ever drafted by the Celtics was Edwin "Bulbs" Ehlers out of Purdue University, the third player taken in the history of the league.

A six-foot-three guard-forward swingman for the Boilermakers. Ehlers wore No. 14 for the Celtics. He played two seasons for Boston and averaged 8.1 points per game. An all-around athlete, Ehlers was also drafted by the Chicago Bears of the National Football League and signed with the New York Yankees, too. He played five seasons of minor league baseball as a first baseman and third baseman with the Yankees and the Chicago Cubs in the majors.

Decades later, in the 1980s, Ehlers was chosen for the Indiana Basketball Hall of Fame and the Indiana Football Hall of Fame. His grandson Scott Dreisbach played pro football in the NFL and in the American Football League.

To the modern fan, Ehlers would be merely the answer to a trivia question, but he was a productive player during his two NBA seasons in Boston.

Boston's No. 1 pick in 1949 was six-foot-three forward Tony Lavelli. He also played just two seasons, averaging 6.9 points a game, but was known for two things: Lavelli possessed a dangerous hook shot, and he entertained Boston Garden fans at halftime by playing the accordion.

Some other early notable Celtics draft choices were Chuck Cooper, a No. 2 pick out of Duquesne in 1950, who was the first African American ever drafted and who later was inducted into the Naismith Memorial Basketball Hall of Fame for his pioneering status; Bill Garrett from Indiana University, who was the first African American star in the Big Ten in 1951; and Gene Conley out of Washington State in 1952, who is one of only a few professional athletes to ever be part of team championships in more than one major North American sport. Conley won championship rings with the Celtics and the Milwaukee Braves in baseball.

Starting with Frank Ramsey in 1950 (although his pro debut was delayed because of military service), the Celtics drafted brilliantly throughout the 1950s, regularly plucking Hall-of-Famers. Following Ramsey, Boston, with Red Auerbach making the personnel choices, spent draft choices on championship contributors such as Jim Loscutoff (1955), Heinsohn (1956), K.C. Jones (1956), Sam Jones (1957), Tom Sanders (1960), and John Havlicek (1962). All but Loscutoff are in the Hall of Fame, Sanders as a special contributor. Loscutoff's No. 18 is retired in Boston.

When the Celtics had to rebuild in the 1970s, after Bill Russell retired as a player and coach and Auerbach was in the front office, the next rounds of No. 1 draft picks included Jo Jo White at guard, Dave Cowens at center, Cedric Maxwell at forward, Kevin McHale at forward, and the great Larry Bird at forward. Later, Brian Shaw, Dee Brown, Antoine Walker, and Paul Pierce were top-notch additions before the 2000s. Since then, No. 1 picks that stand out have been Marcus Smart, Terry Rozier, Jaylen Brown, and Jayson Tatum.

One player seemingly destined for stardom was the 1986 No. 1 draft pick Len Bias out of the University of Maryland. The six-foot-eight forward was a do-everything type of player. An All-American, Bias was viewed as possessing All-Star talent. This was considered to be a coup for the Celtics, who won the 1985–86 title with a dominant team and frontcourt featuring Bird, Kevin McHale, and Robert Parrish. Bias was seen as the upcoming replacement as that group of Hall-of-Famers aged.

Yet just two days after Boston drafted him, Bias shockingly died from cardiac arrhythmia from a cocaine overdose. Bias's death created a scandal at Maryland and set back Celtic development by years. The scandal destroyed careers at his college, as well as being one of the lowest moments in a proud basketball franchise's history.

There was also a period in the 1960s and 1970s when the American Basketball Association challenged the NBA for basketball supremacy. The draft expanded for a time in an attempt to possibly tie up more players and keep them from signing with the opposing league. Some NBA teams drafted top-caliber players already committed to the ABA. Just in case they changed their minds later, they would control their NBA rights.

Over the years, the Celtics drafted two Ron Perrys out of Holy Cross, the father and the son. They also drafted Joe Mullaney, who became a distinguished coach and likewise, Johnny Bach who was an assistant with the Chicago Bulls when they won three titles. John Thompson, the Hall of Fame coach of Georgetown, was a third-round pick in 1964 and spent two years as Bill Russell's back-up at center.

In a gracious gesture, the Celtics made Landon Turner of Indiana their tenth round draft pick in 1982. A star for the Hoosiers who was expected to have a pro career, Turner was partially paralyzed in an automobile accident and had to use a wheelchair.

The vast majority of players drafted by the Celtics never played a regular-season minute for the team. Some may well have decided to not even show up for training camp in the 1950s because they could make more money in other careers. At the least, many of those guys could tell their children they were once drafted by the Boston Celtics.

Bob Cousy

f all the Boston Celtics greats, for all the mystique of the franchise and the tremendous things accomplished, Bob Cousy is in some ways the single most significant individual to play for the team and its most enduring representative.

Bill Russell's addition in 1956 turned Boston into champions. Cousy, who virtually invented the point guard position, gave the club credibility. He helped put fans in the seats at the Boston Garden when the team was struggling at the gate. College basketball's annual point guard award is named after him. As he turned ninety-one in 2019, he was presented with the Presidential Medal of Freedom.

Cousy was born in New York in 1928. He attended Holy Cross in Worcester, Massachusetts and that gave him star power in the Boston area even before he joined the Celtics for the 1950–51 season. He played for thirteen years and one of the most memorable events in team history was Bob Cousy Day when the six-foot-one veteran was honored leading up to his retirement.

Holy Cross won the NCAA title in 1947 and Cousy won some type of All-American recognition in three different seasons. While he was a natural for the Celtics, and owner Walter Brown wanted to see Cousy wearing green, new front office executive Red Auerbach did not initially want him. Auerbach infamously dismissed Cousy as a "local yokel." He added, "I don't give a damn for sentiment or names." He was convinced Cousy's value was overrated by an adoring fan base and felt the Celtics needed a big man more than a guard. This was one time Auerbach was wrong.

The National Basketball Association was in flux during this time period and when franchises folded, the names of some prominent leftover players were written on a piece of paper and placed in a hat. Boston drew Cousy and that is how he became a Celtic. Soon enough, Cousy and Auerbach developed a winning partnership and a great and enduring friendship.

Cousy, often referred to as "Cooz," could score, lead, and pass. His style predated the complete domination of the jump shot, so offensively he unleashed more of a one-hand push shot. Cousy could dribble circles around defenders, leading to open shots for himself or clean passes to teammates. His behind-the-back dribbling was ground-breaking and his no-look passes were ahead of their time and led to a more descriptive nickname: "Houdini of the Hardwood."

Over his lifetime, Cousy averaged 18.4 points a game, but also 7.5 assists and a surprising 5.2 rebounds per game. Cousy led the NBA in assists for eight years in a row. When he made appearances in Boston later in retirement, he was often introduced to fans as "Mr. Basketball."

Cousy came from an unassuming background. He was the son of French immigrants and his first language was French. He also had a minor lisp. Cousy's multi-cultural upbringing with youngsters of all ethnicities and religions later manifested itself in a strong social conscience. He joined the NAACP. From another social justice standpoint, Cousy wielded his star power in the 1950s as the first president of an NBA players union, fighting for, and negotiating for, higher minimum salaries and the players' first benefits.

On the court, Cousy formed half of one of the greatest backcourts of all-time with Bill Sharman, playing together for 10 years. Both men were inducted into the Naismith Memorial Basketball Hall of Fame. The guard position was already set when the Celtics traded for center Bill Russell and drafted forward Tommy Heinsohn in 1956. The roster was complete, the Celtics Dynasty formed, and Boston began winning world championships. A thirteen-time All-Star and winner of the 1957 Most Valuable Player award, Cousy was a member of six of Boston's championship teams until his retirement in 1963.

"I say to people today," Cousy said many years later, "I'm proud of a lot of things we were involved in with the Celtics, and I know legends are made to be broken, but one that will stand forever, in my judgment, is eleven championships in thirteen years."

As remarkable as that stretch was, the addition of free agency to the sport and the unlikelihood of teams staying together for years on end, will make it ever more difficult for that mark to be challenged.

"Given the way free agency works," Cousy said, "that's one that will stand the test of time. That's just not going to happen, in my judgment. I was very proud to be part of that."

One of Cousy's finest games was recorded against the long-gone Syracuse Nationals (who became the Philadelphia 76ers). During the 1953 playoffs, Boston defeated the Nationals, 111–104 in four overtimes in the deciding game. At the end of regulation play, Cousy had 25 points. At the end of the game, he had 50. For whatever reason, Syracuse kept fouling Cousy, and he kept traipsing to the foul line. He made thirty of thirty-two free-throw attempts in that game and mixed in a twenty-five-foot shot at the buzzer to extend the game from three to four overtimes.

"That got us through that round," Cousy recalled much later. "I had a little help. I had four overtimes to do it. I was more pleased with going thirty-of thirty-two from the line under playoff conditions."

The NBA was much rougher around the edges in the 1950s, with less security and more vociferous and physical fans. Cousy made it sound as if suiting up in Syracuse was a bit like stepping into the ring for a World Wrestling Federation match.

"I hated Syracuse," Cousy said. "They would have to pay me more money than exists to live in that town."

Cousy was in his seventh season when Boston won its first title, a never-to-be-forgotten moment.

"I think the first time was the most meaningful," Cousy said. "We had worked six long years in not accomplishing much. You don't remember individual accomplishments as much as [the] teams'."

Cousy's popularity was huge in Boston. Fans admired his style and achievements on the court and his demeanor off the court. It was payback time when Cousy announced his retirement at the age of thirty-four. On St. Patrick's Day in 1963, the Boston Garden was packed with a capacity crowd of 13,909 spectators. Surrounded by his daughters, parents, and his wife Missie, Cousy read a thank-you speech while intermittently wiping tears from his eyes and blowing his nose into a handkerchief. He thanked his teammates for their friendship and allowing him to be their captain.

During a brief silence, a leather-lunged fan yelled from the balcony the memorable summation of the day: "We love ya, Cooz!" It was later revealed that the devoted Celtics fan who made the legendary shout was a guy named Joe Dillon, a water department worker from South Boston. The man had brilliant theatrical timing. Decades later, Cousy said that, when spotted on his occasional visits to games, some fans repeated that verbal tribute.

Not long afterwards, the Celtics won another NBA title, over the Los Angeles Lakers again. Boston won that series 4–2 and Cousy participated in the writing of a book about his last few days leading up to his retirement. Going out as a champion is always a special thing for a player. Cousy had one problem, though. He was dealing with an injury and trainer Buddy Leroux thought he should cease playing. "Let me try it," Cousy responded.

This was a period when Jerry West and Elgin Baylor made the Lakers unbeatable to all except the Celtics. The Lakers won Game Five in Boston with Baylor pumping in 43 points and West 32.

The Celtics wrapped up the title in Game Six and Cousy scored 18 points in the finale.

"If I had any shame, I'd be embarrassed," Cousy said. "It couldn't have worked out better. I had a good year. The team won the championship and – to be honest – the torn ligaments and the return to the game lent the final Hollywood flourish. People like to embellish a good story, and I now find that everybody seems to think I came limping back, my face contorted with pain, and dragged myself up and down the court, scoring key baskets."

A grand memory.

"Oh, absolutely, any athlete wants to go out on top," Cousy said. "Not many do. It was Wyatt Earp walking off into the sunset."

He said he had to use crutches for three weeks afterwards, though.

After leaving the Celtics, Cousy, whose No. 14 jersey was retired, went right on to coach Boston College. He had great success with the Eagles, going 114–38, and in 1968–69 finishing 24–4 and reaching the championship game of the National Invitational Tournament.

For the 1969–70 season, Cousy became coach of the Cincinnati Royals, a stint that did not go as smoothly as things had in the college game. Late in the season, he briefly came out of retirement to give attendance a jump-start. He was forty-one years old when he appeared in seven more games, playing about five minutes at a time. The gimmick did pay off, if only briefly, but the team could not be saved in Cincinnati and became the Kansas City – Omaha Kings. In the middle of his fifth season as head coach Cousy resigned, never leading the club to the playoffs.

In a drastic departure, between 1974 and 1979, Cousy served as the commissioner of the American Soccer League. Then he spent considerable time as a broadcaster on Celtics games.

Still, Cousy's playing days with the Celtics are emblematic of the greatest stretch in the team's history and involved unprecedented achievements by a closely-knit group of men. These players will forever be identified with the city of Boston and the era of NBA play they owned.

In 2019, Cousy, reflecting on those golden days, said that "most particularly, chemistry made you win. We all came with the same motivation. It helped to have a leader like Arnold [Auerbach]. We all had each other's backs. Arnold maintained a certain unity and discipline. In many ways it was like family."

On August 22, 2019, Cousy was awarded the Presidential Medal of Freedom by President Donald Trump in the Oval Office at the White House.

"This acknowledgment allows me to complete my life circle," Cousy said. "I can stop chasing a bouncing ball. The Presidential Medal of Freedom allows me to reach a level of acceptance in our society I never once dreamed of."

Chuck Connors

The actor who starred in the TV western *"The Rifleman"* is the answer to multiple trivia questions. Before he spent some four decades in front of the camera, Chuck Connors managed to play both Major League Baseball and professional basketball with the Boston Celtics for a living.

Few people in history have enjoyed such a charmed trio of careers to support themselves, although certainly only a small percentage of baseball and basketball fans recall Connors in those occupations.

"The Rifleman" can still be seen in reruns on cable television from its first-run days between 1958 and 1963, the iconic role that stuck to Connors. It would be quite the task to find much video of Connors on the field or on the court.

Born in 1921, Connors, whose given name was Kevin Joseph Aloyius Connors, grew up in Brooklyn, New York and, not surprisingly, was a fan of the Brooklyn Dodgers. After high school, he enrolled at Seton Hall, where he played both basketball and baseball and eventually ditched the name Kevin, saying he never liked it, and switched to Chuck.

In the early 1940s, Connors dropped out of college to sign with Brooklyn, playing briefly for a Dodgers minor-league team and then with a New York Yankees farm club before joining the military during World War II.

At war's end, the six-foot-five Connors accepted an offer from the Celtics and played with the club from 1946 to 1948 before giving up basketball to pursue his original dream in baseball. He kept flirting with the majors, regularly being demoted to AAA before finally obtaining his big-league chance with the Dodgers in 1949 and the Chicago Cubs in 1951. On average, Connors batted .238.

In basketball, he appeared in fifty-three games with the Celtics and averaged 4.5 points a game.

Once, later, when the Celtics were in the neighborhood for a game, Connors gave some players a tour of a Hollywood film lot. He acted in about fifty movies.

"I wasn't a bad basketball player," Connors said, "but I wasn't the world's greatest. Good defense, no offense: that was me."

Connors said his greatest value to the Celtics may have been appearing at sports dinners all around New England for $25 or $50 an appearance where he would sometimes recite "Casey at The Bat." During one of these performances, Red Sox star Ted Williams was present and told Connors he was so good he ought to become an actor. Connors followed the career advice.

Kenny Sailors

nly a small portion of guard Kenny Sailors' five-year National Basketball Association career was spent with the Boston Celtics. But in later years, when he lived in Alaska, many people he encountered recalled him as an ex-Celtic. That was because Sailors played in the early days of the fluctuating NBA and his other teams went out of business and were not well-remembered.

Sailors, who stood five-foot-ten, or maybe five-foot-eleven in sneakers, also suited up for the Cleveland Rebels, the Chicago Stags (one game), the Philadelphia Warriors (two games), the Providence Steamrollers, the Baltimore Bullets, and the original Denver Nuggets. Sailors averaged 12.6 points for his career and made one All-Star team.

However, the most notable aspects of Sailors's basketball career took place in the college game and as a pioneer in the sport. Sailors was the captain of the 1943 University of Wyoming team that won the NCAA crown, and he was a two-time All-American wrapped around World War II service with the Marines.

Beyond that, Sailors, who is enshrined in the College Basketball Hall of Fame, is the inventor of the modern-day jump shot; the high-flying, leave-your-feet shot that defines the sport. He employed it when all others were using the two-hand set shot.

Sailors, who died at ninety-five in 2016, began using the jumper in his backyard growing up Wyoming while playing one-on-one with his much taller and older brother Bud. Bud gleefully swatted away most of Kenny's shots in their duets until younger brother developed his new offensive threat. At the time, Kenny was in junior high, standing at about five-foot-six and Bud was 10 inches taller.

"It was just a weapon that came naturally," Kenny Sailors said of his desperate need to work his way around Bud at the hoop. "He was big, but he was fast enough to stop my drive."

It took some years to perfect the jumper, released at the peak of Kenny's jump, with the ball positioned in front of his face, but once achieved, he was able to use it fluidly and effectively in high school and college. When the Cowboys drew nationwide attention, many sportswriters and photographers highlighted his unusual shot.

Sailors brought the jumper with him to the NBA. Only his first coach, Dutch Dehnert, one of the stars of the 1920s Original Celtics and part of Walter Brown's inspiration for using the Celtics name discouraged its use. Dehnert called Sailors's shot showboating and said it had no future in the sport.

Rarely did Sailors end up on a team that had longevity, or a need for his services. When he joined Boston, he played the same position as Bob Cousy, who was anchored in the point guard slot.

"He was an exceptional jump shooter," Cousy said of Sailors. "He got credit for being the inventor of the jump shot. He was an excellent jump shooter. That was basically his weapon."

Sailors did not feel any warmth from coach Red Auerbach.

"He was a tremendous judge of talent," Sailors said. "I never thought of him as a great coach who had knowledge of the science and tactics of the game, but he knew how to get the best out of his ballplayers. There was something about that guy. He could sign up these ballplayers and get great ones."

Sailors is an inductee in the College Basketball Hall of Fame. Many believe Sailors has been shortchanged by not yet being inducted into the Naismith Memorial Basketball Hall of Fame despite lobbying campaigns by the University of Wyoming and having advocates pushing his case such as famed coach Bob Knight and famed broadcaster Dick Vitale.

Among other honors Sailors accrued was the erection of a statue of him, of course taking a jump shot, on the University of Wyoming campus. More recently, he was the subject of a full-length documentary film titled: *"Jumpshot: The Life of Kenny Sailors."* Film-maker Jacob Hamilton said he hopes his portrayal of Sailors's story does aid the quest to get Sailors enshrined in the Hall of Fame in Springfield, Massachusetts.

During his five years in the NBA, Sailors never made more than $7,500 in a season and his only endorsement was prune juice. He was not paid in dollars for that gig, either, but in product, cases of the drink.

Sailors never lamented missing out on a longer career with the Celtics. He was gone from Boston in 1951, several years before the team began winning championships, and he was already thirty years old, just about ready to move on to the next phase of his life.

Bill Sharman

 here have only been four individuals who have been doubly honored as players and coaches going into the Naismith Memorial Basketball Hall of Fame, and Bill Sharman is one of them. That recognition was also extended to John Wooden, Lenny Wilkens, and more recently, Sharman's old Boston teammate Tommy Heinsohn.

Sharman was born in Abilene, Texas in 1926 but lived most of his life in California. He spent his entire National Basketball Association playing career with the Celtics. He gained fame as a coach, the second time around in basketball, like several of his former teammates, while never coaching his former team.

A six-foot-one guard, Sharman played college ball at the University of Southern California from 1946 to 1950 and was picked by the Celtics in the NBA draft in 1951. In some ways, like many of Boston's shrewd moves, it was a risky choice. Not because Sharman did not have the talent to shine on the court, but because he had too much athletic talent. Sharman was also playing professional baseball in the Brooklyn Dodgers' organization. He was making fast enough advancement through the ranks that he easily could have emerged on a Major League roster rather than an NBA roster.

A right-handed thrower and hitter, Sharman was a third baseman. He appeared with three Class A clubs in 1950. Then he moved up to AA Fort Worth in 1951. A steady hitter,

Sharman was a regular high .280s batter.

Famously, Sharman had one of the best seats as a witness to one of the most extraordinary pennant races in National League history. In 1951, the Dodgers had a big lead for the pennant, and Sharman was a late-season call-up. However, as the team's arch-nemesis, the New York Giants, rallied and the Dodgers began losing. Sharman watched up close as the Dodgers blew the pennant and the Giants captured a one-game play-off, without ever playing in a big-league game.

Sharman spent the next season in AAA and hit 16 home runs with 77 runs batted in and a .294 average but did not get summoned to the big club again. He spent a couple more seasons collecting a check from Brooklyn but not advancing. If Sharman had reached the majors, the Celtics would have had two players – Sharman and Gene Conley – occupying spots on professional rosters in two sports at the same time.

When the Dodgers originally brought him to Brooklyn, Sharman thought he was about to experience a different kind of great moment – a Major League debut. He said team executive Buzzy Bavasi telephoned him to give him the news.

"They thought I was a prospect," Sharman said. "He said, 'I want to call you up for the end of the season to our Major League club. As soon as we clinch the pennant, we want you to play four or five games."

The sporting world knows how that went. Sharman never got off the bench – except in a peculiar manner. In one late-season game, a brouhaha broke out and the umpire exiled everyone from the Dodger dugout. So, Sharman had the distinction of being thrown out of a big-league game without ever playing in one.

"It was kind of funny," he said. "Or unique." Funnier in its own way was that, despite his great success in basketball and his near-miss at the majors, Sharman said his best sport when he was young was actually tennis. He won fifteen high school letters and also boxed and weight-lifted, though he weighed about 180 pounds. He really was an all-around athlete.

Sharman was a superior basketball player. A dead-eye free-throw shooter during his ten-year career, making 88.3 percent of his foul shots, he averaged 17.8 points and teamed with Bob Cousy in the Boston backcourt. Some say that tandem, both Hall-of-Famers, constituted the greatest backcourt in league history.

Already twenty-four when he broke into the NBA with the Washington Capitals (because of time spent in the Navy) Sharman played thirty-one games for that club, but then that team went out of business. The league awarded his rights to the Fort Wayne Pistons, but the Celtics acquired him in a trade and he spent the rest of his playing days with Boston. Sharman played between 1950 and 1961. He led the league in free-throwing average seven times, three of those years topping 90 percent, including a career-best season of 93.2 in 1958–59.

One reason the Celtics Dynasty persisted so long was that Red Auerbach was able to find a star fill-in when a player was aging and about to retire. Cousy and Sharman were the best at what they did. Sharman, who was part of four Boston championship teams and made the All-Star team eight times, retired at thirty-four years old. But the Celtics had been preparing. Already coming off the bench were Sam Jones and K.C. Jones, and as Sharman and Cousy ended their tenures, the other two easily shifted into the starting lineup.

"The four of us are in the Hall of Fame," Sharman said. "There's not many teams that have four guards in the Hall of Fame."

The Celtics were the envy of the league when they had Sharman and Cousy together. Sharman made their relationship sound almost like one of brothers and emphasized how their skill sets perfectly complemented one another. Cousy was a passer and dribbler. Sharman was a sharpshooter who could get open. Sharman said he had been a forward when younger, so he did not have the experience to be a point guard – which he certainly would be at his height in the modern era.

"He is maybe the greatest ball-handler of all time," Sharman said of Cousy in 2007. "I could run around and get free. It was just wonderful the relationship we had on and off the floor. We spent 10 years as roommates, and we never had a fight or got mad at each other."

One interesting aspect of Sharman's career was his reputation as a brilliant pure shooter. Yet his lifetime shooting percentage does not that reflect that. The game was different, more physical and slower with teams having fewer offensive possessions. Sharman offered up other obstacles facing shooters.

"When we played in the fifties, the rims were rigid," he said. "We played where the lighting was bad. In some places the rims were a little tilted down on one side. It makes a big difference. One day [in Syracuse] the roof was leaky." In arenas where a pro hockey team shared the building, "the floor would be slippery. The conditions in the fifties were not the same. Even in Madison Square Garden, they were not exact."

Auerbach loved the combination of Sharman and Cousy, believing they brought out the best in one another. "I've always said he was the best pure shooter I've ever seen from anywhere around that foul line," Auerbach said. "Plus, he was just super on defense, the best I ever had in the backcourt until K.C. Jones came along."

Sharman played with Boston through some lean, growing years, and was a member of the first championship team in 1957 after the Celtics added Bill Russell and Tommy Heinsohn.

"The more we won, the better we got," Sharman said. Maybe the more the Celtics won the more the rest of the league appreciated Sharman, too. He was the All-Star game Most Valuable Player in 1955 and seven times was either first- or second-team all-NBA. He was selected as a member of the league's 25th and 50th anniversary All-Star teams, and eventually the Celtics retired his jersey No. 21.

After Sharman retired as a player, he immediately became a head coach. As coach of the Cleveland Pipers in the short-lived American Basketball League, he led the team to the title.

After the Pipers folded, he coached Los Angeles State for two seasons, which was basically a fill-in stop. Sharman rejoined the NBA as coach of the San Francisco Warriors, a two-year job. Then he won another title with the Utah Stars in the fledgling American Basketball Association. When he agreed to coach the Los Angeles Lakers, Sharman had to go through the legal system to be freed from his Utah obligations. Then he promptly won an NBA crown for LA with Wilt Chamberlain and Jerry West. That gave Sharman three championships in three pro leagues, the only one to achieve that. The 1971–72 Lakers won a record thirty-three games in a row in a 69–13 season.

A widespread NBA practice Sharman is credited with introducing is the game-day shoot around. All teams gather together for a light workout, but Sharman dreamed up the strategy when he was still a player with Boston. It all began with Sharman bored sitting around in hotel rooms. He was about six years into his career when, one day on a road trip, he went for a walk and stumbled upon a high school gym. It was devoid of activity when Sharman entered, borrowed a ball, and began shooting free throws. He then turned the event into a regular practice for himself, refusing to quit until he hit 10 in a row and then more. In a letter once, Sharman referred to his decade in Boston as "My [ten] fun, wonderful, exciting years that I spent in Boston and [with] the Celtics."

Sharman became a Hall-of-Famer as a player in 1976 and as a coach in 2004. It was during his most spectacular coaching season with the Lakers that Sharman developed the beginnings of a serious voice problem. First it was a rasp and then, as his vocal chords worsened, he lost the power of speech altogether.

Bill Sharman died in 2013 from the after-effects of a stroke. He was eighty-seven years old.

Howie McHugh

**A** friend of Boston owner Walter Brown going back to the 1940s, Howie McHugh was the Boston basketball team's first publicity man, despite being a college hockey player, not a basketball player, at Dartmouth College. He was a revered figure at the Boston Garden, his first assignment, but he was on the wrong side of lobbying when the team was founded.

Brown was mulling several names for the new franchise, including Olympics, and even Unicorns (that would have been an error in judgment), but when he settled on Celtics, McHugh tried to talk him out of it.

McHugh was the team's public relations man from 1946 until he passed away in 1983, five days after the end of the season. In an era when there were few front-office employees, McHugh did more than keep track of player facts. Sometimes he picked up new players at the airport, too.

McHugh, the all-around Celtics helper, was indeed assigned to pick up Bill Russell at Logan Airport as he arrived to join the team following the conclusion of the 1956 Summer Olympics in Australia. Given that McHugh had public relations in his genes, he arranged for a banner to fly reading "Welcome

Bill Russell to the Boston Celtics."

On November 5, 1946, the Celtics played their first-ever home game at the old Boston Arena, not the Boston Garden. During warm-ups, forward Chuck Connors (the same guy who had western TV acting in his future) broke a backboard. McHugh rushed to the Boston Garden to retrieve a spare so the game could go on.

The National Basketball Association annually gives out an award that includes McHugh's name on it. It is called the Splaver/McHugh Tribute to Excellence Award, honoring McHugh and former Baltimore Bullets's public relations man Marc Splaver. It is given to an NBA executive demonstrating superlative publicity skills.

Bill Mokray

hatever Mchugh did not handle, mostly involving paper and numbers, Bill Mokray supervised as team statistician and historian.

Mokray, born in New Jersey in 1907, developed an affection for basketball statistics as a student at Passaic High School. He got his first taste of public relations at the University of Rhode Island. When the Celtics began play in 1946, he was on the scene.

If not for Mokray, one might wonder if some of the key numbers in understanding what was going on in the earliest days of the league might have been lost. He created the long-running NBA Guide, an essential league reference publication, and was its editor.

Mokray was chosen to tell basketball's story for the *Encyclopedia Britannica*, and then wrote his own in-depth encyclopedia of basketball. He also wrote *Basketball's Best*, an NBA-related magazine, for some seasons, and Converse basketball shoes' annual yearbook. Mokray's record-keeping and input were deemed so valuable that he was inducted into the Naismith Memorial Basketball Hall of Fame in 1965 as a contributor.

Mokray died in 1974 at sixty-six years old.

Arnie Risen

nless one is a true student of Boston Celtics history, Arnie Risen might not be remembered even though he is a member of the Naismith Memorial Basketball Hall of Fame. Risen was a star ahead of the Celtics Dynasty.

He was slender for his height weighing in at 200 pounds and acquired the nickname "Stilts."

Risen originally enrolled at Eastern Kentucky State Teachers College before transferring to Ohio State. In college in the 1940s, the six-foot-nine Risen helped Ohio State reach two Final Fours. His first National Basketball Association team was the Rochester Royals, which ultimately became the Sacramento Kings. For one season, 1951, Rochester was the king of the basketball world. A four-time All-Star, Risen averaged in double figures in seven seasons.

Risen earned his second ring with the Celtics in 1957. He had a lesser role, but was still a contributor, twice averaging more than eight points a game. His playing time decreased once the Celtics obtained Bill Russell.

Prior to Risen's stint with two NBA teams, he played three seasons in the old National Basketball League. Growing up in rural Kentucky though, Risen said, "I didn't know there was such a thing as professional basketball."

Ed Macauley

is nickname was "Easy," and that was only partially because of how Ed Macauley moved on the court, especially on the offensive end. The six-foot-eight Macauley was one of the first accomplished big men in the early days of the National Basketball Association, breaking in for the 1949–50 season with the St. Louis Bombers, a team that stayed around for less time than he did.

Born in 1928, Macauley was a native of St. Louis, and in those early days of the league, teams were able to exercise territorial draft picks to keep homegrown players at home. It was after Macauley's first season, when the Bombers went out of business, that he joined the Celtics. Macauley spent the next six years with Boston and was one of the club's premiere players. He averaged between 17.5 points and 20.4 points per game.

During that time period, Macauley led the NBA in points per game, field-goal percentage, and free-throw percentage once each.

A seven-time All-Star, Macauley won the Most Valuable Player award in the 1951 game, the first one played. He could place the trophy on the shelf next to his MVP award from the National Invitation Tournament, a championship to which he led the St. Louis University. He wore No. 22 for Boston, and that uniform jersey was retired in his honor. Despite Macauley's success and eventual induction into the Naismith Basketball Hall of Fame, he was a great in an era that predated Boston's championship success.

Macauley was happy enough in Boston, but he truly was a St. Louis guy. His mother famously said when he was trying to pick a college that anywhere was OK with her, so to speak. What she literally said was, "You can go to any college you want as long as it is Catholic and in St. Louis."

Macauley ended up a star for St. Louis University, where his number was also retired after he was named a three-year All-American.

Macauley obtained his nickname while playing for St. Louis. He once made the mistake of entering the court too soon when the National Anthem was being played and a strong-lunged fan yelled, "Take it easy, Ed."

Macauley was a staple of the early Celtics, but both he and the team reached a crossroads following the 1955–56 season. The St. Louis Hawks owned a high draft choice and Red Auerbach wanted to pick Bill Russell. Hawks owner Ben Kerner bargained for Macauley, desiring to bring him back to St. Louis as a gate attraction. Auerbach was reluctant.

There were mitigating circumstances. Macauley and his wife Josephine had a baby boy named Pat who had contracted spinal meningitis and incurred brain damage. Not even sure if it was practical for him to be away from St. Louis and continue his tenure with the Celtics, Macauley informed owner Walter Brown and Auerbach they would be helping him out by shipping him home to play in St. Louis.

"We had a one-year-old son whose brain could not function," Macauley said, "and I didn't know if I could play in Boston the next year."

So Macauley went to the Hawks and Russell's arrival in Boston was the cornerstone piece of the Celtics Dynasty. Brown was a great admirer of Macauley's, and he was in his debt – literally for a time. Before the Celtics were a box office success and prior to the days when the NBA became a league where it could almost mint its own money, Brown suffered many financial losses. He later revealed during those lean days Brown was so close to running out of money that he had to write out IOUs in lieu of playoff checks that he could not afford to pay off for nearly a year. Macauley was one of the men who accepted the circumstances without complaint.

That may have been one reason why Brown wrote Macauley a farewell letter of appreciation upon his departure, praising him for his dedication to the franchise and expressing regret over him leaving the team.

Macauley played in every game for the Hawks for the next two seasons at a time when it was a seventy-two-game schedule. His presence helped make St. Louis contenders, and they were stiff rivals to Boston during the first seasons of the Dynasty. In 1957, the Celtics coached by Auerbach defeated the Hawks coached by Alex Hannum 4–3 in the Finals. Macauley, it might be said, was on the wrong side, though he was also joined by Hall-of-Famers Bob Petit and Slater Martin. Macauley had 23 points versus Boston in the opener, 19 in the second game, 16 in the third, 22 in the fourth, 11 in the fifth, but only 4 in the sixth game. His old teammates may have been familiar with Macauley's moves, but they couldn't stop them. In the deciding game, Macauley scored nine points as Boston won, 125–123.

A year later, the same teams found themselves in the Finals again in an equally difficult series. In only one game was Macauley a double-figure scorer. He had been replaced in the starting lineup by young Cliff Hagan, who was also part of the Russell trade, but who had spent two years in the military before breaking in.

The Hawks won the series in six games after Russell sprained an ankle and was ineffective. Even though Macauley had to move halfway across the country, he managed to earn a professional basketball championship ring by beating the team he had departed.

Frank Ramsey

rank Ramsey stood just six-foot-three, and even in the old days of professional basketball, that made him undersized for the forward position he regularly played during his nine-year career with the Boston Celtics. Guard would have seemed more natural, but Bob Cousy and Bill Sharman were already entrenched in the backcourt.

Maybe the real secret of why Ramsey substituted so often at forward off the bench was to relieve six-foot-seven Hall-of-Famer Tom Heinsohn. Ramsey divulged Heinsohn smoked a few cigarettes each halftime, and perhaps that affected his wind and stamina.

Ramsey was one of the foundation pieces of the Celtics Dynasty in the 1950s–1960s era. He was the original model for the sixth-man deployment carried out by Red Auerbach and is formalized today by the National Basketball Association with one of its post-season awards.

By creative use of Ramsey off the bench as a spark, Auerbach instituted a strategy to let one of his best players come into the game when starters from the other team were beginning to tire instead of starting Ramsey himself. No one was using such a game plan when Auerbach introduced it, though now everyone recognizes the wisdom of it as long as they have the proper personnel.

Ramsey was a Kentucky guy all the way. He was born in Corydon in 1931, played for Adolph Rupp's great Wildcat teams at the University of Kentucky, spent his off-seasons in Kentucky, became a banker there after retiring from pro ball, and died in Madisonville at eighty-six in 2018. Some applied the nickname of Kentucky Colonel during his playing days.

Ramsey had a very rural upbringing, mostly on a family farm, not in an environment where colonel ranks were bestowed. He spoke of everyone in the family working twelve-hour days when he was growing up. He plowed and planted and drove a team of mules.

The rest of the time, when he had free time, he competed in sports. Ramsey may have been better at basketball, but he played three years of college baseball, as well, earning all Southeastern Conference honors every season. So he was definitely also pretty talented at that game.

"I may have earned a bachelor's degree in business from UK," Ramsey said, "but I earned a doctorate athletically. I played basketball for one of the greatest coaches ever."

Kentucky won the NCAA basketball title in 1951. The Wildcats were so good they went undefeated one of Ramsey's years and almost never lost games. Ramsey was drafted by the Celtics in 1954, although he faced a military commitment. He was so accustomed to winning all the time at Kentucky that, the first time Boston lost a regular-season game, Ramsey actually broke into tears. He was still getting used to the pro routine where, with so many more games, no team ever comes close to going unbeaten. Two of Ramsey's college teammates were also drafted by Boston, Cliff Hagan and Lou Tsiorpoulus. However, Hagan was shipped to the St. Louis Hawks in the trade that brought Bill Russell to the Celtics. Tsiorpoulous did not have a long pro career.

It was no accident Auerbach drafted all three Kentucky players. "Just knowing they played for Adolph Rupp told me they were motivated and fundamentally sound," Auerbach said.

Wearing No. 23, Ramsey was a mainstay of the Celtics. He played his rookie year in 1954, and then joined the military. When he returned, Ramsey was part of seven straight NBA title teams. As post-season playoffs were about to begin each season, Ramsey developed a routine in the locker room where he made more or less the same speech. He told his teammates now that they had fulfilled their regular-season commitments, and earned the salaries specified in their contracts, they were playing with his money. Players would earn more money the longer the season lasted.

"Yeah, I did that," Ramsey admitted years later. "We all needed the playoff money."

In so many ways, it was a different NBA in the 1950s and into the 1960s. Not only on the court, but in terms of athletes not being highly paid.

"We didn't make a whole lot of money," Ramsey said. "The first year we won the championship, the whole team's salary was under $200,000. I think some of the players today make that much for one game. I was certainly happy with that, though."

The most money Ramsey made in a season, he said, was $20,000.

In the first half of the 1950s, the NBA was still struggling for recognition, many of the teams played in smaller cities, and those affiliations did not last. The arenas were not spanking new and lacked the amenities fans take for granted now.

"The league at that time only had, I think, eight or nine teams," Ramsey said. "I think in Baltimore we were playing in a skating rink, and in Rochester we were playing in a rather old – I don't think it was even an arena – just a gym. The traveling was by train and DC-3s. I guess the camaraderie is what I enjoyed most."

Many years later, Ramsey spoke about his confusion handling the big city of Boston and its traffic patterns, including nearby Cambridge.

"Harvard Square is a circle!" he exclaimed. "You certainly

can get lost because everything they say is a square is like a traffic circle."

Ramsey utilized fantastic planning to compete for Boston as often as he did during the 1956–57 season, appearing in 35 games. He was limited, not because of injury, nor because Red Auerbach didn't want him, but because of his military obligations. Ramsey somehow stitched together one 60-day leave and about 10 three-day passes to play for the Celtics during that campaign.

Ramsey first met Red Auerbach in 1950, when playing basketball in the Catskill Mountains at resorts and being a waiter or some such, was a big-deal college summer job. Bob Cousy once said Auerbach treated everyone the same – gruffly – Ramsey laughed.

"Well, he would come up to you and if he knocked the ashes off his cigar on you, that meant he liked you," Ramsey said.

For that matter, Auerbach had his resemblances to Ramsey's college coach, Adolph Rupp, who once owned the record for most NCAA victories. Ramsey said Rupp had a knack for recruiting rural, naïve, Kentucky kids who dreamed of playing for the state school and turning them into tight-knit units.

"I guess when you played for Kentucky, the coach was a dictator," Ramsey said. "He took boys out of small town... I had never been on an airplane before I went to Kentucky."

Ramsey stood out on the court because of his bright red hair. He also became a constant patient of team trainers, often playing games where his legs were so heavily taped it appeared he was auditioning for a role in "*The Mummy.*" This was done according to a specific plan, Ramsey said much later. He had cartilage problems, but trainer Buddy LeRoux devised a taping system that allowed Ramsey to escape surgery.

Auerbach said he was always happy to have Ramsey on the floor at crunch time. One of the all-time epic games in Celtics history was the seventh game of the 1957 Finals. Boston won its first championship in franchise history, 125–123, in double overtime over the Hawks. Ramsey was a huge factor in both overtimes and nailed the winning shot on a twenty-five-foot one-hander.

"I knew there was no one around to rebound," Ramsey said, "and maybe I shouldn't have taken it. But it went in, so that's all that counts, I guess."

Winning that first crown was memorable. Ramsey remembered Walter Brown providing a team celebration dinner. Ramsey couldn't stick around long because he had to return to Fort Knox for the last two days of his military commitment.

"We had accomplished what we set out to do at the beginning of the year," Ramsey said.

Despite the somewhat unusual manner in which Ramsey received his playing time, he scored in double figures for the Celtics every year he played, except his final one. Ramsey's high point season was the 1957–58 season when he averaged 16.5 points a game and 7.3 rebounds. He averaged more than 15 points a game in four other seasons. Later, Ramsey was inducted into the College Basketball Hall of Fame and the Naismith Memorial Basketball Hall of Fame.

A handful of years after Ramsey retired as a player, he spent one season coaching the Kentucky Colonels of the American Basketball Association. The owners pretty much brought the team to him near his home, or otherwise he likely would not have coached. He was basically a fill-in hired seventeen games into the season. Kentucky went 32–35 under Ramsey's leadership, but squeaked into the playoffs.

Ramsey had come close to becoming Auerbach's successor in Boston when Auerbach moved to the front office, but the timing was not good for him. His father was ill, and he moved into the banking world back in Kentucky instead.

In 2008, a tornado hit Ramsey's hometown of Madisonville. His house was wrecked, and he suffered serious financial losses and could have been killed. However, he was not injured.

When Ramsey passed away from natural causes in 2018, the Celtics' statement of appreciation referred to him as "the original sixth-man" and described Ramsey as a player who helped develop the team's legacy of selflessness that "remains part of the Boston Celtics ethos to this day."

Russell, Ramsey's teammate from the Dynasty era, issued a twitter message lamenting the death of one of his old partners:

> *"I am in shock & deeply saddened of my long-time friend and teammate Frank Ramsey passing. I had the great pleasure to speak with him often. He won 7 NBA and 1 NCAA title & was the 1st true 6th man. He was a great man & father. I will miss him!"*

Frank Ramsey was one of those guys Red Auerbach liked enough to spill those cigar ashes on, and decades after retirement, Ramsey stayed in touch.

"I always called him on his birthday," Ramsey said.

Jim Loscutoff

**O**ne legendary Celtics figure who was adorned with the perfect nickname was Jim Loscutoff. Muscular, six-foot-five, and 220 pounds, Loscutoff's perpetual Marine crew-cut and gigantic biceps gave him a tough-guy image that was real but also purposely cultivated. In the 1950s and early 1960s, the National Basketball Association was a less genteel league.

They called Loscutoff "Jungle Jim" and that was just right. He was the enforcer, the protector of Celtics players with more finesse and better-scoring touches. He was the team bodyguard and you had to go through "Loscy" to get to the others, or, if you were foolish enough to do so, he would retaliate, somehow accidentally knocking you about thirty feet from the lane with a subtle elbow.

The league itself was rougher at the time, and teams needed men like Loscutoff so they would not be pushed around. In nine seasons, Loscutoff, who came out of the University of Oregon for the 1955–56 season, just once averaged more than 10 points in a season. He did average nearly three fouls per game in eighteen-and-a-half minutes of playing time. During his playing career, Loscutoff collected seven championship rings.

Boston Garden fans understood precisely in what role Red Auerbach employed Loscy. Their expectations for him were different than they were for other players. Scoring? Didn't matter. Loscutoff was the guy you called if you were being bullied, and he delivered justice. How much of Loscutoff's image was real and how much was exaggerated?

"I think my reputation helped me," he said. "Of course, a lot of it got blown out of proportion. But I enjoyed it. Put it this way, they knew something was going to happen when I was on the court."

Off the court, Loscutoff was a different person. He was friendly, genial, and chatty. He ran a summer basketball camp and spent years as head coach at Boston State. There he taught X's and O's, not focusing, for the most part, on how he played during games.

"This was an opportunity to stay in the game," Loscutoff said during his Boston State days when he was no longer running up and down the court training for the Celtics.

Later, not wanting to go head-to-head with his players, Loscutoff worked out to keep his weight down somewhat by playing tennis, squash, badminton and handball. "If I didn't exercise, I'd weigh two-eighty," he said, simultaneously making fun of his old teammate Tommy Heinsohn's personal battle of the post-career bulge.

While an all-league player at Oregon, Loscutoff never gave much thought to a pro basketball career. The NBA was still going through growing pains and the league was small, with just eight teams and 10 players on a roster. He was surprised to be a No. 1 draft pick – Auerbach knew exactly what his team needed. Even so, Loscutoff did not expect to make the cut. "It was a thrill in itself making the team," he said. "But my biggest thrill in pro ball was winning that first world championship."

Some years after he retired and was coaching, Loscutoff joked that he would bet some fans in Los Angeles, New York, and Philadelphia still remembered him because of the rivalries and, really, how he could make some players cringe when they had to go up against him.

During the 1972 Summer Olympics, Loscutoff said, he was watching the United States play Russia in men's basketball when some kind of minor fight broke out. The commenting team included his old teammate Bill Russell along with Keith Jackson, and Jackson said, "Shades of Jim Loscutoff." Loscutoff said everyone in the room where he was watching the telecast looked over at him.

"People know me because of that tough image," he said. "I'm remembered, and I can't say that doesn't make me feel good."

The Celtics have numerous retired numbers honored on banners hanging from the rafters above their home court. Loscutoff, who passed away in 2015 at eighty-five, wore No. 18, but that number was not immediately retired. Later, Hall-of-Famer Dave Cowens wore the same number, and afterwards it was retired. To appropriately honor both men, the number is noted on a banner with Loscutoff's nickname "Loscy." Apparently, the space was too small to stencil on "Jungle Jim."

Gene Conley

**F**ew professional athletes have enjoyed the kind of career Gene Conley had, competing in Major League Baseball and in the National Basketball Association while winning championships in both. The six-foot-eight Conley was both a forward-center for the Boston Celtics and a big-league pitcher for eleven years, competing for four teams including the Boston Red Sox.

A small number of athletes have succeeded at the top level in more than one American professional sports league, including Hall of Fame quarterback Otto Graham and long-time catcher Del Rice, both of who also won rings in the NBA. Then there was Bo Jackson and Deion Sanders, both of whom were better football players than baseball players, but who managed to pull off the time-consuming trick more recently than the others.

Conley, who was born in 1930, was a college basketball star at Washington State University before joining the Celtics for the 1952–1953 season. Red Auerbach did not want Conley to tackle baseball and basketball at the same time. For a while, Conley switched to only big-league ball. He changed his mind and defied the objections of pro team officials when he realized he had the opportunity to make far more money in his off-seasons in another pro league than he could as either an insurance or car salesman, as many teammates did.

Guard Bill Sharman, who also excelled at baseball and basketball (spending a month on the Brooklyn Dodgers' bench as they blew the 1951 pennant), was the connector between Conley and Auerbach, telling the coach that his taller friend could really play and help the basketball team.

When Conley shifted his primary focus to baseball for much of the 1950s, he became a four-time All-Star, won a World Series championship with the Milwaukee Braves, and became the winning pitcher in the 1955 All-Star game. He hurled for the Red Sox, the Philadelphia Phillies, and the Boston Braves before they transferred to Milwaukee. Once, during that stretch of his semi-retirement from basketball, Conley was going to take a new offer to rejoin the Celtics, but the Braves actually matched the deal, paying him not to play hoops.

Eventually, Conley returned to the Celtics for the 1958–59 season and mostly served as a reserve center behind Bill Russell. At first, Auerbach was not enthusiastic about taking Conley back. He offered a tryout only, but no guarantees, since Conley had been away from the sport for six years. He told Conley if he got cut, he would have to pay his own way home.

"Somehow, I made the team," Conley said.

He may no longer have been as sharp as he was during his college days when he led the old Pac-8 Conference in scoring, but he still could play. During this stint with the Celtics, Conley was a member of three NBA championship teams in 1959, 1960, and 1961, so things turned out well for everyone.

Due to his early affiliation with the Braves, Conley was the first athlete to represent three professional teams in the same city, the Braves, Celtics, and Red Sox.

"I had such a unique and unusual career," Conley said. "Those two sports, it's a tough one now. I went without spring training for years. They tried to keep me from doing it in those days. Just about the time they'd want me to stop, I'd have a halfway decent year –the timing was perfect– and I'd say, 'See? It really helped me.'"

His baseball team owners became particularly grumpy when Conley chose to stay with the Celtics past the end of the regular season. In the early 1960s, the NBA season was shorter and the playoffs did not run into June, but they did overrun spring training, and the playoffs represented the most important time of the basketball season.

Once, when under pressure to abandon the Celtics for the Braves, Conley expressed his feelings. "I feel I have an obligation to owner Walter Brown to stick with the Celtics and help if I can until the playoffs are over," Conley said.

Conley's heyday with the Celtics was at an awkward time in American society's race relations. Conley, who was white, said Boston's basketball bunch mixed just fine. As tumult infected the outside world, it was all peace and harmony with the Celtics. There were white stars like Bob Cousy, Tommy Heinsohn, and Bill Sharman and African-American stars like Bill Russell, Sam Jones, K.C. Jones, and Tom Sanders.

"The core was the same," Conley said of the long-term makeup of the Celtics. "They didn't break up. Race was not an issue. We were too busy going to the Y and working out and playing the next game. Black or white, the players didn't know the difference."

As a baseball player, Conley won double-figure games four times with a high of fifteen games in a season. The 1954 season was his best earned-run-average year at 2.96. The last year he pitched was 1963.

Conley's basketball role was basically as a back-up, and his career scoring average was 5.9 points a game with 6.3 rebounds a game. Although his hoops career was spread over more than a decade, Conley only actually played in five seasons wrapped around his baseball career.

Conley, who died at age eighty-six in 2017, was probably a better baseball player than basketball player, but he was very useful for the Celtics when they had him. In some ways it is probably a bit difficult to rate Conley as a player in either sport because his career was so fragmented compared to those athletes who devote themselves single-mindedly to one sport.

As a teammate, Conley kept his fellow playmates laughing. Sometimes it was because he became wittier the more he drank, sometimes it was just shooting the breeze, regaling baseball players with tales of the basketball world and vice versa. He stopped the presses once when he enticed Red Sox teammate Pumpsie Green to depart a team bus stuck in traffic with him by suggesting they suddenly head to Israel. They disappeared for a day or two, but never actually made a serious attempt at the overseas foray.

During his fascinating athletic career, Conley was a teammate of Ted Williams and Hank Aaron in baseball and Bob Cousy and Bill Russell in basketball.

"Basketball, to me, was easier to play because it was an instinctive game," Conley said later in life. "You can watch it, and you know instinctively what to do. Baseball is more of a thinking game."

Sam Jones

**D**eadly outside shooting in the clutch was the main thing guard Sam Jones was known for during his long career with the Boston Celtics. Unlike most other sharpshooters, Jones was not known for his swishes, but for his bank shots, precisely firing the ball off the backboard and into the hoop. For his knowledge of angles and use of the glass, Jones could have majored in geometry.

A native of North Carolina, Jones attended tiny, almost-off-the-radar North Carolina Central in the early 1950s, but Red Auerbach found him and made him the Celtics' No. 1 draft pick in 1957. Auerbach knew of Jones through a recommendation from former Boston player Bones McKinney, then coaching Wake Forest. Trusting in this scouting report, Auerbach chose Jones without even seeing him play.

People sometimes forget that in the 1950s, college basketball was not on national television. There was no sophisticated scouting, and a coach without assistant coaches and almost no front office help was pulled in many directions.

"I was so damn busy," Auerbach said. "I didn't know who to draft." He asked McKinney if there was anyone in his area who could play. "Bones told me this kid Sam Jones was as fast as lightning."

Jones was an extraordinary discovery. His magical shooting touch led him into the Naismith Memorial Basketball

Hall of Fame after his playing days. Those playing days were marvelous. Jones won 10 championship rings during his tenure with the Celtics, the second-most in National Basketball Association history after Bill Russell's eleven.

When the Celtics set the record by winning eight world titles in a row between 1959 and 1966, only three players were on the roster for the entire season – Russell, K.C. Jones, and Sam Jones. Sam Jones and K.C. Jones had somewhat parallel careers with Boston, even though they were very different types of players. For a time, they were second-string together, and then they were paired as starters. They were so often lumped together in conversation that announcer Johnny Most regularly referred to them as "The Jones boys."

North Carolina Central is a historically African-American institution, which was at the time, a member of the NAIA, not the NCAA, and its basketball program was not widely known when Sam Jones was setting records there under Floyd Brown and famed coach John McClendon. Jones attended between 1951 and 1954, but then his college days were interrupted by military service. Jones was not a complete unknown. The Minneapolis Lakers drafted him during his first period in school, but he completed his eligibility in 1956 and 1957 and that made him available for the basketball draft again. Jones's college number is retired by his school.

Before Jones established his reputation as an uncanny shooter, teammate Bob Cousy appreciated his speed on the court in practice, saying Jones was "the fastest thing ever seen" when he ran.

K.C. Jones, whose best attributes revolved around defense and passing, may not have been jealous of Sam Jones's superb shooting skills, but he definitely admired them.

"I was totally amazed by his ability to shoot balls," K.C. Jones said. "I recall one time he was about six feet from the basket, and he's saying to the guy going up to block his shot, 'Oh baby, you can't get this.'"

If Sam Jones uttered such phrases during games, he was

a much more vociferous trash talker than fans ever knew. To the public, he was more Serene Sam, not chatty at all, almost-always looking serious on the court rather than playful or outgoing. His demeanor was of a player routinely going about his business without flash.

K.C. Jones agreed with Cousy about Sam Jones's speed. He also described it as somewhat deceptive, his backcourt partner able to accelerate like a sports car.

"He had a way of coming down the sideline with the ball when he was running, but it looked like he was just taking his time," K.C. Jones said. "Then he'd fly by you at eighty miles per hour."

For a time, some fans thought Sam and K.C. Jones were brothers. They were both African-American and shared the same last name, but they did not look alike, and they were only two of thousands of Americans, black and white, named Jones.

The NBA was a shorter league when Jones was breaking in, and his size of six-foot-four and 200 pounds was an asset. He could shoot over six-foot guards and muscle around lighter ones to drive to the hoop.

A terrific scorer, Jones once threw down 51 points in a game for the Celtics, and he was chosen for five All-Star games over his twelve seasons with Boston.

Originally, Jones was a bench player. Both he and K.C. Jones had the problem of being on the roster of a team that already had Cousy and Bill Sharman, two Hall-of-Famers, starting in the backcourt. For a time, Sam Jones averaged less than half a game of playing time, though when the older men retired, he became not only a starter, but a star.

During the Dynasty period of 1957 to 1969, the Celtics had Hall-of-Famers starting at every position. Jones began to truly make his mark during the 1960–61 season, his fourth year in the NBA, when he averaged 15 points a game. His scoring average rose from there, to 18.4, 19.7, and then during the 1964–65 season, Jones hit for 25.9 points per game. That was his career high, but he also averaged more than 21 points a game in three other seasons.

That type of consistent scoring breeds confidence. When it is said shooters are "in the zone," it means they have a hot hand. Sam Jones did not brag about his game, nor did he strut on the court, but his teammates knew other sides of him. Behind the scenes, in the locker room or in practice, he could out-run them in sprint drills and out-play them in card games, dominoes, or pool.

Consistent with K.C. Jones's depiction of Sam Jones zooming past others on the court, at times announcer Most employed "Slippery Sam" as a nickname.

Sam Jones did change facial expression on the court, while also exhibiting his cool in a stressful situation during a game played on April 1, 1962. In a famous incident in Celtics lore, Jones found himself nearly under attack, or at least threatened, by the huge Wilt Chamberlain. Chamberlain, the greatest scorer in NBA history, engaged in numerous memorable duels with Bill Russell. They were the two giants of the game, and any time Boston met one of Chamberlain's teams, including this night against the Philadelphia Warriors, tensions were high and games were intense.

The seven-foot-one, 275-pound Chamberlain versus the six-foot-four 200-pound Jones would have been no contest in a fight. Jones had somewhat piqued Chamberlain's anger, no doubt playing help defense in the low post by harassing the big man, and Chamberlain decided to take action. He went after Jones. Jones retreated, back-pedaling to an end line of the court. Then Jones dipped down and grabbed a little photographer's stool as a shield, just in case. That gave him the appearance of defending himself in the manner of a lion tamer. No blows were thrown, but Jones's instinct in grabbing a potential equalizer weapon is the enduring image from the scene.

"He wanted to break my arm," Jones said of Chamberlain's intent. "If I'm going to fight him, I'm not going to fight fair." As

Jones well knew, Chamberlain possessed enormous strength and there had been talk of the big basketball player entering the ring to fight heavyweight champion Muhammad Ali. That publicity-gimmick bout never came off, but neither did Jones-Chamberlain. "So I grabbed the stool. Naturally, I wasn't going to tangle with a guy that size, so I made sure I had some protection."

Jones particularly excelled in the playoffs. He competed in 154 playoff games for the Celtics, and his scoring average almost always went up during those big games. For seven consecutive seasons, Jones averaged a minimum of 20 points per game in the playoffs. In 1965, he averaged 28.6 points for the team's twelve playoff games while averaging 41.3 minutes played per game, as well.

In 1966, he averaged 24.8 points and in 1967 he averaged 26.7. The Celtics were very much a share-the-ball team during the regular season, but those offensive options seemed to narrow in the playoffs when it was must-win time. Jones got more shots and made more shots. It is not always remembered that Jones retired at the same time as Russell, most likely Jones recognizing a fallow period coming for the team.

During that last Finals against the Los Angeles Lakers, Jones hit the winning shot in one game, one last dagger through the heart for the Celtics' chief rival of the time to remember him by. It was not unusual for Jones to take the last shot when Boston was in a tight game, but this was one he almost missed.

Jones's number was called on a play practiced, but never before used in a game. The ball went to him for a twenty-two-foot jump shot. Just as he released his normally picturesque shot, Jones slipped, throwing himself off-balance. His aim was affected and Jones's shot caromed off the front rim, the backboard and the back of the rim. Still, it went in and Boston was victorious.

"I was lucky," was Jones's basic analysis of that shot.

Jones turned thirty-six shortly after retiring in 1969. He

had started pro ball late because of his two-year military commitment during college, so he felt the time was right. Jones did try coaching in various forums, spending 1969 to 1973 at Federal City College and then 1973–74 at North Carolina Central. He returned to the NBA briefly, as an assistant coach for the New Orleans Jazz, 1974–75.

As a professional, recognition had come only gradually to Jones, but he received his share once he gained full-time playing status.

In later years, he was even more greatly rewarded. Jones's No. 24 uniform was retired by the Celtics.

Jones, who passed away at eighty-eight years old in December of 2021, was voted as a member of the NBA's 25th and 50th anniversary teams and was inducted into the Hall of Fame.

K.C. Jones

One of the greatest defensive guards in basketball history, K.C. Jones is one of the greatest winners in the history of North American professional sport. Most of those triumphs came with the Boston Celtics – first as a player, then as a coach – but even more were generated dating back to college when he first became a teammate of Bill Russell's.

The soft-spoken Jones, born in 1932 in Taylor, Texas, was a six-foot-one, 200-pound guard with muscle. He was a slick playmaker with exceptional smarts running an offense. Long removed from Texas, Jones played his high school ball in San Francisco before enrolling at San Francisco University in 1952.

Jones and Russell headlined the high points of the program, leading the Dons to consecutive NCAA championships in 1955 and 1956. He was the Celtics' No. 2 draft pick in 1956. Jones and Russell postponed signing with Boston that year because of the opportunity to play in the Summer Olympics for the United States. The Games were held in Melbourne, Australia, from November to December, so they delayed beginning their National Basketball Association careers.

Then Jones volunteered for the Army, so he did not suit up for Boston until 1958. For a short time after college, Jones, who had the strength to be a defensive back, considered becoming a professional football player. He tried out for the Los Angeles

Rams, but after a surprisingly good showing in the defensive backfield in training camp, a calcium deposit in his leg sidelined him. In the end he stuck with hoops, departing the Rams and asking Red Auerbach to try out for the Celtics long after they drafted him.

Jones was not even a surefire college basketball prospect. He was quick, but he was short until his senior year when he spurted four inches. He was also a mediocre outside shooter. But Jones had the intangible of being a winner, and other talents. Being so strongly identified with Russell, San Francisco's championships, and an Olympic gold medal outweighed any liabilities. In addition to his two-year military stint, Jones sat out one season in college because of his appendix. By 1958, he might have been an old rookie at twenty-six, but he was ready.

Jones believed his time spent in the Army helped him in the pros. He thought he was a better player later and felt "that if I had gone to a tryout with the Celtics straight from college, I would not have made the squad."

It was true that, even when he did at last become a Celtic, Jones was a little rough around the edges. It was also accurate that, for a small man in a big man's game, Jones was not a good outside shooter. But Auerbach appreciated Jones's passing and the same kind of hard-nosed defense that the Rams liked. He was also not being counted on as an instant starter. The Celtics had Bob Cousy and Bill Sharman at the time, so Jones was really being groomed for the future. He was elected to the Naismith Memorial Basketball Hall of Fame with a lifetime scoring average of 7.4 points per game, so his other attributes had to be major-league impressive.

Ultimately, Jones spent nine years as a pro player, all with Boston, and won eight championship rings. The only other players in NBA history who won more were his teammates Russell (eleven) and Sam Jones (ten). K.C. Jones later added to his collection during his long career as an assistant coach and head coach.

One reason Jones thought his late move to the Celtics was fortuitous was because the passage of time for others. Cousy and Sharman were well into their careers, so it was obvious that, soon enough, Boston would need backcourt help.

"A team loaded with great players was getting older," Jones said. "I made the squad. I'm sure it was by the skin of my teeth." Jones said Auerbach later told him that the Celtics seemed to play better when he came into games, even if it was not because he lit up the scoreboard. "If we were behind when I walked in, we were closer when I got out. If we were ahead when I came in, we increased our lead by the time I came out."

Well, maybe not at first. His rookie year, the 1958–59 season, Jones played just over twelve minutes per game in forty-nine appearances and averaged 3.5 points. As he gained experience, Jones contributed more. His second season he played in seventy-four games while averaging 6.3 points. After that, Jones played more and more. He never averaged more than 9.2 points per game in a single season, but his assist totals kept growing, as well as playing time. Eventually, there came the day when with both Cousy and Sharman were retired and he and Sam Jones constituted the starting guard tandem for the Celtics.

Not only did the Celtics have great players during the Dynasty years, running in player after player who became a Hall-of-Famer but Jones said the club had unbelievable chemistry. He quoted Auerbach as saying, "The Celtics aren't a team – they are a way of life" and concurring with the sentiment.

"It's almost impossible to describe the feeling that the players on our teams had for one another," Jones said. "Every player on those winning teams supported his teammates. We had great personal ties on the court and off the court and possessed a sense of togetherness that you could feel."

Jones was part of the remarkable stretch of eight NBA titles in eight seasons when the Celtics ruled the world between 1959 and 1966. He chose to retire after the 1966–67 season when the streak was interrupted. He was playing at about the same level with 6.2 points a game and 5.0 assists on his resume in seventy-eight games, but Jones recognized he was aging as a basketball player and when a feeler was sent his way to become a college coach, he mulled it and accepted.

"It was time to step away," Jones said. "During the 1965-66 season I started thinking about life after basketball."

It turned out there was life after the Celtics, but not life after basketball. Brandeis University, in nearby Waltham, Massachusetts sought Jones as a coach. He said he consulted with Auerbach, who recommended that he play one more year. During that time, Jones was able to recruit players for his first team. Jones coached the NCAA Division III program from 1967 to 1970, kicking off a long and fruitful coaching career with many stops and rewards.

Jones spent one season as an assistant coach at Harvard University before being summoned back to the NBA by, of all teams, the Los Angeles Lakers, the Celtics' chief rival. The job offer was to become old teammate Bill Sharman's assistant coach.

"I felt comfortable with Bill," Jones said. "We'd spent so many years beating each other up during practice, and we'd been through the playoff wars together. It was an easy decision to make."

It was also a serendipitous decision. Jones joined the great Lakers squad of 1971–72 that won the championship. A new ring for his collection. That was Jones's only season with LA. As often happens for assistants with title teams, other teams wished to poach him, and Jones gained his first professional head coaching job with the American Basketball Association's San Diego Conquistadors.

That was another short-lived position, but again Jones was moving up. From 1973 to 1976, Jones was the coach of the Capital Bullets, later renamed the Washington Bullets. The 1974–75 Bullets finished 60–22, featured such stars as Elvin

Hayes and Wes Unseld, and reached the Finals.

"The Bullets were a good team when I got there, and they got better," Jones said.

When Washington dropped off by twelve games and finished second in its division the next year, Jones was done there.

He spent a year with the Milwaukee Bucks as an assistant coach, and then returned to Boston as an assistant between 1978 and 1983. He once joked that this job could be described as "The kid comes home."

Jones succeeded Bill Fitch as boss of the Celtics and led his old franchise to two more NBA championships in 1984 and 1986, spanning the team generations from the days of Bob Cousy and Bill Russell to the days of Larry Bird and Kevin McHale.

When Boston won the '84 crown under Jones he was quietly ecstatic. He had gone through some tough times being fired in Washington and Milwaukee and now was back on top of the NBA, adding to the legend of the team he played with as a coaching leader.

"Celtic Pride was back," Jones thought as he sipped his champagne.

When Jones was coming out of high school, he admitted to almost terminal shyness. He and Russell have told the story of how he practically never uttered a word during his first month in college in San Francisco. His confidence level on the NBA bench was a million times higher but he was not a demonstrative head coach. He was not a yeller. He had a gift for getting strong-willed stars on board for his program without alienating them.

In Boston in the 1980s, that was exactly what was needed for a team loaded with strong-minded stars. He provided the overriding guidance. This was especially true for the 1986 title team, which is regarded as one of the best ever. Key players were Bird, McHale, Robert Parish, Bill Walton, and Dennis Johnson.

Jones was aggrieved when critics suggested this meant he was a do-nothing coach. They wanted fire, but he was ice.

"Many people ask me why I never seem to lose my cool during a game," Jones said at the time. "Once in a while I do. I boil over. When that happens, it's usually directed at the referees."

The results, though, were Jones's real rebuttal. As a player, assistant coach, and head coach, Jones was part of twelve NBA championship teams. He was inducted into the College Basketball Hall of Fame and the Naismith in Springfield, Massachusetts. The track record is enviable.

Boston Celtics Chief Rivals

1. Los Angeles Lakers. Forever.

The first time the Celtics and Lakers met in the National Basketball Association Finals with the championship at stake, the Lakers were still located in Minneapolis. The last time the Celtics won the NBA crown in 2008, the foil was also the Lakers. Eight other times in-between, Boston and Los Angeles met in the championship round. This crossed different eras, but only twice did the Lakers best the Celtics when the title was on the line.

The first era encompassed the Celtics Dynasty years with Bob Cousy, Bill Russell, Tommy Heinsohn, and the other Boston stars of the late 1950s and early 1960s. Although the Celtics won three titles in the 1970s, none came over the Lakers. The intense rivalry was rekindled, however, in the 1980s when Larry Bird was the signature star for Boston, and Magic Johnson was the alpha star for the Lakers. During that decade, Los Angeles won five championships and Boston three. On two occasions, LA beat Boston head-to-head, and Boston beat LA head-to-head once.

Throughout the course of NBA history, the Celtics had registered the most titles with seventeen, but recently, the Lakers, who represented the NBA's first dynasty in Minneapolis, equaled that total.

2. St. Louis Hawks. 1957–1961.

During the earliest days of the Celtics dynasty, the second-best team in the league was St. Louis. Once the

Tri-Cities Blackhawks, and eventually the Atlanta Hawks, the St. Louis Hawks met the Celtics three times in four years in the Finals, winning the 1958 NBA crown when Bill Russell sprained an ankle. The Hawks were led by the terrific trio of Hall-of-Famers Bob Pettit, Cliff Hagan, and Clyde Lovellette, who at the end of his career joined Boston as Russell's backup.

3. Philadelphia 76ers. Mid-1960s.

For the 1966–67 season, the 76ers were about as good as anyone in history. They established a then-record finest mark of 68–13 and won the title over the San Francisco Warriors. That club featured Wilt Chamberlain, Billy Cunningham, Hal Greer, Chet Walker, and Lucious Jackson, as well as veterans Larry Costello and Dave Gambee.

That was one of the two seasons in the midst of Boston's eleven titles in thirteen years streak that the Celtics did not win the championship. All of the teams' games, regular-season and playoffs, during this period were rugged affairs, and the game where John Havlicek stole the ball to preserve a Celtics playoff victory took place during this era.

4.   New York Knicks. 1970–1974.

Except for this narrow window of time, the Knicks were not truly a serious Celtics rival beyond the proximity of the two teams' home arenas. Since New Yorkers felt they had pretty much invented basketball, this was to the team's chagrin. The Knicks were just not very good for long periods of time. That semi-perpetual doormat status was alleviated by a talented group of players in the early 1970s. Willis Reed, Walt Frazier, Bill Bradley, Earl Monroe, Dave Debusschere, Jerry Lucas, and Dick Barnett led the Knicks to the 1970 and 1973 crowns under coach Red Holzman.

5. **Cincinnati Royals. 1960–1970.**
    One of the most unusual franchises in NBA history, this
    club began life as the Rochester Royals (and won a title
    in 1951), became the Cincinnati Royals, made a stop in
    Kansas City and plays on as the Sacramento Kings.

    For the decade of the 1960s, the Royals featured Oscar
    Robertson. If there is any other legitimate claimant to
    the best basketball player who ever lived besides Michael
    Jordan, it is Robertson, aka "The Big O." Robertson could
    do anything on the court. In addition to scoring, he was
    a brilliant passer and a strong rebounder at six-feet, five-
    inches.

    Even supplemented by stars Jack Twyman and
    Wayne Embry, Robertson could never lead the Royals
    past the Celtics in the Eastern Division playoffs. It took
    a trade to the Milwaukee Bucks for Robertson to win a
    championship in the twilight of his career.

Tommy Heinsohn

ommy Heinsohn was the only man that has been officially connected to the Boston Celtics longer than Red Auerbach. He was a championship player for the organization, a coach of the team, and a broadcaster. Still on the air in 2020, he began his playing career in 1956.

Heinsohn saw it all: all seventeen world championships, somehow participating in one way or another, as well as the other four times Boston reached the National Basketball Association Finals and did not win the title.

In its own way, Heinsohn's career was one of the most astonishing runs in professional sport. That type of longevity for anything is remarkable. Through every stage of his adulthood, Heinsohn was connected to the Celtics, spanning generations of fans.

As a player, Heinsohn was listed on rosters at six-foot-seven, and he weighed about 220 pounds. Born in Jersey City, New Jersey, Heinsohn attended Holy Cross College, Bob Cousy's alma mater, in 1953. Holy Cross is located in Worcester, Massachusetts, about thirty-five miles from Boston.

In some ways, Heinsohn outdid Cousy for the Crusaders. When he departed Holy Cross, he was the school's all-time leading scorer, and, in one game against arch rival Boston College, Heinsohn scored 51 points. Auerbach did not have to go far to scout Heinsohn. In the 1950s, when the NBA was still a fledgling league and teams sought every advantage to increase attendance, clubs could draft local stars with so-called territorial picks. Boston made Heinsohn such a choice in 1956.

Unlike center Bill Russell, who was late to join the Celtics that season because of his commitment to the United States Olympic team, Heinsohn attended training camp and won a starting position immediately. That leg up on Russell enabled Heinsohn to be chosen rookie of the year. Heinsohn averaged 16.2 points and 9.8 rebounds a game in his first season.

It was often said that, during his playing days, Heinsohn never met a shot he didn't like. Hence, one of his nicknames was "Tommy Gun." A variation nickname was "Ack Ack." Rare enough for a forward, Heinsohn possessed a hook shot, usually in the arsenal of centers who patrolled the foul lane. Heinsohn, though, regularly surprised defenders – and even Boston fans – by wielding a hook from the corner. Most would consider that a low-percentage shot, but somehow Heinsohn made enough of them to keep defenders wary. He was so closely identified with the hook shot that, later in life when he wrote a book about his life in basketball, Heinsohn titled it *"Give 'Em The Hook."* Those who recalled his career chuckled at that. There was a story behind why Heinsohn even developed a hook shot. When he was a youngster on the playgrounds, he went up against many taller and older kids.

Heinsohn was a key member of the Celtics' first championship team in his first season. In a nine-season playing career, Boston won eight world titles. He was a six-time All-Star selection. Following his rookie season, Heinsohn went on a scoring binge, recording higher figures and going from 17.8 points to 18.8 points to 21.7 points in consecutive seasons. His career high was 22.1 points per game in 1961–62.

With another team, Heinsohn might well have scored

more, but Boston had reliable depth. The most playing time Heinsohn ever averaged in a season was about thirty-two minutes per game, which is about two-thirds the length of an NBA game. In that different era, athletes generally did not take as much care of their bodies, and Heinsohn was a regular smoker. He may have needed those rest periods on the bench.

Surprisingly, Auerbach did not object to Heinsohn's puffing. It was before the Surgeon General's warning reports came out, though later Auerbach was sarcastic about Heinsohn and cigarettes. "If Heinsohn wanted to kill himself, that was OK with me," Auerbach said. "As long as it didn't make him run any slower."

Auerbach was the personnel maven, as well as the coach on the sidelines during Heinsohn's playing days. He built the Dynasty and perpetuated it. "Red Auerbach was a management genius," Heinsohn said. "He banded us together. Eight guys went into the Hall of Fame. One way or another, we had exceptional talent."

While some fans and basketball observers assume the talent was not as developed during the 1950s–1960s era compared to now since everything improves over time, Heinsohn notes that there were only eight teams in the league with ten players each, meaning, "Only eighty players were making a living from a pool of basketball players."

There are currently thirty NBA teams, with five starters each, for 150 players alone in those roles.

"All of a sudden, seventy or so of those guys wouldn't have made the league," Heinsohn said.

Boston was primed for a breakthrough in 1956–57, and that year, with Heinsohn, the Celtics won their first crown over the St. Louis Hawks in the Finals. It was a tone-setting championship.

"We came in with a boatload of confidence," Heinsohn said. "The veterans were so anxious to win. We talked basketball all the time. We tried to get off to a great start so everyone understood what we were capable of doing. We were driven to win. The Boston Celtics of that era were not ego-driven. We wanted to be the best."

Certainly one of the greatest games of Heinsohn's career – and most important big-game performance – was the seventh game in that Hawks showdown series when he scored 37 points and collected 23 rebounds. In fact, Heinsohn was the team's high scorer throughout the playoffs that year.

In the first half of the 1950s, players were lucky to command $10,000 salaries. Auerbach felt the responsibility to owner Walter Brown to keep the payroll down. The games were not all sellouts, and Brown lost a lot of money in his early years running the team. Only Heinsohn (and teammate Frank Ramsey) waited until Auerbach was out of town to try to negotiate with Brown "because they knew he was a softie," Auerbach said. "I finally had to tell Walter he wasn't allowed to negotiate contracts anymore without me in the room."

Speaking of the issue of money, while NBA players in the modern age make millions upon millions per season, any type of movement to get owners to share their wealth in the past was a tug of war. The beginnings of the NBA players union were initiated by Bob Cousy. Cousy believed in the cause, but he was such a big star and so popular in Boston, it was understood the team could not dump him because of his labor activity. Gains were minimal, and then Heinsohn became the second union president.

Heinsohn took over and again only small gains were made in negotiations. The biggest names in the league decided to take a stand at the 1964 All-Star game. The game, scheduled for the Boston Garden, was scheduled to be nationally televised. The players said they would boycott the game, hurting the league's image and costing quite a bit of money, if the owners did not immediately agree to establish a pension plan for which they had been lobbying for ages. The owners, Brown included, were furious, much of the anger directed at Heinsohn as the front man, but the agreement was sealed.

The Celtics kept winning, and Heinsohn kept scoring,

but no one from the Celtics came close to leading the NBA in scoring. The attack was too diversified.

"I wasn't afraid to shoot, but I wasn't a ball hog," Heinsohn said.

He established a reputation as a jokester in the locker room and tricked Auerbach into lighting up exploding cigars.

Heinsohn's NBA career was not especially long. He retired after nine seasons when he was only thirty years old. When Auerbach announced he was giving up coaching and moving full-time to the front office, he initially asked Heinson to succeed him after 1965. Heinsohn wanted to do so, but realized the only person besides Auerbach who could motivate Russell was Russell. Russell became player-coach.

Instead, Heinsohn handled radio work from 1966 to 1969 – Auerbach's suggestion – and then became Celtics coach when Russell retired. Heinsohn took over in 1969 and stayed in the role through 1978. His biggest problem was that Russell and Sam Jones retired, so the talent level was thin at first. Heinsohn's first season was a losing one, but Boston rebuilt quickly, and the Celtics won two more championships on his watch in 1974 and 1976. Jo Jo White, Paul Silas, and Don Nelson were the biggest contributors.

Auerbach informed Heinsohn that Cowens might be small for a center, but was a special player. "I didn't know what he was capable of until I saw him play," Heinsohn said. "I immediately said, 'Wow, this guy is the perfect bundle of energy and ferocity."

Heinsohn's lifetime coaching mark was 427–263, or just about a .620 winning percentage.

After coaching, Heinsohn resumed broadcasting on television and radio. He has a raspy voice, not what schools would call stylish for the work, but he brought his status as Celtics legend to work with him, and the jokester that was in him as a player stayed alive on the air. One of his trademark phrases include "Tommy Points," verbally awarded to players for showing extra hustle on the court.

As he aged, Heinsohn's role diminished slightly. He gave up road games, though he worked as a studio analyst when the team was traveling. Heinsohn had a health scare during the 2018–19 season, but rebounded and rejoined the team before season's end.

After his playing days ended, the Celtics retired Heinsohn's No. 15 jersey. He was inducted into the Naismith Memorial Hall of Fame as a player in 1986. Then he cracked the small fraternity of basketball figures inducted twice, honored again as a coach in 2015.

"It was totally unexpected, to tell you the truth," Heinsohn said of the coaching recognition.

Bill Russell

The greatest winner in professional sports history, two numbers define Bill Russell's thirteen-year career with the Boston Celtics in a way not even his intangibles did. During Russell's playing career, the Celtics won eleven world championships. Russell was selected Most Valuable Player of the NBA five times.

It is less precise how to explain to the modern fan how Russell revolutionized his sport, but overall defense and shot-blocking are two places to start. Russell stood just under six-foot-ten, not tall by current pro basketball standards, but he was a center and nothing but, with tremendous jumping ability and timing. A one-time track and field high jumper, Russell was able to apply that leaping talent to rebounding and playing defense.

Until Russell came along, the tallest players in basketball employed their height to block the shots of smaller men, but a typical blocked shot would sail into the stands, and the offensive team retained possession. Russell changed the dynamic of the play by not only blocking the shot, but often tapping it to himself rather than swatting it over the horizon. It was very demoralizing for the shooter and his team.

Russell, who was a left-handed shooter, was born in Monroe, Louisiana in 1934. His early life, and the manner in which he saw African-Americans treated in a racist society, made a major impact on him. This stayed with him even after his family moved to Oakland, California when he was eight. The Russells were not well-off, and Bill experienced severe poverty during his upbringing.

Although blessed with fundamental athletic talent, Russell was no basketball prodigy. He barely made the cut as a freshman on his high school team, but by the time he graduated, he was an all-star. Even so, Russell suffered the discrimination of being unwanted by schools hesitant to take on a black player. He stayed local, signing on to the University of San Francisco. There, Russell teamed with future Boston teammate K.C. Jones as the Phil Woolpert-coached Dons won two straight NCAA titles. After college, Russell represented the United States in the Summer of Olympics of 1956, adding a gold medal to his trophy shelf.

Red Auerbach, the astute judge of talent, understood that Russell possessed the exact skills the already-strong Celtics needed to become a great team. Auerbach targeted the St. Louis Hawks for a trade that gave Boston Russell. He was the missing piece in what developed into the Dynasty that dominated the league from the late 1950s to the late 1960s.

Russell was a fabulous defensive player and rebounder, but not a major force on offense, although he did seem to always deliver in the clutch. The important element was that Russell was surrounded by tremendous offensive players, so the Celtics did not need him to be a leader on that side of the ball. For his career, Russell averaged 15.1 points a game, which is quite solid, but he also averaged 22.5 rebounds a game, which is unbelievable.

The vast majority of current NBA players go through their entire careers without once collecting as many as 20 rebounds in a single game. Russell averaged more than 20 per season ten times. He led the league five times, and the only reason he did not lead it more often was the presence of seven-foot-one Wilt Chamberlain. This never-ending duel under the backboards was one reason why their confrontations were epic.

Chamberlain averaged 22.9 rebounds a game for his career, and he led the NBA in rebounds eleven times. Chamberlain owns the single-game rebounding record of 55. Russell has the next three highest totals, 51, 49, and 49. In the context of the modern game, those numerals are fantastical, reading like fiction. Many times, those Russell rebounds on the defensive end helped jump-start the Celtics' fast break. His one-handed pass would catch players streaking downfield, as if he was a quarterback. The Russell-Chamberlain rivalry is one of the greatest and most prominent pitting of individuals in the history of sport, ranking alongside Muhammad Ali–Joe Frazier in boxing, but few others.

Russell contended rivalry was a misnomer.

"It was never a rivalry, it was a competition," Russell said. "I once told Wilt, 'I'm probably the only guy on this planet who really knows how good you are because I get to see it up close every time we play.'"

Chamberlain posted better overall statistics, but Russell had the advantage in wins and losses, especially in terms of championships won. It was always acknowledged during Boston's Dynasty years that Russell benefited from a superior supporting cast, except for the single season Chamberlain and his Philadelphia 76ers grabbed the crown in 1967.

There was always a big newspaper buildup to the Celtics games against Chamberlain's teams. The men themselves felt affection for one another, going out to dinner together and operating on friendly terms when not on the court.

Russell's image away from the court was of an aloof man. He was not a mingler. For years, he declined to sign autographs. Even when fans embraced him in Boston, Russell did not always feel comfortable there. He complained of racism and never made his home in the city. He quietly nursed his hurts, which he turned to fire in competition. Russell was close with his teammates, white and black, but that locker room was very much guarded by a closed door.

Bob Cousy, the most visible and revered basketball

player in Boston before Russell even arrived, had a social consciousness and became a member of the NAACP. He was sensitive to the slights Russell endured, yet he always felt an internal nagging that he had not done enough to assist Russell by extending enough friendship to better understand him. In 2019, with both of them old men, Cousy cooperated on a book that discussed that very issue. A sense of Cousy guilt pervaded it, a second-guessing operation indicating that he felt in the 1950s and 1960s, a period of American societal upheaval, he could have taken stronger stands.

"Bill is a very complex person," Cousy said. "He suffered from racism and discrimination in so many ways that most people could never imagine. It was very difficult to be an African-American at that time, and being a famous athlete only complicated the situation."

As a player, Russell was at his best in the biggest moments. Many times, he played the full forty-eight minutes in key playoff games. He was dripping sweat, but his lean, wiry frame, carried by long legs and a purposeful stride, still made him the first man downcourt on defense.

The seventh game double-overtime win over the St. Louis Hawks in 1957 for Boston's first title was one of Russell's finest hours early in his career. A rookie that season, Russell scored 19 points, grabbed 23 rebounds, and had five blocked shots. He established that he was a winner from the get-go.

Although at times Russell and Tom Heinsohn could have a prickly relationship, most of the time Russell put being a good teammate at the top of his priority list. His laugh was often termed a cackle and was notably high-pitched. At all times, in basketball, in public, and as a proud man Russell demanded respect. He became an outspoken African-American spokesman, not afraid to take a stand when he felt it necessary.

In those turbulent times, Russell made militant statements about white people, one controversial *Sports Illustrated* article quoting him as saying that he hated most whites. But those did not include players who wore the green and white, nor Red Auerbach. Russell referred to Auerbach as the greatest coach in American professional sports history, and the men liked and appreciated one another.

Before he even retired, Russell became a head coach in the NBA. Auerbach made him player-coach of the Celtics, a daunting task. Once a somewhat regular happening, the player-coach model has pretty much disappeared across North American professional sports. There hasn't been a player-coach in the league since Dave Cowens held the title during the 1978–79 season. Pete Rose is the last player-manager in Major League history, dating back to the mid-1980s. There hasn't been a player-coach in the National Hockey League since 1969, Russell's last year with Boston. For a time in the 1920s, the Chicago Bears' George Halas was a player-coach-owner of the National Football League franchise.

This made Russell a pioneering African-American head coach in North American professional sport, although Fritz Pollard had the distinction of being the first black coach in any pro sport when he supervised the NFL's Akron Pros in 1921.

Russell was a success as a coach. His first team could not keep up with Wilt Chamberlain's Philadelphia title team in 1967, but the Celtics won two more crowns under Russell. The combination of playing and coaching did take a toll on Russell, and in 1969, he felt he was just losing some of his sharpness due to age.

"A thousand adjustments in my game helped the Celtics to our eleventh championship that year," Russell said, "but there were some factors no amount of tinkering could fix. The grades I gave myself consistently went down, and the spells of inspired basketball [plays] became less frequent. I knew that sometimes this happened because I was coaching as well as playing, so I couldn't allow myself to let go as much, but a lot of it was that I just couldn't keep up."

Russell stepped away from basketball after the 1968–69 season and did not return for five years. Beginning in 1974, he coached the Seattle SuperSonics for four seasons with limited success. Twice Seattle made the playoffs, and twice the team did not. Russell gave coaching one last try with the Sacramento Kings in the 1986–87 season, but the team was 17–41 when he was let go.

The Celtics retired Russell's No. 6 jersey in 1972, but unlike all other such ceremonies, Russell wanted to have it done in private. So the team conducted the event in an empty arena, an hour before the gates opened for a game. Twenty-seven years later, there was a redo, in a packed Fleet Center with many NBA stars present.

A member of the Naismith Memorial Basketball Hall of Fame and the College Basketball Hall of Fame, the NBA Finals Most Valuable Player Award is named after Russell. William Felton Russell was honored again in Boston in 2013 when a statue of him was unveiled at Boston's City Hall Plaza.

When Russell passed away at 88 after a long illness on July 31, 2022, the world took notice. He was feted for his greatness and accomplishments on the basketball court and praised as a Civil Rights pioneer, a leader in the African-American community, and as a humanitarian.

Former President Barrack Obama, who had awarded Russell the Presidential Medal of Freedom, and President Joe Biden, joined basketball figures in acclaiming Russell as an extraordinary man. They proclaimed Russell a winner as an athlete and man.

Shortly after his death, the NBA announced that it was retiring the No. 6 jersey for every team in the league to honor Russell in the manner Major League Baseball did with the No. 42 for Jackie Robinson.

Johnny Most

**R**adio broadcaster Johnny Most's famous "Havlicek stole the ball!" call has resonated with Celtics fans forever. Sometimes it can be lost in the shuffle of that 1965 Eastern Division playoff game excitement that he ever said anything else. It may be the term "gravelly voiced" was invented for Most, but one of the basic thrills he provided to his long-time listeners was his simple nightly game opener for home games, "This is Johnny Most, high above courtside at the Boston Garden."

Most was a Boston and Celtics institution. He was the radio voice of the team from 1953 to 1990, and even though so much time has passed, fans of a certain age still tune in half-expecting to hear his game calls. It is in some ways ironic that a born New Yorker – those 200-miles-apart can be a yawning barrier – became so beloved in Massachusetts.

Curt Gowdy, better known later as a national sports broadcasting figure, had been doing Celtics play-by-play when Most got word that the team needed a new guy. After Most's audition, owner Walter Brown's only concern was whether or not Boston fans would accept a New Yorker in the role. Red Auerbach was involved in the process from the start and assured Brown it would work out, so they hired Most.

"I was on my way to Boston Garden," Most said, while also admitting he did not anticipate staying the rest of his life.

Interestingly, Most, who lived in a Boston hotel during his first season on the job, did not think he was bringing enough emotion to his work (something that would be hard to believe among future listeners) and thought it might be because the in-house crowds were small and not vociferous. Sam Cohen, one of the local sports editors, urged Most to juice up his broadcasts.

Most decided he was being too objective and the fans wanted to hear more enthusiasm in his voice about their guys. That's when Most changed his approach. "For the first time, I saw that there was nothing wrong with rooting for the team you're covering." Most said.

Most was born in 1923, and during World War II, before he became a sports broadcaster, he served with the Air Force, flying twenty-eight combat missions as an aerial gunner and being awarded seven medals.

Although likely forgotten, Most did broadcast for the New York Giants baseball club in the early 1950s before they moved to San Francisco. Of course, that was before he moved to Boston, too. By then he had also gained some pro basketball experience in New York broadcasting Knicks games. In Boston, although more loosely linked to that team, Most did post-game Red Sox baseball shows for a period. Lesser known about Most was that he wrote poetry at times.

There was no questioning Most's allegiance to the Celtics. Since they captured sixteen world titles on his broadcast watch, except for a few drought periods, there wasn't much to criticize. Still, even a close listener and supporter of his style would never state that Most was anything but a blunt "homer." In his eyes, Celtics players never really did anything wrong. A pattern did emerge, though, of his readiness to lambast visiting players, no matter how great, if only with the tone of his voice. He definitely raised the sound to a higher level if he thought a rival coach or opponent seemed to be getting away with anything. And if a Celtic player bit the dust on the hardwood, Most would be informing the listeners, who had not witnessed the play, just how badly one of their favorites had been abused.

During the late-1950s–1960s Dynasty years, Most saw and commented on it all. He defended and befriended the players, a crew of Hall-of-Famers.

He once said that people were mistaken about Bill Russell being a pure dynamic leaper. He was a perfect timing leaper.

"When it comes to shot blocking, I doubt there will ever be a player who matches Russell," Most said. "Russell, with his superhuman reflexes, was a basketball genius."

Most also got to watch firsthand as Bob Cousy embodied a revolution at the point guard position with his clever passes and untouchable dribbling. "Cooz was, and is, the greatest passer the game has ever had," Most said. "He invented so many different ways of getting the ball from Point A to Point B. What further set him apart from all the other good point guards was that he only called a play for himself as fifth option."

Those who believed in more restrained objectivity did not particularly like Most calling Lakers point guard Magic Johnson, "Crybaby Johnson" during the 1980s rivalry between the clubs. More humorously, and perhaps more accurately, he had nicknames for two Washington Bullets in the early-to-mid-1980s. Jeff Ruland and Rick Mahorn earned Most's animosity. He called them "McFilthy" and "McNasty" interchangeably.

Only a few years later, when the Detroit Pistons were seen as the bullies of the league, getting away with extremely physical play as they won championships in 1989 and 1990 and reveled in the name "bad boys," Most called six-foot-eleven center Bill Laimbeer "Big Baby."

Likely, Most would have preferred calling Celtics games indefinitely, but he retired in 1990 because of his self-described declining health. Most, who was known to be a voracious smoker, suffered a stroke February 8, 1983, on what he called the scariest day of his life. He became ill on the ride to the airport for an away game in Maryland that night. He lost his voice in the terminal, and immediately Most thought he was finished in broadcasting. Most lost considerable weight and went through extensive rehabilitation, but he returned to the air. His first game back the announcement to the crowd produced a three-minute standing ovation and Most had tears running down his cheeks.

Ten years later, and three years after he retired, Johnny Most died from a heart attack. The Naismith Basketball Hall of Fame bestowed the Curt Gowdy Media Award on Most for his contributions to basketball. And the Celtics installed a permanent display honoring Most that featured a silver microphone. Perhaps silver was more appropriate than gold for Johnny Most because no one ever said he had a golden voice, only a very informative and loyal one.

Tom Sanders

**I**f one talks to Tom "Satch" Sanders about basketball long enough, he will let slip a point of pride that is almost always overlooked when his pro basketball career with the Boston Celtics is discussed.

"I had a good offensive game in college," Sanders says about his time spent at New York University before being drafted by the Celtics and becoming renowned as one of the finest defensive forwards in history.

It was Red Auerbach, naturally, who reshaped the six-foot-six front-courtman to take advantage of what may have been unseen abilities beforehand.

"Well, he just knew what his team needed and that was on defense," Sanders said.

Sanders was born in New York City in 1938 and starred at New York University, playing well enough for the Violets to be named a third-team All-American. At a time when there were only eight teams in the National Basketball Association, Sanders was the last pick in the first round in 1960. He was just happy to get a chance to play professionally, no matter what Auerbach wanted from him.

"I looked at it as an opportunity to play with the Boston Celtics, and you worry about the other things once you get in the door," Sanders said.

Even after college, and even as a native of New York City, young Tom Sanders was still skittish about the bright lights and bigger arenas featured in pro ball. He was even hesitant to sign with Boston at first, but later recalled a pep talk from Auerbach that convinced him to commit to a contract.

"He talked to me like a father," Sanders said. "He said a job was something I could always get, but that the chance to play ball comes just once in a lifetime. That made sense to me. Then he said Loscy's [Jim Loscutoff] back was hurting and [Gene] Conley was getting tired of two sports, and he kept stressing there was room on the team for me. By the time he got done, I envisioned myself rushing to the rescue of the world champions. Then I got to training camp and found fifty forwards fighting for my job!"

Famously, it was said that Sanders showed up for his first Celtics training camp wearing glasses and bulky knee pads that made him look gawky and innocent ripe for veterans to verbally assault. However, that exterior appearance was quite misleading. While the fifty contenders for the job was an exaggeration, Sanders did beat out all other fresh candidates for a roster spot.

Once he became established inside the team circle, Sanders was regarded as the hippest guy in the club, knowledgeable about jazz and other music, and as someone with a great sense of humor. Although not known to be a chatty guy, Sanders was viewed as Mr. Laidback. Sanders issued probably the most famous utterance of his career in a public forum, not in the locker room.

The year was 1963 and the Celtics were invited to meet President John F. Kennedy at the White House. This was before it became routine for sports championship teams to receive such invitations. In this case, it did not hurt the moment any that Kennedy was from Boston and had been a fan of the team for many years.

"Well, certainly having the opportunity to meet the president of the United States and having him be an enthusiast was a good feeling," Sanders said. "He laughed a lot. He had some stories to tell about when he was a kid admiring the

Celtics and he took about twenty-to-thirty minutes with us. That didn't make his staff very happy because that was a lot of time, but he was happy and he was a good conversationalist and we had a lot of laughs."

Sanders recalled the meeting in 2017, and his reference to JFK as a childhood fan of the Celtics could not be strictly accurate because the team did not exist until after Kennedy returned to Massachusetts following his World War II service.

As an indication of how cool Sanders was under pressure, when the team and the president were parting ways, Satch said, "Take it easy, baby." That familiarity was probably uncommon in diplomatic circles.

That nickname was one borrowed from the great pitcher Satchel Paige, a connection any athlete would be proud to share.

Boston was already established as the best team in the league with three championships recorded. Sanders played for thirteen years with the Celtics and was part of eight more title teams. Indeed, during Sanders's seasons, Boston went 8-0 in the Finals competition. Sanders wore No. 16 during his stint with the Celtics, and the team retired that number in appreciation.

"You look at a team that's won two or three championships and you probably find a team that's very close," Sanders said.

Auerbach placed a premium on good defense and, with Bill Russell at center, K.C. Jones at guard, and Sanders at forward, he had the best defensive players in the NBA at each position for years. Leading up to games, Sanders knew exactly what was expected of him. His job was to shadow the opponent's highest scoring forward.

Defensively, Sanders was assigned to cover a who's who of Hall-of-Famers, players who, judging from their statistics, could really never be stopped, only slowed down. Elgin Baylor, Rick Barry, Dolph Schayes, and Bob Petit were only some of the All-Stars Sanders put the clamps on, if only briefly. His job was to annoy them; make it more difficult for them to catch passes, put the ball on the floor, and dribble to the hoop; and force them into a slightly deeper outside range for jump shots.

Petit was one of the greatest scoring forwards of all time, and Sanders admired him and knew how tough he would be to cover when the Celtics met the St. Louis Hawks.

"Bob Petit was a player who got the most out of his talent, which was an awful lot," Sanders said. "He was going to bring the ball up-court and go around his back [dribbling]. He focused on what he could do well, and that's why he did so well."

Sanders was hardly the Celtics' first option on offense. He picked up his points in the flow of the game. Although his lifetime points-per-game average was just 9.6, it might surprise fans to learn he averaged in double figures nine times with a high of 12.6 per game. If he made star foes record seven fewer points in a game than their average, and scored 10 himself, then Sanders was effectively neutralizing the foe.

Of course, this type of work did not often draw headlines. Sanders was underrated by anyone who believed box score numbers revealed all. It came with the territory. In fact, Auerbach called Sanders "the unsung hero" of the Celtics Dynasty teams, an apt description for such an integral part of the big victories, but one who contributed with less flash than the team's All-Stars.

There is little doubt if Sanders had played for another NBA team, he would have scored more, received more accolades, and might be better-remembered as an individual player by latter-day generations of fans. But he also would not be the possessor of eight championship rings.

When he retired in 1973, Sanders was able to stay in basketball by becoming the coach at Harvard University. This made him the first African-American coach for any sports team in Ivy League history. He was the face of the Crimson for four years. He sported a dashing look, wearing bow-ties with his sport coats or suits.

In 1978, Sanders's coaching career took a surprising turn.

Then a Boston assistant, he was tapped as a mid-season replacement to lead the Celtics when the team fired Tommy Heinsohn. Boston was not particularly strong at the time, and it was a short stint for Sanders.

Sanders also remained in basketball after coaching. He went to work for the NBA as vice president and director of player programs under then-commissioner David Stern. From league headquarters, he initially developed programs to help rookies and young players adjust to the professional lifestyle. Then the programs expanded to offer services to all players. This included counseling on anti-drug and anti-drinking matters, how to deal with fame as a celebrity-athlete, and more.

"Basically," Sanders once described his work, "we're still trying to help players make that adjustment coming into the game and, certainly, while they are here, but also on the way out –their departure time. So, we are working with players on 'adjustments.'"

Sanders is often asked about his Celtics days, a special time in his life.

"Well, I tell you, fond memories come about every single time I take a look at that parquet floor, OK? No matter where it is, the Garden or here in the Fleet Center, it's meaningful to me and it brings back a rush of memories. Now the problem is trying to put those memories in the right place, OK? I can't seem to get some of those championship games together. I know there were quite a few, but I can't seem to put them together."

That's what happens when you win eight world championships.

Fans always assume the caliber of play is better when they follow a team in the present-tense, as opposed to the sport in its past. That applies to basketball, as well as football and baseball. When historians go back far enough, there are obvious differences in how games are played, especially before rules were changed. Sanders sees some differences, but believes at its core basketball is the same as it always was.

"The only thing that really has changed is the athleticism of the players," Sanders said. "Obviously, the dollars have changed. But the game is, pretty much, a lot of it the same, as it was when I was playing. The fact that there is so much individual talent here means you see a little bit more of the one-on-one game, but it's a fun game to watch and I still enjoy it immensely."

Although Tom Sanders was shorted on attention when he played for the Boston Celtics, that did not mean he was forgotten. In 2011, he was inducted into the Naismith Memorial Basketball Hall of Fame as a contributor.

John Havlicek

 million times. John Havlicek laughed about it. Just about everyone he ever met in retirement said something. They said they were either there to see it live and in person or they heard Johnny Most's most famous yell. "Havlicek stole the ball!"

Forever linked to one play by the broadcaster's raspy and exceptionally loud voice in this instance, more than a half century after the occurrence, Havlicek could only chuckle about such a popular moment that did not define him on the basketball court during his National Basketball Association career with the Boston Celtics.

When the six-foot-five Havlicek broke in with the Celtics in 1962 as the team's No. 1 draft pick out of Ohio State, Boston was in the midst of its Dynasty. Initially, Havlicek became the club's sixth-man, the role originally improvised for Frank Ramsey. Then he became a swing man, shifting between forward and guard. Then he became the team leader when all of those older star players from the 1950s and 1960s began retiring. His nickname was "Hondo," because of an alleged resemblance to cowboy star John Wayne in the movie of that name.

During a sixteen-year career ending in 1978, Havlicek outlasted everyone, and was part of the reconstituted 1970s Celtics champs with their transformed roster, too. Of all the greats, of all the Boston Hall-of-Famers, it is Havlicek who is the franchise's all-time leading scorer with 26,395 points.

Havlicek was a terrific high school athlete from Bridgeport, Ohio, and one of his frequent companions as a youth was Hall of Fame pitcher Phil Niekro. Ohio State won one NCAA title with Havlicek in the lineup, in 1960, and his Buckeye teammates included star center Jerry Lucas, future Celtics teammate Larry Siegfried, and Bob Knight, who went on to a legendary college coaching career.

Highly regarded as a skilled athlete, the 200-pound Havlicek was drafted by the Cleveland Browns of the National Football League even though he did not play college football.

"I was flattered," Havlicek said. The Browns gave him $15,000 and a car and, at what today would be called a mini-camp, he impressed Cleveland officials with his hands. "I had unlimited confidence in my ability to catch."

Havlicek got into one exhibition game and was hit so hard by the legendary "Big Daddy" Lipscomb he emerged from the contact with his helmet turned around. Havlicek did love football, and he had a lofty plan.

"My goal was to play both and make a decision [between the sports] after a year," Havlicek said.

He did not get the chance to make such a choice. He nearly made the Browns as a receiver after his four-year layoff from football due to his college years, but was cut and spent the rest of his athletic life with the Boston Celtics. Interestingly, this was one time in the draft room that Auerbach worried the man he wanted would not still be on the board when it was his turn to pick near the bottom of the first round.

"I wasn't a hundred percent sure Havlicek would still be there when we picked," Auerbach said because Ohio State had received great exposure. "I needed to figure out an alternative, just in case." That alternative was forward Chet Walker from Bradley. Although team history may or may not have read differently, Walker would have been a worthy Plan B. The six-foot-six forward was a seven-time All-Star who, at 18.2 per game, scored almost as much as Havlicek.

It is appropriate that so many of Havlicek's hoops memories revolved around championship achievements.

Going back to "Havlicek stole the ball," which became the name of a record album collecting Most's broadcast highlights, in some ways the phrase is better known than the circumstances that spawned it.

The occasion was a Celtics–76ers Eastern Division playoff game in 1965. The Celtics led the deciding game, 110–109, and seemed to have neutralized the 76ers because Boston had possession of the ball. But Bill Russell made an errant pass that led to it being Philadelphia's ball. Philadelphia star guard Hal Greer tried to make the pass-in for a quick basket on his own end. Russell had Wilt Chamberlain blanketed, so Greer had to throw it deep. K.C. Jones was fronting Greer, who saw forward Chet Walker. But when Greer threw long, Havlicek stepped in and tipped the pass away.

Most shouted, "Greer is putting the ball into play. He gets it out deep. Havlicek steals it! Over to Sam Jones. Havlicek stole the ball! It's all over! Johnny Havlicek stole the ball!"

As the game ended, fans mobbed the Boston Garden court, lifted Havlicek on their shoulders, and began ripping off his Celtics shirt.

"At the time, I thought I was just doing what I was supposed to do," Havlicek said of getting his hand on the pass. "But he [Most] made it into a memory. I had my shirt torn off my back. Fans come up to me and say, 'I was there,' or 'I remember.'"

No Celtic fan ever forgot that moment.

Another playoff victory Havlicek always cherished was winning the triple overtime game over the Phoenix Suns on the way to the 1976 world title.

"The triple overtime game was special," Havlicek said.

No Celtic fan ever forgot that one either. Many basketball fans consider that June 4, 1976 finals game the best in NBA history. Boston won, 128–126, following a series of dramatic plays. Havlicek appeared to win the game on a jump shot near the end of the second overtime. But two seconds remained, and in the pandemonium, Suns forward Garfield Heard hit a near-impossible, turnaround from the top of the key to force the third overtime.

"If there would have been a three-pointer," Havlicek said of the rule not yet in effect, "we would have lost."

After attending Ohio State, Havlicek joined a fully formed Celtics team so loaded with talent he was really just a young fellow learning and blending that rookie year of 1962—63. Havlicek got into eighty games and played twenty-seven and a half minutes a game, contributing 14.3 points, so he made an impact right away. During this early era of his Boston career, Havlicek marveled at Red Auerbach's personnel acumen and how he always seemed to find the right guy to replace a retiring key player while still coaxing the best out of the others.

"We never had that much turnover," Havlicek said of the core group of players from the Dynasty period. "Red Auerbach kept everybody together and didn't make too many trades. Today it would never happen because of free agency."

Havlicek was one of the most prominent of Celtic stars who did not go into coaching. Although Havlicek never desired to be a coach, the closest he came to fulfilling the job in the NBA was as an unofficial assistant to Bill Russell during the years when Russell was a player-coach. Russell said he relied heavily on Havlicek's advice. When Russell and Sam Jones retired in 1969, Havlicek became the clear team leader on the court. There were some trying times ahead, but Havlicek spanned the lean years until the Celtics became champs again in the 1970s.

"He inspired us," said guard Jo Jo White

One way he did so was by being indefatigable. When the Celtics were essentially short-staffed with quality depth, Havlicek practically never came out of games. He had seasons where he averaged forty-five minutes per game in scheduled forty-eight-minute contests. He led the NBA in minutes played both of those years.

A versatile scorer, Havlicek was faster than he looked, a better outside shooter than some defenders thought, and slippier driving to the hoop than some gave him credit for, all adding up to seasons like 1970–71 when Havlicek averaged 28.9 points a game and 1971–72 when he averaged 27.5. His career mark was 20.8 points a game and Havlicek was a thirteen-time All-Star. In eight seasons, Havlicek was either a first- or second-team all-defensive league selection.

An all-around player, Havlicek also averaged 6.3 rebounds and 4.8 assists a game for his career, adding to his reputation as a do-everything guy. Havlicek never seemed to run out of energy and he never failed to give 100 percent.

"A player's player," teammate Tom Sanders once proclaimed.

Another epic playoff series was the 1974 Finals against the Milwaukee Bucks featuring Kareem Abdul-Jabbar before he joined the Los Angeles Lakers and Oscar Robertson at the end of his phenomenal NBA career. That was a tremendous back-and-forth seven-game series. It was 1–0 Boston, 1–1, 2–1 Boston, 2–2, 3–2 Boston, and 3–3. The Celtics won the seventh game, 102–87. Havlicek was the Finals Most Valuable Player.

"The one I remember most was against the Milwaukee Bucks and against Kareem and Oscar Robertson," Havlicek said. "Nobody could win at home."

While Havlicek recalled how the Celtics would have lost to Phoenix if Gar Heard's shot counted as a three-pointer, he frowned on how the powerful offensive weapon has taken over the sport.

"I think it's become too much," Havlicek said near the end of the 2018–19 season. "But it is exciting at the end of a game."

Havlicek wore a tuxedo to the arena for his farewell game in 1978, and then scored 29 points in a Celtics victory. He addressed the Boston crowd at halftime. "Thank you, Boston," he said. "I love you."

A member of both the Naismith Memorial Basketball Hall of Fame and the College Basketball Hall of Fame, Havlicek's

No. 17 Celtics jersey was retired. Havlicek was selected as a member of the NBA's 35th and 50th anniversary teams.

In late April of 2019, Havlicek passed away from the effects of Parkinson's Disease at age seventy-nine. Havlicek's Hall of Fame career with the Celtics spanned two distinct eras with the club, both very different from each other.

When Havlicek died, the Celtics' official statement spoke about him as a man and player, saying in part, "His defining traits as a player were his relentless hustle and wholehearted commitment to team over self. John was kind and considerate, humble and gracious."

Clyde Lovellete

**W**hile Clyde Lovellette was not among the greatest of Boston Celtics players, he is an honored inductee of both the Naismith Memorial Basketball Hall of Fame and the College Basketball Hall of Fame for the rest of his career.

Lovellette was a high school star in Indiana, was part of an NCAA title winner at Kansas where he led the nation in scoring, won an Olympic gold medal, and had an eleven-year NBA career starting with the Minneapolis Lakers in the 1953–54 season and finishing with Boston in 1963–64. Lovellette averaged 17 points a game in the NBA, though his role at the end of his career was as a back-up for about ten minutes per game to fill in for Bill Russell at center.

Twice an All-American, the six-foot-nine Lovellette won three NBA championship rings, including one with Minneapolis and two with Boston, and was a four-time All-Star.

Lovellette was contemplating retirement when Red Auerbach wooed him to Boston. Even though he knew it was going to be in a secondary role after his years of stardom, the idea of joining a ready-made championship club was irresistible.

"I had never been a backup in my life," said Lovellette said, who was coming off an injury that may have left some teams hesitant to reach out with a contract. "But that didn't matter at that moment. "My first thought was, 'I'm going to play for Boston, the champions.'"

Lovellette knew he was not going to replace Russell in the starting lineup, but felt if he showed enough remaining talent, it would add some years to his career and he might even be coveted by another team later.

As a player who had been part of the backbone of the St. Louis Hawks when the Hawks stood in the way of Boston's title aspirations, plus being the kind of hard-nosed, physical player who did not always make friends in opposing arenas, Lovelette wondered how his reception would be in the Boston Garden. That turned out OK. Now he was one of the good guys.

"I had to make the shift from being an enemy of the Celtics on the court to a teammate," Lovellette said. "I used to get booed and razzed a lot at the Boston Garden, but now I was family to the fans."

Bill Russell and Wilt Chamberlain

**P**robably the greatest one-on-one rivalry in American sports history outside of the boxing ring was Bill Russell versus Wilt Chamberlain. Literally giants of the hardcourt, the men overlapped in pro basketball in dramatically opposing ways. Russell virtually invented defense and Chamberlain was the greatest scorer of all time.

Russell, who was born in 1934, is regarded as the greatest winner in team sport. With the six-foot-nine-and-a-half-inch two-time NCAA champion and Olympic gold medal winner, the Celtics won eleven titles in thirteen seasons. The seven-foot-one Chamberlain, born in 1936, a player for Kansas, was a member of two NBA championship teams while once scoring 100 points in a game and averaging 30 points a game for his career.

Russell won five Most Valuable Player awards and Chamberlain won four. Russell triumphed more often in big games, but he clearly had a superior starting lineup surrounding him by far. They were the two greatest rebounders of all-time. Chamberlain won the single-season rebounding title eleven times, Russell four times.

Russell was in the NBA between 1956 and 1969, Chamberlain between 1959 and 1973. The first time Russell and Chamberlain faced each other as opposing centers was November 7, 1959 at the Boston Garden and the pre-game publicity was already of significant magnitude, particularly for a regular-season game. Despite the Celtics' grand success, not every game was being sold out for the perennial world champions, but the first meeting between Chamberlain and Russell was an advance sellout of 13,909 fans.

Chamberlain was representing the then-Philadelphia Warriors before that club moved to San Francisco and was replaced in Philly by the 76ers. That night, Chamberlain scored 30 points and grabbed 30 rebounds. Russell scored 22 points and collected 35 rebounds. Boston won the game.

Before Red Auerbach was aware of Bill Russell, he knew about Wilt Chamberlain, who set the high school scene aflame in Philadelphia. Auerbach operated a summer basketball program in the Catskill Mountains at Kutsher's Country Club. Young players acted as waiters and entertained guests with their basketball prowess. Long before shoe companies sponsored showcases that brought together the top talent in the nation, the best players in the Northeast would play in the Catskills.

Auerbach marveled at Chamberlain's size and his athletic ability and felt he could become the Celtics' man in the middle. He actually said, "Why don't you go to Harvard, kid?" Then Chamberlain could have become a Boston territorial NBA draft pick. Although he did not graduate from the school, the heavily recruited Chamberlain chose Kansas before dropping out to play for the Harlem Globetrotters and make money for a year before joining the NBA.

In his rookie year, Chamberlain performed at a higher level than anyone following the NBA had ever seen. He averaged 37.6 points per game and 27 rebounds. That was the first of six straight years Chamberlain led the league in scoring. His high-water mark – and the still-standing all-time record – was 50.4 points per game in the 1961–62 season. That is such an outlier of a statistic it is almost unbelievable. Only a tiny percentage of NBA players will ever score 50 points in a game once. Chamberlain averaging that much across an entire season is one of the most astounding feats in the history of sport. Almost overlooked is that a year later, Chamberlain averaged 44.8 points.

Against most players, Chamberlain seemingly scored at will. Whether it was on fierce dunks, fallaway jumpers, or short shots, Chamberlain, stronger than any other man in the game, could impose his will most of the time. Chamberlain was hardly ever whistled for fouls and opponents who sought to guard him routinely fouled out.

Chamberlain's ultimate showpiece game, undertaken with the cooperation of his teammates and coach, was hanging 100 points on the New York Knicks at a neutral court game in Hershey, Pennsylvania on March 2, 1962. When there were about five minutes left in the forty-eight-minute game and Chamberlain already had 89 points on the scoresheet, New York coach Eddie Donovan told his players, "There's no way that big S.O.B.'s going to get a hundred on us." The Knicks sought to slow down play, but nothing interfered and Chamberlain recorded the point total for the ages.

The only one who seemingly possessed the capability of slowing down Chamberlain was Russell.

Russell and Chamberlain's face-to-face battles were legendary and represented drama of the highest order. From outside the game, Russell and Chamberlain were viewed as enemies, and in the buildup to games, tall headlines implied as such with Chamberlain assuming the role of Goliath.

However, Russell always maintained the men had no animosity for one another away from the court.

"Wilt Chamberlain and I carried on a friendship the entire time we played basketball together," Russell wrote in one of his memoirs, Second Wind, "even though the newspapers portrayed us as mortal enemies. There's a certain amount of show business in professional basketball and the two of us were a promoter's dream. You would have thought we were heavyweight boxers going at each other because our respective teams were largely ignored."

While Russell was spoken of more for his team play, rebounding, and defensive contributions, Chamberlain was a statistical machine. Over the course of his career, Chamberlain also led the league in scoring seven times and in field-goal percentage nine times. He was so tall and strong, complementing his athleticism, Wilt revolutionized shooting accuracy, hitting 54 percent of his shots for his career.

"Wilt was by far the toughest center I ever played against," Russell said. "He was awesome, and no matter what anyone says about his lack of team play, his teams always ended up in the playoffs staring at us. He always out-scored me by huge margins."

Johnny "Red" Kerr, another first-rate center of the Russell-Chamberlain era, took beatings from both men.

"Chamberlain had good scoring games against everyone and Russell was the best defensive player," Kerr once said.

It is no surprise that long-time Boston coach Red Auerbach picks Russell over Chamberlain as the better of the two. This was Auerbach's argument: "Russell was the greatest rebounder who ever lived – and don't give me any of that stuff about Chamberlain's statistics. Those are just numbers. When the game was on the line and the ball was up for grabs, Russell had no equal."

Controversy surrounded the last game of Russell's career when Boston again bested the Lakers for a championship, winning 108–106, in seven games. Chamberlain hardly ever came out of games (one season, because of overtime play, he averaged forty-eight and a half minutes per game, more than a full regularly-scheduled contest), but was taken out with five minutes to go with a tweaked knee. It was later said Chamberlain asked out. But Chamberlain claimed LA coach Butch van Breda Kolff kept him benched, although he requested to be reinserted. "I asked about ten times."

Russell was soon asked what he thought about Chamberlain's injury, removal from the game, and failure to return. Essentially, he said if Chamberlain was hurt so badly, he should have gone right to the hospital. In part he also said, "You can't quit like that and win championships."

Many years later, well after both had retired from playing, a scene that neither would have imagined in the 1960s played out at Boston College High School. The giants of the game were paired together signing autographs for hire, and Auerbach was there, too. When the men were in their heyday in the game, there really was no such thing as an autograph market. It was kids who collected autographs at arenas.

But the world changed and professional athletes' signatures – the bigger the name, the more desired the example of penmanship – discovered they could make a good income by scribbling their names for adult collectors who coveted the souvenir and enjoyed meeting players they had watched when they were younger and whom they still admired.

"Without sounding egotistical," said Chamberlain, who had never worried about that trait being exposed before, "this kind [of rivalry] doesn't come along but once in a lifetime. I don't know if there's been anything else like it, or if anything else like that will happen."

Again, with the possible exception of a few boxing rivalries, Chamberlain was correct. It was reported that Russell, who had eschewed signing autographs for most of his life, was paid $120,000 for the appearance and signing five hundred items. Chamberlain, who had been more generous with his name, was said to be raising $40,000 for charitable causes by signing one thousand times.

With Chamberlain having passed away at sixty-three in 1999 and Russell living into his eighties until 2022, it is now Chamberlain's autograph that is rarer.

Celtics-Lakers Rivalry First Time

The first time the Boston Celtics defeated the Lakers in an NBA championship round, the 1958–59 conclusion to the season represented the end of one era and the beginning of a new one. They were still the Minneapolis Lakers that season, a team that in the early 1950s had captured five world titles, but was about to abandon Minnesota for Los Angeles

It was a fluke that the Lakers reached the Finals that year after a 33–39 regular season. The vestiges of the great Lakers teams of the past had one more run in them, guys like Vern Mikkelson, Larry Faust, Bob Leonard (who would later become a Hall-of-Famer for his work as coach with the Indianapolis Pacers), and Dick Garmaker.

Guard "Hot Rod" Hundley was a member of that team with the great Elgin Baylor, the forward who helped raise the level of the sport with his fantastic moves. Both would accompany the team to LA with the reward of constant heartbreak at the hands of the Celtics in the 1960s.

That first year in Los Angeles was superstar guard Jerry West's rookie year. Guard Frank Selvy joined the club with forward Rudy LaRusso.

The Lakers reached their first Finals from the West Coast in 1962 and in that year, 1963, 1965, 1966, 1968, and 1969, the tremendous one-two punch of West and Baylor allowed the Lakers to dominate the Western Division and reach the championship round. The Celtics were there waiting for them every time, and every time Boston won.

"If it had been six different teams we'd lost to, perhaps the pain would have been diluted," West said many years later. "But the same team, over and over? You felt as if you were being taunted, like when you are a kid, and someone says something about your being too skinny, or too fat, or your buck teeth, or your big ears. But when you're a kid, it would usually be one-on-one. Here, it was ten-on-ten and you had to take it like a man."

Sometimes West was the best player in the series. He even won a Most Valuable Player trophy in the Finals – on the losing team.

"Those losses scarred me," he said, "scars that remain embedded in my psyche to this day. The thing about scar tissue is that it keeps building, and pretty soon it's awfully sizeable."

At least West stayed around with the Lakers to eventually win a championship. Sadly, for Baylor, who was a couple of years older, he retired after the start of the 1971–72 season when the Lakers, with Wilt Chamberlain, romped to the crown. Baylor's body gave out just months too soon to enjoy the spoils.

Years later, looking back at 1962, Baylor lamented the title loss to the Celtics in seven games, thinking perhaps if the Lakers had pulled out that series then things may have been different later when the Celtics kept building upon their glory and taking out the Lakers so many times in the 1960s.

"It could possibly have changed things," Baylor said. "We

always thought that we could win. We never thought we were going to lose."

As great as the Lakers were, and as great as West and Baylor were, the Celtics repeatedly came out on top because Boston had more Hall-of-Famers. Bob Cousy, Bill Sharman, Bill Russell, Tommy Heinsohn, Frank Ramsey, Sam Jones, K.C. Jones, and Tom Sanders were all on the roster at the same time. Soon after Sharman retired, another Hall-of-Famer, John Havlicek, joined the team.

There were times, as the Celtics aged, Boston was occasionally written off when they came up against the Lakers. Naturally, when Cousy retired after the 1962–63 season, he went out as a champion, and also naturally enough, after a triumph over the Lakers.

As Cousy's career came to an end, coach Red Auerbach said, "I guess Los Angeles isn't the basketball capital of the world yet."

So the man for whom the annual college point guard award is named, played his last game as a Boston Celtic as a victor over the Los Angeles Lakers. Six years later, so did Russell. That was the night the Celtics traipsed into LA's home arena and stumbled across the prepared script for how the post-game celebration would go "when" the Lakers won the title. Only they didn't. Boston did again.

"They had champagne back there on ice, too, you know," said Celtics backup guard Emmette Bryant. "We made note of it."

Celtics
Key Trades

1. The most significant trade in Boston Celtics history was
    engineered by general manager-coach Red Auerbach
    and took place on April 30, 1956 when he obtained Hall
    of Fame center Bill Russell. The brilliant Russell led Bos-
    ton to eleven world championships in thirteen years. For
    Auerbach to get Russell, he had to trade star center Ed
    Macauley; newcomer Cliff Hagan, a future star; and the
    seventh-round pick in the draft for the St. Louis Hawks'
    second-round choice. As a side aspect to the deal with
    St. Louis, Walter Brown, who also owned the Ice Capades,
    agreed to bring that show to Cincinnati so the Royals
    would not take Russell with the first pick.

2. Another magnificent deal for the Celtics was the June 9,
    1980 trade of the No. 1 choice in the NBA draft to the Gold-
    en State Warriors for center Robert Parish and the num-
    ber three selection. Parish blossomed into a Hall-of-Famer
    and Boston grabbed Kevin McHale, another Hall-of-Famer,
    with the draft choice.

3. On September 1, 1966, Boston obtained future Hall of
    Fame forward Bailey Howell from the Baltimore Bullets
    for back-up center Mel Counts. Howell was deep into his
    career, but gave the Celtics four very productive years,
    the first three averaging right around 20 points a game.

4. Ray Allen, one of the greatest three-point shooters of all-time, was acquired by Boston by general manager Danny Ainge along with Glen "Big Baby" Davis from the Seattle SuperSonics for Jeff Green, Delonte West, and Wally Szcerbiak, plus a second-round draft pick on June 28, 2007.

5. Boston's Danny Ainge swapped Ryan Gomes, Gerald Green, Al Jefferson, Theo Ratliff, Sebastian Telfair, and a future No. 1 draft pick for Kevin Garnett on July 31, 2007. The price was high, but paid off with an NBA title.

6. Charlie Scott was in the vortex of drafting acumen and complex trades. A star guard from the University of North Carolina, he was leaving school when the NBA and the American Basketball Association were warring over players. Although Scott joined the Virginia Squires of the ABA, Red Auerbach selected him anyway. That way, in case Scott wanted to join the NBA someday, Boston would own his rights. That day did come, but Scott signed with the Suns. Boston demanded compensation, and on March 14, 1972 received All-Star forward Paul Silas. Then, May 23, 1975, Boston acquired Scott for Paul Westphal and two second-round draft picks.

7. Red Auerbach, as he did with Bailey Howell, had a knack for convincing other teams to part with former All-Stars when they still had some good days remaining, and he blended them into his own championship lineups. Center Wayne Embry, a five-time All-Star for the Cincinnati Royals, was acquired on September 15, 1966 in exchange for the inexpensive price of a third-round draft selection.

8. On June 27, 1983, guard Dennis Johnson was picked up by Boston in a trade with the Phoenix Suns, and the opportunity to solidify a championship lineup gave him a chance to shine. Johnson, a first-round draft pick, and a third-round draft picks went to the Celtics for Rick Robey and two second-round draft picks. Johnson ended up in the Hall of Fame.

9. On July 12, 2013, the Celtics traded away Kevin Garnett, Paul Pierce, Jason Terry, and D. J. White to the Brooklyn Nets for Keith Bogans, MarShon Brooks, Kris Humphries, Kris Joseph, Gerald Wallace, and three No. 1 draft picks. Made by general manager Danny Ainge, the trade represented the dismantling of a championship team's featured players due to age and the start of a rebuilding effort.

10. Also on the negative side of the ledger, it was universally agreed that Boston gave up too much for high-scoring Bob McAdoo on September 6, 1979 when the Celtics traded the New York Knicks three first-round draft choices and a player named Tom Barker.

Bailey Howell

One of Red Auerbach's great transactions was the acquisition of future Hall-of-Famer Bailey Howell. The six-foot-seven forward who came out of Mississippi State was a star with the Detroit Pistons and the Baltimore Bullets, but was turning thirty, so when the Celtics offered a younger seven-foot Mel Counts straight-up, the deal was arranged.

It turned into a steal. Counts never quite fulfilled his potential, though he was one of those near-the-end-of-the-bench guys for the Celtics for a few years. Howell, a six-time All-Star, kept right on playing at a high level for Boston for four more seasons. In his first three years with the Celtics, Howell averaged just about 20 points a game. He finished with career averages of 18.7 points and 9.9 rebounds. Howell helped the Celtics win two more National Basketball Association titles.

None of this should have been a surprise. In Tennessee, Howell had set the state high school scoring record, and at Mississippi State he was a two-time Southeastern Conference player of the year.

It did not exactly break Howell's heart when he moved from Detroit to Baltimore to Boston. He went from struggling teams to a perpetual champ when he joined the Celtics for the 1966–67 season.

"It was the biggest break I could have had in my career," Howell said. "With the Pistons and Bullets, we had some decent teams. But everybody would like to have that ring."

Howell, who was also always known for his flat-top haircut, came to Boston at an intriguing transition time. Auerbach had given up the reins as coach and became a full-time executive. Bill Russell became head coach, as well as a player, and the Philadelphia 76ers, with Wilt Chamberlain, put together their best team to win the crown.

"Red had retired that spring, and we lost it my first year," Howell said. "Everyone was saying Boston was dead."

Not quite. That was one of the two seasons during Russell's playing career when Boston did not win the championship. But the Celtics regrouped and captured their tenth and eleventh titles immediately afterwards, giving Howell his coveted jewelry.

"It's the biggest thrill you can have," Howell said of winning championship rings. "To play on the best basketball team in the world."

As a player, Howell had excellent, all-around offensive skills. He not only possessed a sharp outside shot, but was such a ballhawk that rebounding it provided he and his team repeated bonus shots inside. He ended up with a 48 percent lifetime field-goal percentage during a time period when only centers shot that well.

The best basketball is still played in the United States, despite the rise of the quality of competition around the world in a steady arc since the Summer Olympics of 1992 and the large influx of talent into the NBA. The NBA is still the best league on the planet and most certainly was when Howell played. It was no exaggeration to state that the team which won the annual NBA crown was the best team anywhere.

"When you really stop to think about it, it was, 'We're the best team in the world,'" he said.

In the decades since Howell retired, there have been other great NBA teams. The Chicago Bulls with Michael Jordan won six championships. The Los Angeles Lakers keep rising and now have won seventeen titles in all, equaling Boston, which also added its share after Howell's departure. Recently, the Golden State Warriors had a nice run.

"Now they're saying San Francisco [Golden State] is the best team of all-time," Howell said, "but none of them have approached what the Celtics did."

Eleven titles in thirteen years stands alone in pro basketball as unapproachable.

When the Celtics of his era reigned, Howell noted, rosters were put together through the draft and some trades. Now, with free agency, the best players can play out their contracts and make themselves available to the richest teams and form alliances picking their spots to join other All-Stars.

"They can assemble a great team much more quickly," Howell said. "It's easier today to try to assemble a great dynasty."

Teams try to do that all of the time, but sometimes even being able to capture one title, never mind repeated championships, eludes them, even by spending big or trading often.

One thing those championship Celtics had, Howell discovered quite quickly, was a special chemistry.

"It was just the joy of winning," Howell said. "There wasn't any bad blood. Since I was an experienced player, it didn't take long to get comfortable."

Before becoming a Celtic, Howell had no fondness for the Boston Garden.

"I didn't like it as a visiting player," he said. "It was so cold in there. The locker rooms were so small. You just had a nail to hang your clothing on."

Whether, as it was said, Auerbach just wanted to make things uncomfortable for the visiting team on purpose or not, the real challenge was facing up to the high-caliber team Boston put on the floor.

"Before you knew it, Russell was blocking a shot and throwing it to [Bob] Cousy and they've got a basket," Howell said.

By the time Howell shifted to the Celtics, Cousy was retired and Howell was stepping in for some of the other greats. He said when Russell assumed control of the sidelines, he addressed the team with, "We're not changing anything."

As seasoned a veteran as Howell was, there was one constant to his post-game routine after night games. He could not calm down for hours after the final whistle. He may have been physically whipped after playing, but his mind kept rolling. He could not fall asleep easily.

"I can never fall asleep after a game," Howell said. Ruminating over losses was not the cause. Savoring victory was not the cause, either. "No matter what the score is, I can't sleep for those first two or three hours in bed. I'm all right the night before a game, but the night after it's terrible. Some of these stretches when we play three straight games are rough."

He just went on counting sheep or staring at the ceiling in his room.

Russell knew there was not much reason to change things on the court. The pronouncement of the death of the Celtics was both exaggerated and premature, home or away.

"For a real pro, the home-court advantage is not that significant," Howell said. "You're self-motivated. If you are a real pro, you come to play every night. The superstars are stronger mentally than the stars. The stars are stronger than the regular players."

Howell's favorite game as a Celtic was the sixth game of the 1968 NBA Finals when Boston won the crown – the first of his career – by beating the Lakers, 124–109. Howell scored 30 points.

"We won it in LA," Howell said of the special moment. "It was one of the best games I had in the playoffs."

Howell was pleased he played a role in the Celtics Dynasty, one that no one expects to see equaled.

"Teams have come part of the way," Howell said.

Despite all of the great players who contributed, Howell believes Auerbach was the most important cog.

"Red was the architect," Howell said. "He really knew how to handle people. Coaching is a lot more than just having talent."

Mel Counts

ne of the tallest men in Boston Celtics history, Mel Counts was atypical, especially for his time period. He was a seven-footer with a jump shot more than a low-post style. Everyone taking a look at Counts's size would assume he might well dunk, but he could hit from long-range.

Counts starred at Oregon State University and won a gold medal as a member of the United States team in the 1964 Summer Olympics in Tokyo. The Celtics made him their No. 1 draft pick that same year.

The Olympics was a cherished experience and that group of Americans was seen as a bunch of overachievers that was unlikely to win the championship, then did. The United States beat the Soviet Union, 73–59, in the title game. Among Counts's teammates were Bill Bradley, the future US Senator; Jeff Mullins; Walt Hazzard; and Larry Brown, later a championship coach.

"Our goal was to represent our country to the best of our ability and that's what we did," said Counts, who noted coach Hank Iba had the team practice together for a few weeks at Pearl Harbor in Hawaii. "We won the gold medal and proved everybody wrong."

Counts always remembered his first Celtics training camp as being intensely demanding, even though he was not present for all of it. Red Auerbach wanted to make sure his players were in top shape for his fast-break style. He also had some pet peeves and phobias about what was permitted.

"That was like boot camp," Counts said. "Red would say, 'I'll fine you.' He said, 'We don't do pancakes or carbohydrates.'"

Some credit Auerbach to bringing a fast-break style to the NBA, which may have been an overstatement, but was definitely a trademark.

"Oh, they'd push the ball," Counts said. "They were cracker jacks. Not all teams did that. They were ahead of their time. Heart, fire, passion: that's what the Celtics had. Everybody was trying to knock you off, but it didn't happen. They won those eleven championships in thirteen years. A lot of people talk. They may believe they were arrogant. They were just darned good. I think it takes more than just talent."

Although he had a fan following, Counts, who made $12,000 a year, joined the Celtics at the height of Bill Russell's career, so he was never going to get into the starting lineup and mostly spectators' views of him, especially his rookie season, were of him wearing his warm-up jacket. Counts appeared in fifty-four games at a rate of just more than ten minutes per showing his first season. His second year in Boston, though, Counts received a bit more playing time, which made his statistics of 8.4 points and 6.4 rebounds per game fairly impressive.

Just when it seemed Counts might have a break-out season, however, Red Auerbach traded him to the Baltimore Bullets for future Hall-of-Famer Bailey Howell. Counts may have been younger with potential, but Howell was an established star who brought 20 points per game to the starting lineup.

That is why giving up Counts in this circumstance was one of the best swaps in team history. Counts only played a few months for the Bullets before being traded again to the Los Angeles Lakers. Counts put together three straight double-figure scoring years for LA and another for the Phoenix Suns. Counts was on three Laker teams that also went to the Finals, but all lost to Boston. He also suited up for the Philadelphia

76ers and New Orleans Jazz.

Although Counts played 10 years in the National Basketball Association and only two for the Celtics, he is surprisingly well-remembered in Boston. One reason is because he participated with two Celtics teams that won NBA championships, in 1964 and 1965.

"At the time, you don't really take it all in," Counts said. "But as time goes on, it becomes more meaningful. Now I can look at my Celtic ring, or my Celtic watch, and say, 'Hey, I was on a world championship team.' I've been very blessed and very fortunate to play on those teams."

After retirement, Counts returned to Oregon, where he was fondly remembered from his college days, and went into the real estate business in Woodburn, about forty-five miles south of the capital of Salem.

Willie Naulls

One of UCLA coach John Wooden's first great players on the West Coast, Willie Naulls was a starting forward in the 1950s, before the run of Bruins NCAA titles. Naulls was a powerfully built six-foot-six and 220 pounds, but also an excellent shooter. In one college game, Naulls took down 28 rebounds. He also played on a squad that upset the San Francisco team of future Celtic teammates' Bill Russell and K.C. Jones when it was on a long winning streak.

Naulls was originally from Dallas, Texas before his family moved to California to avoid the racial segregation there. In two ways as a professional, Naulls became part of pioneering desegregation developments.

While with the New York Knicks, in 1960, Naulls was the first African-American named captain of any American professional sports team, not only in the National Basketball Association. With New York, Naulls was a four-time All-Star and averaged nearly 20 points a game. For the 1961–62 season, Naulls averaged a career-high with 25 points per game. Naulls was one of the players on the other side of the box score when Wilt Chamberlain notched his record 100-point game for the Philadelphia Warriors in 1962. Naulls hit for 31 points that night, rather dramatically overshadowed.

Naulls became a Celtics for the 1964–64 season. In three seasons with Boston, his scoring average dropped to about 10 points a game because he received less playing time. However, Naulls won three championships with the Celtics.

Also, while playing with the Celtics, Naulls was one of the five players who took the court for the first all-African-American starting lineup for an NBA game. The regular starting lineup for Boston during the 1964–65 season had Russell at center, K.C. Jones and Sam Jones at guard, and Tom Sanders and Tommy Heinsohn at forward. Heinsohn, the only white player in the group, was injured and Red Auerbach plugged Naulls into the starting lineup for a game against the St. Louis Hawks on December 26, 1964. The Celtics won, 97–84.

Auerbach, who was still coaching before turning to the front office full-time, later said he did not use Naulls as the starter to make any kind of a statement and he did not even realize a special nature of the occasion.

"First of all, I had no idea that I started five black players until a writer pointed it out to me a few weeks later," Auerbach claimed. "It didn't make any difference to me what color any of my players were. I was putting the five best players on the court so that we could win."

It would be difficult to believe that Auerbach, who seemed to know exactly what he was doing every minute, would be unaware of what he had done, but certainly believable that he did not dwell on it.

Naulls died at eighty-four years old in 2018.

Don Nelson

**O**ne of the most distinctive aspects of Don Nelson's style on the court was his one-handed foul-shooting method. It was less picturesque than functional. For the most part, that could describe the way Nelson looked while playing. He did not appear to have an athletic gene in his body, but somehow beat opponents off the dribble, made outside shots that seemed to have no business going in, and out-hustled foes.

Nelson played 1,053 games in the National Basketball Association, spread over fourteen seasons, eleven of them with the Celtics. He then coached in another 2,398 games, winning a record 1,335 of them. The six-foot-six forward was born in Michigan in 1940, went to high school in Rock Island, Illinois, and college at the University of Iowa. Two seasons in a row, junior and senior years, Nelson averaged 23-plus points a game.

In the early 1960s, Nelson was briefly a member of the expansion Chicago Zephyrs, then was given new life by the Los Angeles Lakers where he spent two seasons as a bench player. LA also seemed to have little faith in Nelson's future, and he was let go, but he was signed as a free agent by the Celtics, pounced on by Red Auerbach.

"I was home for a couple of weeks when I got a call from Red, who was looking for a player," Nelson said.

Auerbach is the one who invented the sixth-man role in the NBA, now an acknowledged award. Nelson was the third Celtic to fill the job.

He immediately became a double-figure scorer for Boston and kept up that pace. For much of that time Nelson was distinguished by a blond, flat-top haircut, though he grew his hair out later. Nelson's contributions were appreciated promptly and, although always a sixth-man, he scored in timely ways, as many as 15.4 points a game during the 1969–70 season. He always showed court savvy and came through at crunch time. Nelson played for five Boston world championship teams and the franchise retired his No. 19 jersey. Nelson was overshadowed by the Celtics' Hall-of-Famers, but he was a team winner.

One of his shining moments came at the end of the 1968–69 season. Bill Russell was player-coach and about to retire, although his teammates did not know it until the Finals. As they did several times during the Dynasty years, the early championship Celtics faced the Lakers for the crown. Not only was Los Angeles favored, but the seventh game was scheduled for the West Coast. This title finale was the famous contest where the Celtics players discovered the Lakers had set up for a grand championship ceremony, with balloons falling from the ceiling and a choreographed party. Boston won the close game, 108–106. Nelson made the game-winning shot on a jumper, one that seemed to make its own travel arrangements to the hoop. A loose ball came to Nelson, standing just inside the foul line. He rose up with his one-hand push shot and fired it at the Lakers' basket. The ball hit the front rim, bounced in the air, and dropped through the hoop. Some might call the shot ugly, others may call it fate. Later, Nelson even called his shot a poor one, saying he was only in the right place at the right time when John Havlicek lost control of his dribble. The ball found Nelson, most assuredly in the right place.

"That was the luckiest shot I ever made in my life," Nelson said. But it counted just as picture-perfect ones did.

This was against the team that ditched Nelson, so it was the ultimate payback. Nelson must have felt vindicated taking a championship right out of the Lakers' hands. He did not speak in gloating terms, however, only saying that because it was his first title, it felt sweeter than the others.

That victory represented the break-up of the old gang, the end of the period when the Celtics won eleven championships in thirteen seasons. The last of the original group of the 1950s retired. Havlicek was still around and so was Nelson. The holdovers helped the Celtics rebuild and contributed to next generation titles in 1974 and 1976. Indeed, Nelson was still a member of the Celtics for the incredible, three-overtime playoff win over Phoenix in 1976, a game with so many twists and turns it defied probability. And it was the turning point in giving the Celtics the impetus for another crown.

"That game had everything," Nelson said. "We jumped to an early twenty-point lead, but the Suns came back and forced overtime." And more overtime. And still more. But Boston survived. Nelson retired as a player after that series.

Nelson did not leave pro basketball behind for another profession. It seemed only minutes passed before he accepted an assistant coaching job with the Milwaukee Bucks. And only minutes later became head coach of the team when the club dismissed Larry Costello eighteen games into the 1976–77 season.

That began one of the most distinguished of NBA coaching careers. Nelson coached the Bucks, the Golden State Warriors, New York Knicks, Dallas Mavericks, and Golden State for a second time. He coached from 1976 through 2010 before retiring to Hawaii. His overall record was 1,335–1,063. In some stops, he was also the general manager. All but a handful of his teams qualified for the playoffs, but Nelson never won a championship as a coach.

Nelson's nickname was "Nellie," and as a coach his style was often referred to as "Nellie Ball." When he was a player, Nelson was referred to as a "point forward," a position not in the traditional starting five but one which meant a forward who saw plays unfold the way a point guard did and who could make the same type of passes. Nellie Ball emphasized the type of quick-paced offensive game the Celtics played and Nelson relied on smaller, quicker athletes to execute, "I learned everything that I knew about coaching from Red Auerbach," Nelson said. "Not only did I play for him, we struck up a friendship, and he became a close personal friend."

When he was still on the Celtics roster, Nelson said he arrived early enough for games to just talk hoops with Auerbach for an hour a night.

"I learned so much just listening to him – how he handled the players, his coaching philosophy," Nelson said. "Things like that. And I basically adopted what he imparted."

For that matter, Nelson owed almost his entire playing career to Auerbach's acumen. He had cleared waivers, meaning no other team wanted him, when Auerbach summoned him to Boston.

"I believe he sees things in certain players that no one else sees, or maybe that no one else bothers to look for," Nelson once said. "It's something inside a player, something other than talent alone." In 2012, Nelson was elected to the Naismith Memorial Basketball Hall of Fame.

While attending a Golden State game in 2019, Nelson had completely discarded his old, conservative look. He had wavy long hair and sported a beard. He also told people he was smoking pot in his leisure and that as he approached eighty years old, he was inhaling his own crop since he was a marijuana farmer in Maui.

Boston Celtics Famous Games

1. On April 13, 1957, the Boston Celtics defeated the St. Louis Hawks, 125–123 in two overtimes to win the franchise's first world championship.

2. June 4, 1976 was the date of the fifth game of the NBA Finals between the Celtics and Phoenix Suns, a game so improbable that many believe it is the greatest game in NBA history. Boston won, 128–126, in triple overtime and then captured the championship in Game Six.

3. Although the NBA championship was not at stake, it felt as if it was when the Celtics outlasted the Philadelphia 76ers in the seventh game of the Eastern Division finals, 110–109, on April 15, 1965. A Boston mistake had given Philadelphia a last-gasp chance, but when the 76ers sought to inbound the ball, John Havlicek tipped it away, sending Celtics team announcer Johnny Most into his most famous call, shouting, "Havlicek stole the ball!' The line is so ingrained in Celtics lore that a record album was made with that title.

4. The Celtics' eleventh title in thirteen years was solidified in Los Angeles, the last night of Bill Russell's glorious playing career. The series was tied, 3–3, with the Lakers hosting Game Seven. Phenomenal guard Jerry West was at his peak, averaging 37 points a game in this Finals, desperately hoping to finally beat Boston. When the Celtics arrived for the game, they learned the Lakers had

stashed balloons in the ceiling for a celebration and left instructional sheets on seats telling fans how to react. Boston won, 108—106, to spoil the party. West won the MVP, and the Celtics won the team trophy.

5. Boston had not won an NBA crown since 1986 when the club put an end to the drought, besting the Lakers in six games. The championship was earned on June 6, 2008, with the core players Kevin Garnett, Paul Pierce, and Ray Allen leading the way.

6. After the Hall of Fame crew of Bob Cousy, Bill Sharman, Bill Russell, Frank Ramsey, Tommy Heinsohn, Sam Jones, and K.C. Jones retired and the Dynasty Celtics completed their run in 1969, neither Boston fans nor the basketball world had any inkling when the Celtics would rise again. They got their answer on May 12, 1974, when the new-era Celtics led by holdover John Havlicek, Dave Cowens, and Jo Jo White polished off the Milwaukee Bucks in a seventh game.

7. Some fans believed the Celtics of the 1985–86 season may have been the greatest Boston team of all. The Celtics, anchored by Larry Bird, beat the Houston Rockets in six games in the Finals, the last win coming on June 8 by a 114–97 count. Kevin McHale and Robert Parish completed the Big Three, Hall-of-Famer Bill Walton was a supersub for Boston. This was the capper for the 1980s group of Celtics that won three NBA titles in the decade.

8. On December 26, 1964, the Celtics became the first NBA team in history to have five African-Americans in the starting lineup. Coach Red Auerbach opened the game with Bill Russell at center, Sam Jones and K.C. Jones in the backcourt, and Tom Sanders and Willie Naulls at for-

ward. Tommy Heinsohn was a regular starter at forward, but was injured that night and Naulls filled in.

9. Larry Bird set the single-game Boston Celtics scoring record on March 12, 1985 with 60 points. The barrage came in a 126–115 victory over the Atlanta Hawks on a neutral court in New Orleans. Bird made just one three-point shot that night and hit fifteen out of sixteen free-throw attempts. The Celtics had five other players in double figures that game, including Kevin McHale, who only nine days earlier had set the club record with 56 points. This was a Bird take-that bit of one-upmanship.

10. Before the Celtics Dynasty began, the team engaged in one particularly memorable playoff game against the Syracuse Nationals. On March 21, 1953, guard Bob Cousy scored 50 points in a four-overtime Celtics 111–105 victory over Syracuse in an Eastern Division series. Cousy made thirty out of thirty-two free-throw attempts – still an NBA playoff gamer record. This was the year before the twenty-four-second shot clock was introduced.

Luck Of The Irish

he mascot symbol of the Boston Celtics is a cartoon-like figure named "Lucky." This faux individual is an impish-appearing character wearing a green-tinged bowler, bow tie, and vest. He's a winking leprechaun who has a brown basketball twirling on one index finger while leaning on a shillelagh. Lucky has a pipe in his mouth as well.

When the Celtics first began playing in the late 1940s, Boston was regarded as an Irish town with its politicians rooted in the old country. The team colors became green and white, and the connection to Ireland and winning with the luck of the Irish was ingrained.

The mascot himself, and the team logo where he is superimposed on a green circle with white lettering reading "Boston Celtics," was actually an artistic creation by Red Auerbach's brother Zang who designed the figure in the 1950s. Originally a one-dimensional figure, Lucky's role was eventually expanded and real-live people auditioned for the job of becoming Lucky in the flesh to help entertain children at games during the season. Apparently though, once along the way, one Lucky was not so lucky, being fired for not showing up for scheduled charity events.

Some Luckys are athletically gifted enough to make acrobatic moves and dunk. Good thing there have been replacements along the way, because Lucky is around sixty-five years old and eligible for Medicare.

Back to attire: the green swatches on Lucky's hat, bow-tie, and vest are all three-leaf clovers. There is no apparent reason for Lucky wearing black pants or black buckle shoes. His waist line is even a tad larger than athletic looking, as if he may have imbibed a few too many beers beyond doctor's recommendations.

Certainly, the look on Lucky's face goes beyond a basic smile. He seems to be smirking, as if he knows something you do not, or perhaps because he has listened in on the huddle and knows the Celtics' next strategic move is bound to pay off.

At one point, the Celtics team website ran a question-and-answer session with Lucky. In this interview he revealed such personal opinions as his favorite meal being green eggs and ham, his favorite number being eighteen because when the Celtics win it all again that will be their total number of championships, and that his favorite holiday (no surprise here) being St. Patrick's Day.

John Thompson

**W**hen he strode onto the court to coach his Georgetown Hoyas to considerable glory in college basketball, John Thompson was using his mind more than his body in his favorite sport. But when he was much younger, first at Providence College, and then with the Boston Celtics as Bill Russell's back-up center for a short period of time, he did have success as a player.

A second-team All-American for the Friars, where one season he scored an average of 19.2 points a game, Thompson was second team all the way with Boston, one of the many big men who gave Russell a breather here and there and played some forward. He averaged 3.5 points a game and 3.5 rebounds. His reward was collecting two NBA championship rings.

Never the star he was in college, Thompson admitted he had difficulty adjusting: "When I fill in at center for Bill, I find I have to change from the style I played in scrimmages with the Celtics where I oppose Bill in the pivot."

He played two seasons between 1964 and 1966 after being a third-round draft choice. Left unprotected in the expansion draft, Thompson was selected by the new Chicago Bulls, but never played for them.

Instead, Thompson went into coaching. Long-forgotten was his tremendous success at St. Anthony's High of Washington, D.C. between 1966 and 1972, where he finished nearly one hundred games over .500 and rarely lost.

Following that stint, Thompson became much better known for his twenty-seven years on the Georgetown bench. Thompson won 596 games, became the first African-American coach to win an NCAA title, coached in the Olympics, and was inducted into the Naismith Memorial Basketball Hall of Fame in 2006. During his days on the sidelines at Georgetown, one of Thompson's trademarks was carrying a towel draped over his sport coat.

Regarded as outspoken, especially on issues of racial sensitivity, Thompson was viewed as running a tightly controlled program that often seemed unfriendly to sportswriters. When he retired from coaching in 1999, however, he joined the media as a sports commentator.

One of Thompson's sons, John Thompson III, eventually became the Georgetown coach.

Larry Siegfried

hen it came to nicknames Larry Siegfried answered to "Ziggy." His real nickname should have been Scrappy because that's the way he played 100 percent of the time on the court. The six-foot-three guard spent seven seasons with the Celtics in the 1960s, and his career average was 10.8 points per game. During that time Boston won five world championships, so Siegfried earned a ring for every finger on one hand.

A member of one of the greatest college basketball teams of all-time – the early 1960s Ohio State Buckeyes – Siegfried was a teammate of future pros Jerry Lucas, John Havlicek, Joe Roberts, Mel Nowell, and a sixth-man named Bob Knight, later the Hall-of-Fame coach.

In Boston, Siegfried was just a back-up because the Celtics' backcourt was cluttered with Hall-of-Famers. Red Auerbach called on him for quick offense from his jump shot and clamp-down defense. Siegfried, who died in 2010 at age seventy-one, prided himself on his hustle. He said his mindset was built around the theme, "A loose ball was my ball."

That epitomized his constant movement and opportunistic

style. Siegfried represented the kind of guys Auerbach coveted: guys who could contribute in spurts, play unselfishly, and make things happen.

Siegfried understood from the first moment what Auerbach demanded from his players. Those demands were intense, but the rewards significant. When he first showed up to training camp, Siegfried said Auerbach virtually ran the players into the ground.

"We pressed, man-to-man, from one end of the court to the other during that whole scrimmage the first day of camp," Siegfried said. "If someone got sick, that person would come out, and you'd play five-on-four. Red wanted to find out who was in shape and who really wanted to be there."

Big talk could not substitute for stamina and Siegfried showed his stuff.

Henry Finkel

rafting the big man was a good idea in theory, but his outside shooting seemed to be at odds with his listed height of seven feet. Still, Henry, or Hank, Finkel was a popular player with the Celtics for several years, although he was never viewed as an important cog in building a winner.

With his size, Finkel was somewhat of a curiosity during his stay in Boston between 1969 and 1975 after stints with the Los Angeles Lakers and San Diego Rockets. A star player at Dayton University, a college that has seemingly almost always enjoyed prosperity, Finkel could maneuver near the hoop, but also deliver from outside, unusual for a player so tall during that era and before the three-point shot was adopted. In that sense, his style resembled that of Mel Counts, another Celtics seven-footer.

Finkel, who grew a distinctive, dark mustache, had great success in Ohio. He averaged 23 points and 13 rebounds per game as a sophomore, 25.3 points and 14.9 rebounds as a junior, and 22.7 points and 12.1 rebounds as a senior. Finkel had one 44-point game for the Flyers and was named to some All-American teams.

Finkel did not make a quick impact in the National Basketball Association with his California teams, though in his second season in San Diego, he averaged a career-high 11.6 points. His first season in Boston Finkel was player-coach

Bill Russell's back-up at center. However, Finkel was tutored in finer points of pivot play, and a year later, with Russell in retirement, Finkel scored at a 9.7 clip.

As a starter, while the Celtics went into a losing tailspin with a record of 34–48, for the first time since the mid-1950s, Finkel took heat from fans.

"Henry Finkel is not the reason we're losing," coach Tommy Heinsohn defended him. "It's not fair for him to be singled out as a symbol for the team's problems. You lose a Bill Russell and there are going to be consequences."

Although Finkel was sometimes irked by his situation, he seemed to understand the outsized expectations.

"People said I was acquired to be Russell's replacement," he said. "That bothered me because everyone knew no one in the NBA could 'replace' Bill Russell. Heck, I was just an average reserve player. Before I even put on the Celtics uniform I knew I wasn't a legitimate starting center in this league. I didn't kid myself. I didn't have great talent, so I just made up my mind to try and outwork whoever was matched up against me."

After Boston drafted Dave Cowens and Finkel again served as a bench player, he became more popular. Just as often happens in high school and college basketball, spectators warmed to one of the last men to get into games. The biggest reward Finkel received for his six-season perseverance with Boston was a championship ring for the 1973—74 season.

Finkel's career NBA averages were 5.1 points and 3.9 rebounds a game in nine seasons.

After retiring, Finkel stayed in the Boston area and did some broadcasting of Celtics games.

Dave Cowens

he fiery redhead Dave Cowens was one of the most unusual of Boston Celtics stars. Not only was Cowens an undersized All-Star center at six-foot-nine, but he temporarily walked away from the National Basketball Association for a time out, and when the mood struck him, he filled in as a taxi cab driver.

Yet Cowens was also the cornerstone of some great Boston teams that won championships in the 1970s with him in the middle, and he later coached in the NBA. Born in 1948, Cowens was from Newport, Kentucky and played his college ball at Florida State. In high school, he shot up in height by about five inches between his sophomore and junior years, which transformed him from a guard to a pivot man.

At FSU, Cowens still owns team records for rebounding. He was an All-American pick, and the school has retired his jersey.

When he joined the Celtics in 1970 after being their first-round draft pick, Cowens became the league's rookie of the year. In 1973, he was chosen as the NBA's Most Valuable Player and twice, in 1974 and 1976, Cowens was a key figure on world championship teams. Ultimately, he was elected to the Naismith Memorial Basketball Hall of Fame in 1991.

Playing center at Cowens's height in the NBA was rare even back then. Long before many other big men had mastered the trait though, Cowens was an excellent outside shooter. At that time, pivot men were expected to use their bodies to gain position in the low post and take short-range shots. Cowens disrupted defenses with this added skill. How much it helped him was impossible to discern, but he was also a left-handed shooter.

Hall-of-Famer Bill Russell, who nearly revolutionized center play on defense while being only slightly taller than Cowens gave Cowens a plug.

"Nobody is going to tell that kid he can't play," Russell said.

Cowens proved that immediately. As a rookie, he averaged 17 points and 15 rebounds per game. In a rarity, Cowens did share rookie-of-the-year honors with Geoff Petrie of the Portland Trailblazers. It was the first time that happened.

In ensuing years, after the 1994–95 season when Grant Hill and Jason Kidd tied, and for the 1999–2000 season with Steve Francis and Elton Brand splitting the vote, there were also two rookies of the year.

Another way Cowens surprised opponents was his uncanny knack in getting to the ball for rebounds. Other players were taller and had longer arms. Cowens, who weighed a powerful 230 pounds, wisely used his bulk for positioning and had textbook blocking-out skills. Eight times, Cowens averaged between 13.9 and 16.2 rebounds a game during the regular season. That last figure led the league. Cowens may have been mobile, but sometimes his lack of size cost him in the NBA against seven-footers. Cowens fouled out regularly and collected more fouls than any other player on the Celtics for several years in a row. "I had the mentality that I could guard anybody," Cowens said. That is the proper mindset, but reality has to play a role as well.

The rookie-of-the-year attention represented only the beginning of the awards accorded to Cowens. He was an eight-time All Star (and won the game's MVP award once), a three-time defensive team player, and he repeatedly showed off his all-around game as a scorer, rebounder, and defender.

It did not take long for people to overlook that Cowens was supposed to be too short to line up at his position. His relentless hustle and style always defined his game.

It was during the 1976–77 season that Cowens asked for a leave of absence from the team. The request startled management and fans. Cowens played in just fifty games that season. Saying he wished to see how others lived, he briefly took a job driving a cab. This was Cowens's personal walkabout. He returned to the Celtics for the next season exhibiting his same high level of play, averaging 18.6 points per game.

During one of the Celtics' down periods, the 1978–79 season when the team did not make the playoffs, Cowens took the reins as head coach. He became one of the last player-coaches in professional sports but quickly returned the keys to the car. Cowens appeared in sixty-six games, starting just fifty-five of them, during the 1979–80 season. His scoring dropped to 14.2 points a game, and he decided it was time to retire.

"I have sprained my ankle at least thirty times over the duration of my career," Cowens said, "broken both legs, and fractured a foot." He said he had visited squadrons of doctors, and specialists told him he was lucky to be walking, never mind continuing a pro basketball career. Yet Cowens then changed his mind and announced he would like to give playing one more whirl for the 1982–83 season. By that time, however, the Celtics had reloaded in the front court with Larry Bird, Kevin McHale, and Robert Parish. Sizing up the situation, Cowens said it would probably be best if the Celtics traded him.

Boston still held Cowens's NBA rights. It was unknown exactly what his worth was then – that was not something he could really estimate either – so it was not clear what other team might want to sign him and at what price. In the end, the Milwaukee Bucks, then coached by Don Nelson, who had played alongside Cowens with the Celtics, made a deal. Boston acquired guard Quinn Buckner, who starred for Indiana University's 1976 NCAA champion team.

Buckner played a few seasons for Boston coming off the

bench and was a member of the 1984 championship team. Cowens played in just forty games for the Bucks. He averaged 8.1 points, 6.9 rebounds, and 2.1 assists a game. That was much lower than his usual output, but he also played many fewer minutes per game. After that season, Cowens retired from playing for good.

However, Cowens was in demand as a head coach in the NBA. He led the Charlotte Hornets for two-and-a-half years. The first season, the club won fifty-four games and reached the playoffs twice in a row. Cowens resigned after just fifteen games the next year when the team started 4–11. In-between the Hornets and accepting the Golden State Warriors head job, Cowens was an assistant for the San Antonio Spurs. He coached Golden State during some lean years. The Warriors went 17–65 in his first season, and he was fired after a slow start during the 2001–02 season. That ended Cowens's NBA head coaching career.

In 2005 and 2006, Cowens served as head coach of the Chicago Sky of the Women's NBA. Between 2006 and 2009, he was back in the men's NBA as an assistant coach for the Detroit Pistons.

Cowens came to the Celtics as a player at just the right time. The Dynasty days were over. After the eleven titles in thirteen seasons ending in 1969, there was a void and the team faced a great unknown. It was not as if the magic had run out, but the never-ending stream of star players had been interrupted. Cowens was the fresh tonic for the next generation to join John Havlicek as a signature player to uplift Boston back into the title hunt.

Cowens was the key man who helped Boston regain its footing, the fresh bridge player (Havlicek couldn't do it all alone) between Bill Russell and Larry Bird.

"No one could replace Bill Russell," Cowens said in an understood understatement. "All I could do was come in, be me, and hope that it was enough." It very much was so. How could anyone count on the team drafting another Hall-of-

Famer to play center immediately after Russell's retirement?

The Celtics had been known for making hay with the fast break during the Dynasty years. With Tommy Heinsohn as coach when Cowens arrived from Florida State, he wanted to employ the same style he had thrived with as a player, and Cowens knew it and suited it.

"I'd played up-tempo in high school and college, and my conditioning was at a very high level," Cowens said. "I was used to pushing through various thresholds of pain and fatigue, even when other players were having trouble."

Run, run, run. It seemed Cowens was ready to compete in a ten-thousand-meter race. But he was also a tough guy who used his body to shove around foes who wanted to shove him out of rebounding range. He admitted he was a little bit of a wild man during the early days of his career.

"I was very much a Dennis the Menace on the court," Cowens said. "My attitude was to play all out and to just let it rip. I stayed in constant motion and tried to wear my opponent down. If I looked a little crazy doing it, that was part of the package."

The center nobody was quite sure about played for eleven professional seasons, ten of them with the Celtics, and his work warranted his admission to the Hall of Fame. Cowens was one of Boston's main men during the 1975–76 season that ended with a world title and what may have been described as the greatest NBA game ever played in the play-offs versus Phoenix. Boston won the triple overtime game in the Finals.

"There's never been another game like it," Cowens said. In some ways there may never have been another player like Dave Cowens either.

Jo Jo White

ou could count on Jo Jo White being there, every game, every night, and in the clutch. A major figure in the Celtics' resurgence of the 1970s after the original Dynasty group aged into retirement, the six-foot-three guard out of Kansas helped Boston win two more National Basketball Association titles during his ten seasons with the club.

The Celtics' No. 1 draft pick in 1969, White was a collegiate All-American and a member of the United States' 1968 Summer Olympic basketball squad. That American team was not favored in Mexico City, but White emerged as one of the leaders and the US took home the gold medal. A seven-time NBA All-Star, White was elected to the Naismith Memorial Basketball Hall of Fame in 2015.

The son of a minister, who grew up in St. Louis, White established a national name for himself in hoops while a Jayhawk. He was always thankful for the coaching he received at Kansas and whenever he talked about his basketball roots, he praised those who helped him there.

"He was a KU legend," said Kansas coach Bill Self. "When you talk about KU greats and you're trying to fill that five of the best who ever played here from a talent standpoint, most of the old-timers put Jo Jo in that group."

Although he was known for his basketball skill, White was also drafted by the Dallas Cowboys of the National Football

League and the Cincinnati Reds in baseball. However, he stuck with hoops. Actually, he nearly spent two years in the military instead of starting his career with Boston. Red Auerbach, the man who chose White and believed in him, somehow used his influence to place White in the Marine reserves, and that minimized his time away from the team.

"Red's fingerprints were everywhere when I got to Boston," White said. "From the banners overhead to the shrewd roster moves, to him being there during training camp and at practices. And the cigar smoke. If you were ever around Red, you know what I'm talking about. Red Auerbach was a true genius."

White joined the Celtics when he was very much needed. He teamed with veteran John Havlicek and newcomer Dave Cowens in 1974 to bring Boston its first crown since Bill Russell retired. In 1976, when the Celtics won it all for a second time during the decade, White was the Most Valuable Player in the Finals.

Besides his obvious skill, one thing that set White apart during his stay in Boston for most of his pro career was his ability to stay healthy and avoid missing games. White played in 488 consecutive games for the Celtics, a team record. White played in all eighty-two regular-season games for five seasons in a row.

The most vivid memories of White on the floor revolved around his smooth outside jump shot. White's highlight lifetime stats include averaging 17.2 points, 4.0 rebounds, and 4.9 assists per game. White's finest season was the 1971–72 campaign when he averaged 23.1 points per game. In his second highest-scoring year, White hit for 21.3 points a game.

"With Jo Jo White, if you were a Celtic, that personified cool," said teammate Cedric Maxwell. "He did everything so cool. He walked cool. He talked cool."

Although White was unhappy to be traded, and played elsewhere for his final two NBA seasons, he did eventually reconcile with the Celtics. In 1982, his No. 10 jersey number was retired.

White began suffering from serious health problems in 2010 when a brain tumor was discovered. While the surgery to eradicate the cancer threat was deemed to be successful, it accelerated the process of dementia. White died from complications of pneumonia at seventy-one in 2018. At the time he died, White was working for the Celtics front office as a community relations official.

When White passed away, the Celtics issued a statement summing up his connection to the team and as a player and a man: "We are terribly saddened by the passing of the great Jo Jo White. He was a champion and a gentleman, supremely talented and brilliant on the court, and endlessly gracious off of it."

Greatest Game Ever

The greatest National Basketball Association game ever played may have been the June 4, 1976 Game Five Finals showdown at the Boston Garden between the Celtics and the Phoenix Suns, won by Boston, 128–126, in triple overtime.

It was not just the circumstances, being part of a championship series and lasting three overtimes that made the game so special, but the manner in which each round of overtime played out. This was the fifth game of the seven-game title series with the teams being tied at 2–2 at tipoff. Boston was a decided favorite over the Suns, which had not been a powerhouse in the Western Division that year, but maneuvered through the playoffs.

The Celtics led early, but the Suns eroded the lead in a low-scoring second half and regulation ended at 95–95. The triple overtime meant the game had sixty-three minutes of playing time rather than the usual forty-eight minutes. It was 101-all after the first overtime, and 112–112 after the second overtime.

There were several unlikely elements in the contest, too. The Suns put all five starters in double figures – and no one else. Phoenix forward Garfield Heard played sixty-one minutes, the most of anyone, while Boston's Jo Jo White played sixty minutes. White, later a Hall-of-Famer, was the game's high scorer with 33 points.

"We had quite a few characters on that team, and we had a lot of smart players," said forward Paul Silas of the makeup of that Celtics roster.

The iron man Heard also made a miracle shot to keep the Suns alive at the end of the second overtime. Phoenix led by one point with four seconds left when Boston's John Havlichek dribbled down-court and hit a 15-point jumper. It appeared to be the game-winner as the buzzer sounded. Fans mobbed the parquet court at the Garden, and some Celtics even retreated to the locker room.

They had to be retrieved when officials put one second back on the clock and it was Phoenix's ball. Guard Paul Westphal, a former Celtic also headed to the Hall of Fame, called timeout. This was a ploy.

The Suns had no more time outs, so were assessed a technical foul. Boston made the shot for a two-point lead. However, that gave Phoenix the ball near mid-court instead of under its own basket. The pass-in went to Heard, who hit a long-range turn-around jumper for the tie. This was prior to the approval of the three-point shot rule, or Phoenix would have won at that point.

As players began fouling out or getting into foul trouble, the Celtics employed deep bench player Glenn McDonald more than usual. McDonald scored 8 points total, six made during the third OT, for his greatest stretch as a Celtic.

"That game had everything," said forward Don Nelson, who later became an esteemed coach and who gave McDonald much credit for the win. "It is without a doubt the craziest game that I ever played in."

Boston center Dave Cowens had 26 points and 19 rebounds, Havlicek scored 22, and forward Paul Silas added 17.

"No two teams ever shot so well in overtime," White said. "That's the kind of game that you'd like to have to end a series."

Only it did not. The Celtics then led 3–2. Two days later, Boston won the championship with a seven-point victory, the opportunity set up by the triple overtime triumph.

Paul Silas

ven though he wasn't the biggest guy in the world, Paul Silas put the power in power forward as a rebounder. He was a monstrous rebounder in college at Creighton, especially for a six-foot-seven player, with his 220-pound bulk helping him to edge competitors out of the way.

Even though he was a native of Arkansas, Silas attended high school in California and college in Nebraska. Over a three-year period, Silas averaged 20.6 rebounds per game. If the ball was bouncing off the rim or backboard, Silas would go get it for his team. He set NCAA records while playing in the early 1960s. He earned All-American recognition for those exploits, but not first team. Later, Creighton retired his No. 35 jersey.

Although Silas did not attain instant stardom when he broke into the National Basketball Association with the St. Louis Hawks for the 1964–65 season, he had a long career and played a pivotal role with the Celtics for four seasons in the 1970s. Two of his three championship rings were collected with Boston, and Silas took home another one with the Seattle SuperSonics.

He competed for sixteen seasons in the NBA and, while never a truly great scorer, Silas averaged in double figures for points eight times, four of those with Boston.

Silas's hustle, defense, and rebounding always gained him respect from teammates, and his strength under the hoop made him very valuable to the Celtics during those 1974 and 1976 title runs. A two-time All-Star, Silas was honored with five mentions on all-league defensive teams.

"We had a lot to prove in 1976 since we weren't able to repeat as champions in 1975 like we thought we should," Silas said.

To obtain Silas, Red Auerbach traded the rights to guard Charlie Scott to the Phoenix Suns. At that point, Scott had never played for Boston. When the Celtics drafted him, Scott signed with the Virginia Squires of the American Basketball Association. This essentially meant Auerbach got Silas for nothing. It was only later that Scott became a true member of the Celtics. In-between, Silas was tearing up the boards for Boston. At one point, frustrated Phoenix management sought to buy Silas back from the Celtics, going as high as $250,000 in its offer. Auerbach said no.

Going to the Celtics was big for Silas, who up until he experienced the workings of the organization up close was a skeptic about some of the things he heard indicating it was a great club.

"Prior to winning the championship, I didn't believe in all the Celtics pride and beliefs," Silas said, "and little elf (presumably Lucky the Leprechaun) and that kind of thing. But I became a believer. It was special." Of Auerbach, Silas said, "He started this whole thing and without him, it just couldn't be."

Although several Celtics players went on to coach the big club, Silas never got his chance despite following his playing days with a very lengthy NBA coaching career, from 1980 to 2012. In addition to serving as an assistant coach for several franchises, Silas spent periods as a head coach for the San Diego Clippers, Charlotte Hornets, New Orleans Hornets, Cleveland Cavaliers, and Charlotte Bobcats.

When he was with Cleveland, Silas was assigned to mentor LeBron James during the early days of his career.

"I didn't have a point guard," Silas said, "so I made him my point forward."

Those days really helped James improve his passing skills at the highest level of the game.

Clarence Glover

**A**fter a career at Western Kentucky, six-foot-eight Clarence Glover was drafted on potential, making the Celtics roster for the 1971–72 team as a first-round draft pick.

But Glover was a seldom-used player during his single season with the team. He appeared in twenty-five games, averaging just under five minutes of playing time and 2.6 points per game. Sometimes, during blowouts, Boston Garden fans hollered for Glover to be inserted into games.

Glover gained considerable late-season attention the season before his pro season when he helped lead the Hilltoppers to the NCAA Final Four. The exposure at the right time gave him his chance at the NBA. Glover was a dominating rebounder during the tournament. Western Kentucky took third place after falling in the semi-finals in double overtime to Villanova. It was a grand showcase for him.

One reason Glover's stay in Boston was brief was the club's acquisition of All-Star Paul Silas at forward to step in. The Celtics did not truly give up on Glover. In a different era of pro ball, when options were limited, they arranged for him to play for Hartford in the Eastern League in the hopes that he would continue to improve and become a key asset later. That would be like a team sending a player to the G League now.

"I've been playing very well," Glover said after making a mark in Hartford. "My defense and my rebounding have been improving real well. And my scoring has improved, too. Playing in Hartford has been a good opportunity."

Still, Glover took some heat in Boston as a No. 1 draft choice who did not contribute immediately. He said the level of talent in pro ball shocked him and he was not ready. The year at Hartford made him determined to get back to the Celtics.

"I'm at the peak of my talents," Glover said, "and I'd like to put them in action for the people in the Boston Garden."

Glover got his second shot with Boston the next season, but did not make the cut coming out of training camp and left pro basketball to become a teacher and coach. He is enshrined in the Western Kentucky Athletics Hall of Fame.

Chris Ford

**G**uard Chris Ford came to the Celtics from the Detroit Pistons a few games into the 1978–79 season, already well into his career. He was known as a solid, if not great player, with good size at six feet, five inches and the owner of an excellent outside shot.

As he approached his 30th birthday, Ford, who attended Villanova, finally got enough opportunity to average in double figures. His best years, though, lay immediately ahead, and his scoring output increased to more than 15 points per game in his first year with Boston.

In June of 1979, the National Basketball Association voted in the use of the three-point shot as a weapon. The American Basketball Association had introduced the play in the mid-1960s.

The Celtics opened that season on October 12th with a game at the Boston Garden against the Houston Rockets. Boston won, 114–106, with the aid of a Ford three-point shot, the first one made in NBA history, although Rick Barry also made one in the same game.

Ford scored 17 points in that game. Both Larry Bird and Dave Cowens attempted one three-pointer as well. Coaches and teams had not quite embraced its use and were still experimenting with the shot.

Ford's make was not a designed play because the team did not yet have designed plays for trying the long-distance shot. Bird, who became very proficient throwing down threes, joked of Ford's shot, "Well, actually, they were double- or triple-teaming me and he was out there with nothing to do, so I passed it to him."

Ford hit 42.7 percent of his three-point attempts that first year, though he never exaggerated his talent:"If you saw me playing in a pick-up game over there, you'd wonder how I was a professional basketball player. You'd say, 'No way.' But if you put me in a team setting where there's a clock and there are fouls being given out and the score is being kept, and all those things, then I can hold my own."

In addition to the distinction of making the first-ever three-point shot in NBA history, after his playing days, Ford became the Celtics' head coach. He led the team for five seasons, though his teams never advanced beyond the conference semifinals.

Always intense, Ford always wanted to become a coach. Some wondered if he would blow a gasket because he seemed so close to the boiling point as an assistant under K.C. Jones. One former teammate who was surprised was forward Kevin McHale.

"Chris has an unbelievably good bench demeanor," McHale said. "I really thought he'd be a psycho when he became head coach because all he ever did was yell at us when he was an assistant. But he's pretty cool."

Ford won a championship ring with the Celtics as a player and won fifty-six games as a coach the year McHale talked about. Later, Ford coached the Milwaukee Bucks, Los Angeles Clippers, and Philadelphia 76ers.

Scott Wedman

**A** seven-year National Basketball Association veteran by the time he joined the Boston Celtics for the 1982–83 season, the six-foot-seven Scott Wedman was a dangerous outside shooter.

Already thirty years old, he was approaching the downside of his professional career, yet Wedman spent five more seasons in the league with Boston.

Much in the manner Red Auerbach always seemed to find the savvy performer who had shown well for other teams but was looking to extend a career and willing to back-up the next generation of stars, Wedman fit the Boston mold.

Wedman played college ball at the University of Colorado and had twice become an all-conference player for the Buffaloes. The Kansas City-Omaha Kings made him a first-round draft pick in 1974 and their instincts about Wedman's pro future were correct. He was a National Basketball Association All-Rookie selection his first season.

During seven seasons with his original franchise, Wedman scored in double figures every year. Twice, near the end of his stay in Kansas City, Wedman averaged exactly 19 points a game. He was twice chosen for the All-Star game while affiliated with Kansas City. Wedman spent a year-plus with the Cleveland Cavaliers and became a Celtic before the end of the 1982–83 season. He was making one million dollars a year with Cleveland, but his production dropped due to injuries.

The Celtics acquired Wedman in a trade in January of

1983, giving up Darren Tillis and a first-round draft pick. Wedman's stay in Boston resulted in a career compromise. He became a bench player for the first time in his career, spelling the star trio of Larry Bird, Kevin McHale, and Robert Parish in the Boston front-court, yet being rewarded with two championship rings at the end of the 1984 and 1986 seasons.

Off the court, considering the time period more than thirty years ago, Wedman was a rarity; he was a professional athlete and a vegetarian. This resulted in merciless teasing from teammates.

While his playing time declined, Wedman earned critical minutes on the court. His sharp shooting – a career level of 48-plus percent – made him valuable in re-energizing the team when he entered games and catching opposing teams off-balance.

"Ironically, my first game as a Boston Celtic was against the Cavaliers in Cleveland," Wedman said. "I remember how strange it felt to dress in the road locker room."

At the time, he said, the Celtics wore green basketball shoes and he only had white with him after his quick team transition. Wedman said he had to paint his sneakers green that day.

Although Wedman was primarily someone who entered games to relieve the Big Three, on occasion, he made the moment his. Perhaps his most famous Celtics game came in the first contest of the 1985 Finals against the Los Angeles Lakers. Wedman shot a perfect eleven-for-eleven from the field for 26 points.

After his playing days, Wedman twice had coaching stints with minor league teams in Kansas City and Great Falls, Montana.

It was obvious to Wedman upon arriving in Boston that his days as a starter were over given the future Hall of Fame group of stars ahead of him as front-court men. But he showed the organization and coaches Bill Fitch and K.C. Jones, he still had skills.

"I had no illusions when I was with the Celtics," Wedman said. "They had the best player in basketball. Who could have realistically thought of taking Larry Bird's job away?"

Nate Archibald

lthough his nickname said differently, guard Nate Archibald was not really "Tiny." He may have been slender at 160 pounds, but he stood six-feet, one-inch, which fails to meet the definition of tiny. And in his own way, Archibald played basketball like a giant.

Despite only part of his fourteen-year National Basketball Association career being spent in Boston, Archibald made an impact everywhere he went. He played well enough in his multiple-team stops to reach the Naismith Memorial Basketball Hall of Fame.

A New Yorker, Archibald was a brilliant point guard out of Texas-Western who played for the Cincinnati Royals, then Kansas City when the franchise relocated, the New York Nets, the Buffalo Braves, the Celtics, and the Milwaukee Bucks. To clarify, Archibald never actually played a game for Buffalo because he tore an Achilles tendon that changed his game.

Once just about the fastest man in the sport, who could slither around big men to reach the basket and hit the outside shot to throw them off-balance, Archibald did have to adapt a bit after being hurt. He was a seven-time All-Star, who averaged 34 points a game and 11.4 assists during the 1972-

73. That made him the only player to ever lead the league in both of those categories in the same year.

Archibald spent five years with the Celtics and was a member of the 1981 NBA championship team, the only year he won a professional title. Even though he was not counted on as heavily as he had been by other teams earlier in his career, Archibald always averaged in double figures for Boston and twice averaged at least 8 assists a game for the Celtics.

Tiny joined the Celtics at a precarious time in his career. He had missed the entire previous season with injury and was not sure if his recovery would allow him to remain a star player:

"Fortunately for me, Red [Auerbach] was completely in my corner from the start." Archibald had gained weight and was not in top playing shape. But Auerbach understood. "Before training camp," Archibald added, "he just looked me right in the eyes and said, 'Look, there's no sense in pushing yourself too much and risking a setback. I want you back at a hundred percent, not seventy or eighty percent."

While Archibald was not pleased with his first season wearing green and white, he did average 11 points and 4.7 assists in comeback mode – and he stayed healthy. That was critical to his future and allowed him to be fully healed without worrying in the back of his mind about the next year.

Archibald was a full-fledged partner when a revamped Boston team, for which he played eighty games, captured the championship at the end of the 1981 season. That was a 13.8-point and 7.7-assist campaign for him.

"Without a doubt, the greatest moment in my career," Tiny said. "To be a part of that team with all of the great players we had, is something I am very proud of."

Cedric Maxwell

In some ways one of the Celtics' most underrated great players, Cedric Maxwell is probably as well-known to the team's fans now as he was when he was at the peak of his game. Maxwell, whose nickname was "Cornbread," named after a movie character by a college teammate, broadcasts Celtics games on the radio.

A teammate of Larry Bird, Kevin McHale, and Robert Parish when the 1981 Celtics won the National Basketball Association crown, Maxwell was the fourth guy in what came to be called Boston's first Big Three. Yet he averaged 14.8 points a game. An injury actually cost Maxwell his spot in the starting lineup. McHale had been a sixth-man honoree, but took over when Maxwell was sidelined.

The six-foot-eight forward came out of the University of North Carolina Charlotte, after leading the 49ers to the Final Four. Maxwell was a Celtics' No. 1 draft pick in 1977 and made a quick impact on a bad team before those other players were gathered together. Maxwell earned two championship rings with Boston and was the Most Valuable Player in the 1981 NBA Finals.

Maxwell, who was not terribly fond of his nickname, at

least at first, had to put up with Cornbread because it stuck for others. He played eleven years in the NBA, eight with the Celtics, finishing with a 12.5 points-per-game scoring average. Maxwell was not a particularly strong outside shooter, but possessed very slick moves near the hoop that often faked out defenders or caused them to foul.

Maxwell's No. 31 jersey was eventually retired by the Celtics.

Periodically, on his live radio calls, Maxwell has uttered phrases that gained attention, bad and humorous. The bad came when he took exception to some whistles on the Celtics made by female referee Violet Palmer and said she should "go back to the kitchen." He apologized for that one.

Another time, when James Harden committed two offensive fouls near the end of a game when the Celtics came back from 26 points down to win, Maxwell declared to Harden (actually via twitter), "Take that wit yo' beard!"

Another memorable call was, "Ahhhh, this puppy is over," Maxwell said. "Sorry Jazz. Go home and find some more music to play."

Larry Bird

**I**t didn't take very long in Larry Bird's 1979–80 rookie season with the Boston Celtics for the basketball world to realize just what a rare bird he was. Many All-Americans enter the pros with grand reputations and can't-miss labels, but Bird was better than advertised almost from the first minute he stepped on the Boston Garden court.

After the Celtics had sunk down near the bottom of the National Basketball Association at the end of the 1970s after a mid-decade resurgence that included a couple more world titles, Bird was the chosen one by Red Auerbach, the player designated to lead the Celtics to the promised land once again. Which he did in proving he was one of the greatest players in basketball history.

Bird was born in Indiana in 1956, and played at six feet, nine inches and 220 pounds. He originally enrolled at Indiana University, but felt uncomfortable and transferred to Indiana State in Terre Haute, leading the Sycamores to the finest finishes in school history. After nearly going undefeated, Indiana State lost in the 1979 NCAA championship game to Michigan State and Magic Johnson. The two would become professional rivals and ultimately friends.

Under the league draft rules in place at the time, Bird was eligible to be drafted as a junior because his class had graduated (he lost a year due to his IU–Indiana State switch) and the Celtics took the chance and picked him a year before he would play for them. It turned out to be worth it, beginning with him winning the rookie-of-the-year award. While Bird did not advertise what he said on the court, opponents considered him to be just as prolific at trash talking as at scoring. He sometimes said it helped pass the time during the long season and that's why he indulged in locker room pranks with teammates, too.

Bird became a twelve-time All-Star for Boston during his thirteen NBA seasons, won three Most Valuable Player awards, and aided the Celtics to three world titles. Somewhat withdrawn in public and a proud country boy, Bird was often called "The Hick from French Lick" early in his career. But he was smarter and shrewder than many gave him credit for being, as well as being more multi-talented than it was originally thought.

"Anyone [that] tells you they knew Bird would be as good as he turned out – including me – is a liar," Auerbach said. "I thought he was good, very good. But did I know he had one of the great work ethics ever? No. Did I know he had a genius IQ for the game? No. Smart yes, genius no." As to why Auerbach picked Bird a year in advance of his availability, he said, "I knew this was my shot at him, and I was thinking long-term."

While Bird lacked pure speed, he had tremendous basketball instincts. He rebounded well, had a deadly outside shot, an on-court arrogance that he imposed on opponents, and the passing skills of a point guard.

Bird had confidence when he turned pro, but not even the best players in the world will know how things will play out when they make the leap from college. It didn't take Bird long to realize he was going to do just fine, indeed by exhibition games his rookie year.

"I was able to get my shots, make my cuts, things like that," Bird said. "When the season began, the game slowed down for me. I was able to think my way around the court and see plays develop before they actually happened. Then I realized I could play at a high level and be successful."

Bird was complemented by great players, but he could also put the team on his shoulders and light up the scoreboard, employing off-balance shots that swished and left opponents astonished. He did not particularly care about numbers, but he knew what he needed to do for his team to win.

Over the course of his career, Bird averaged 24.3 points, 10 rebounds, and 6.3 assists per game and nearly two steals, as well. Bird's lifetime foul shooting percentage is 88.6. His career-high game of 60 points is still the Celtics record, but was equaled by Jayson Tatum.

In the early 1980s, the Celtics had a strong rivalry with the Philadelphia 76ers within the Eastern Division. There was a lot of back-and-forth between the clubs that led to who would advance to the NBA Finals. Philadelphia was very tough at the time. Their preeminent player was Dr. J., Julius Erving. At one time, a poster was produced that showed Bird and Erving in the air going against one another.

During that era, the 76ers reached the Finals and lost to the Los Angeles Lakers in 1980. To get to the ultimate series, they had to get past the Celtics. That year, the Celtics were one of the highest scoring teams around, averaging more than 113 points a game. The 76ers blitzed Boston in five games, holding their opponent to 94 points a game. Bird had just 12 points on five-for-nineteen field-goal shooting, which did not please him, in the deciding game.

"I felt great," Bird said. "I came out good, but I missed some key shots. I don't have any excuses to make."

He never did.

The Celtics won it all in 1981. The 76ers lost to the Lakers in the Finals in 1982. The 76ers won the title in 1983. The Celtics also won championships in 1984 and 1986. Several times Boston and Philadelphia had to get past one another. Bird considered coming back from a 3–1 deficit in 1981 as a highlight and not being able to bounce back from 3–1 down again in 1982 to be a lowlight.

Bird had a 31-point game versus Philadelphia in the 1980 playoffs as a rookie. Coach Bill Fitch rode Bird's sharpshooting. "We went to Larry as long as they were going in, we thought we should stay with it," Fitch said.

Bird shrugged off who was covering him on defensive.

"I don't worry about who's guarding me," he said. "I just run the plays and do what the coach wants. If I'm open, I take the shot. It doesn't matter if it's Dr. J or Bobby Jones. I just took what was available. I tried to get my moves down."

One of Bird's most famous and clutch plays came in 1987 in a showdown against the Detroit Pistons. The teams met in the Eastern Conference finals and the game count was 2—2. Detroit led, 107—106, in the closing seconds of Game Five. Bird attempted a shot, but the ball was knocked out of bounds. Most felt it should have been Boston ball, but it was given to Detroit. Hall-of-Fame guard Isiah Thomas inbounded with five seconds to go.

However, Bird slid in front of Detroit center Bill Laimbeer, swiped Thomas's pass and quickly fed a cutting Dennis Johnson for a lay-up that won the game. That was an iconic NBA playoff moment. "For me, it was the greatest play I was ever involved in," Johnson said.

Bird always gave credit to Johnson for being in the right place to react to his own steal. "The steal doesn't matter if DJ doesn't have the presence of mind to cut to the basket," Bird said. "We lose that game."

The Celtics of the 1980s, three-time champions, often had their legendary front-court praised. Bird, Kevin McHale, and Robert Parish together were nicknamed the Big Three. They all went into the Naismith Memorial Hall of Fame, and they each contributed mightily to Boston success. They were dynamite together, impossible for most teams to stop. The Celtics were on an upswing as the 76ers began a downswing and no longer were the two teams always battling for eastern supremacy.

"It got progressively harder as Bird came along," said Jones, the outstanding Philadelphia defender. "Then came Robert size and ability."

That all-star cast of Celtics peaked for the 1985–86 season. Boston romped through the regular season, 67–15, and in four playoff series lost only as many as two games against any other team. "We simply had to have that championship," Bird said. "It was our best team. By far."

Bird seemed like one of those guys who would have loved to play forever. Human frailty is what caught up to him, though. Bird averaged a career-high 29.9 points per game for the 1987–88 season, but the next season he only appeared in six games. Bird had bone spurs removed on both feet. That was a signal of the beginning of the end approaching with what soon developed into chronic back problems.

Trying to keep things together, Bird did have back surgery after sixty games of the 1990–91 season. The operation was not a cure-all. Bird played in just forty-five games the next season, though he did still average 24.3 points a game when active. That was Bird's final playing time for Boston.

However, in a dramatic change in Olympic rules, for the first-time professional players were welcomed into the basketball competition in Barcelona in 1992. Nicknamed the Dream Team, a signature moment in basketball history, the United States was represented by such luminaries as Bird, Michael Jordan, Magic Johnson, Karl Malone, John Stockton, Patrick Ewing, Charles Barkley, Clyde Drexler, David Robinson, and others. The gold medal was a gimme.

Bird played in all eight games, but fewer minutes than the other stars. By then his back was bothering him so much he had spent bench time with the Celtics and the Olympians lying on the floor to ease the pain of sitting up straight.

Larry Bird made his retirement from the Boston Celtics official on August 18, 1992.

"A lot of tears that night," Bird said after he made up his mind and was going public. "And a lot of flashbacks, too. I woke up throughout the night thinking about it and knowing it's finally going to be over with." Later, Bird said "it was one of the happiest days of my life" because he was in such pain he was certain he could play no more.

Bird did not leave basketball, however. He followed up his spectacular playing career with a winning coaching career with the Indiana Pacers, earning a coach-of-the-year-award. Then he became a front office official and also won the NBA's executive-of-the-year award. In 2019, he was presented with the NBA's Lifetime Achievement Award.

If Bird wished to coach again, it is a sure thing any NBA team with an opening would take him in the blink of an eye.

Robert Parish

If anyone ever called him Bob, it remained a secret. It was always Robert Parish, full length. And Parish, at seven feet tall, pretty much always looked full length, even when standing next to other National Basketball Association tall guys.

Parish's frontcourt partners, Larry Bird and Kevin McHale were chattier, Parish more inscrutable, but without him there was no Big Three in Boston Celtics, no successes that defined the franchise's championships of the 1980s.

Playing twenty-one seasons, Parish had one of the longest careers in NBA history. He appeared in 1,611 games, and for a time it seemed he would never retire. Parish was born in Shreveport, Louisiana in 1953 and, in addition to being verbally quiet, his game was on the quiet side. He could score when he needed to, but his prominence revolved around contributions rebounding and playing defense.

Parish's lifetime scoring average was 14.5 points per game. Although he came close in several seasons, he never hit for more than 20 points per game in his long career. One of his main weapons was a perfect-looking jump shot released high above his head.

Always tall for his age, Parish reached six-foot-six in the seventh grade. Until then, he had never played basketball. Urged to take up the sport by his junior high coach Coleman Young, Parish still refers to the man as possibly the most influential person in his career. Learning basketball was the right move for him. After high school, Parish enrolled at Centenary College in his hometown. The tiny school was no basketball power. Even now, decades later, the school has just 600-some students, including graduate students.

Parish is listed as one of the notable alumni for the school, which features athletic team nicknames of Gentlemen for the men's sports and Ladies for the women's sports. The heyday of the basketball program was the 1970s when Parish played there. Caught up in changing NCAA academic eligibility rules, Parish's career was played under a cloud. Ultimately, he and the school were vindicated, his playing stats were acknowledged, and he was a first-team All-American as a senior.

The Golden State Warriors made Parish a first-round draft pick in 1976, and he played in California until 1980. Boston's acquisition of Parish in a trade, that also included a No. 1 draft pick that became McHale, is one of the best in team history. Already a developed player by the time he joined the Celtics, Parish blossomed into a Hall-of-Famer, selected in 2003. He was also honored as one of the fifty greatest players in NBA history.

Although he got into most games, Parish did not play huge minutes as a rookie for Golden State, nor did he start his second season. But by his third and fourth seasons on the West Coast, Parish was scoring more than 17 points per game. His last season with the Warriors, he also averaged 12.1 rebounds. The Celtics knew exactly what they were getting. It's just that the Warriors wanted the younger Joe Barry Caroll, and they drafted him with the Celtics' former pick.

"It was a good time for me," Parish said of his tenure with the Warriors. He said he learned a lot about the pro game and appreciated the tutoring he received from veteran Clifford Ray.

Parish said he did not even think he would become a starter when he joined the Celtics, but everything changed when center Dave Cowens retired. That pushed him into the role alongside Bird and McHale and what became known as an iconic front line. "So once we started playing together, I realized that we could be something special," Parish said.

Being swapped to Boston also rejuvenated Parish. As his time was running out with Golden State, he felt he was being made a scapegoat for some of the Warriors' problems. "The trade gave me incentive," Parish said, "and I was motivated to play basketball again. I considered cutting my career short before the trade because I was being blamed for the Warriors' demise."

Instead of a career ending early, Parish had one of the longest in NBA history. He spent the next fourteen seasons with the Celtics.

His first season in Boston, Parish went from a bench player with Golden State to starting seventy-eight games. He averaged 18.9 points and 9.5 rebounds. The team went 62—20 in the regular season under coach Bill Fitch and the combination of Bird, McHale, and Parish led the Celtics to the world championship. That was Boston's fourteenth banner.

It was early on in his stay with the Celtics that Parish had his memorable nickname bestowed on him. Parish was forever-after called "Chief." That was not because of Native-American heritage or because he held a leadership post in the local fire department. Teammate Cedric Maxwell began calling Parish chief based on a character in the famous movie *"One Flew Over the Cuckoo's Nest."* In the film, one figure called Chief, feigning being deaf and mute, always stayed calm, said little to nothing, and kept a blank look on his face as he absorbed the scene.

"Cedric said that I was stoic like the Chief," Parish said. He didn't deny it. It wasn't as if Parish was unfriendly, he was just a quieter, lower key guy in the locker room than many of his more voluble teammates.

Once the Celtics captured that 1981 title, they were solidified as contenders each year in the 1980s. Boston won its second title of the decade – with Parish in the middle – in 1984 during a seven-game endurance contest versus the Lakers.

By then Fitch was out as coach and K.C. Jones, a member of the old guard, was in. Parish loved playing for Jones, whom he said had a knack for making everyone on the roster feel important, even if they could not all be starters.

Jones greatly admired Parish, not only for his skills, but for his attitude as a team player. "Robert was special because he knew his place on the team," Jones said. "He knew that there were only so many basketballs to go around and that Larry and Kevin were going to get the majority of the shots. Robert embraced his role on the team, which was to rebound, play tough defense, and to be a force in the middle."

That was said by a coach whose playing career was much like Parish's. Jones was less of an offensive threat, but made the Hall of Fame and won championship rings because of his defense and passing abilities.

As tough a defender as Parish was, his most difficult match-up came around to haunt him somewhat when one of those Celtics-Lakers games showed up on the schedule. While many talked of Boston being a Bird-led team and the Lakers of that period being a Magic Johnson-led team, the Lakers were unstoppable to many opponents because they had Kareem Abdul-Jabbar playing center. Abdul-Jabbar remains the NBA's all-time leading scorer.

Parish called the seven-foot-two Abdul-Jabbar the best player he ever went up against. "No one was ever able to devise a defense to stop Kareem," Parish said. "He exploited every defense that was ever thrown at him. He was smart. He was intelligent. He was an extremely gifted athlete, and the only player I'd ever played against that I could never change his shot."

Indeed, Abdul-Jabbar's hook shot, dubbed a skyhook, was viewed as unstoppable. It was released so high and from such a deeply removed angle, no defender, not even another seven-footer like Parish, could reach it or block it.

Once the NBA realized just how good the trio in Boston's front line really was, Parish gained more and more recognition.

He ended up a nine-time All-Star. Immediately after the first championship, Parish began a string of three consecutive 19-plus-point-per-game seasons. He tip-toed to the absolute edge of 20 during the 1981–82 season when he finished at 19.9 points per game.

Boston won its third crown of the 1980s in 1986. Most fans believe the 1985–86 Celtics were one of the best ever. Dennis Johnson had been added to the backcourt and Bill Walton was coming off the bench. The roster seemed to be a perfect blend of stars and hungry back-ups. "In my opinion, the 1985–86 Celtics are one of the top five teams of all-time," Parish said.

But that high point was the beginning of the end of the ride for that group. The often-injured Walton was reinjured the next season. No. 1 draft pick Len Bias died of a drug overdose almost immediately after being selected, and other players were aging. The Celtics began a slide and did not win another championship for twenty-two years – even Parish, who played until he was forty-three, was retired by then.

The 1993–94 season was the last that Parish hit double figures in scoring (11.7) and the last that he was an NBA starter. He was forty when he departed Boston, signing as a free agent with the Charlotte Hornets. He spent two seasons in North Carolina and saw some time with the Chicago Bulls, winning another title with the 1997 Bulls just prior to retirement. Since he had turned forty-three, that made Parish the oldest player ever to win a championship in the league.

Looking back more than two decades later, Parish's longevity has only ever been rivaled by a few players in different ways. He is first on the games-played list, appearing in fifty-one more than Abdul-Jabbar. His twenty-one seasons was eclipsed during the 2019–20 season by Vince Carter in his twenty-second year.

"I will always treasure my time in Boston," Parish said. "All of the hard work, the championships, everything."

Parish always wore the distinctive No. 00 on his jersey. The Celtics retired his number in 1998.

Kevin McHale

**I**n the Old West, Kevin McHale would have been called "a long, tall drink of water." He stood at six feet, eleven inches, with long arms and legs. He had little fat on his body, weighing 210 pounds. He was a light pole with limbs. As a basketball player, he possessed quick footwork, tremendous instincts, and a slickness around the basket that combined with his soft touch to allow him to run up big point totals.

A native of Hibbing, Minnesota, population sixteen thousand in the state's iron range, McHale hails from a small town that has produced the famous before. It is the home of iconic singer-songwriter Bob Dylan (born Zimmerman). McHale wasn't even the first National Basketball Association player from Hibbing; so was earlier hoopster Dick Garmaker. Also, baseball star Roger Maris was born in Hibbing.

Born in 1957, McHale was a Minnesota Mr. Basketball in high school in 1976 and attended the state's flagship university, the University of Minnesota, ultimately being named the best player in Golden Gophers history. His No. 44 was retired by the school. McHale was the third player taken in the 1980 NBA draft, and the Celtics' first-round selection. When he was picked by an NBA team, McHale had not yet seen an NBA game in person.

Initially, McHale played the heralded sixth man role with the Celtics, the spark-plug off the bench who could give the team a lift. Twice, McHale won the award as the league's best sixth man while backing up forward Cedric Maxwell. Eventually, though, Maxwell was traded and McHale teamed with Larry Bird and Robert Parish in the frontcourt. The trio was dubbed "The Big Three." They were big in size and big on talent, and all three were voted into the Naismith Memorial Basketball Hall of Fame.

At first, McHale wanted more money than the Celtics were willing to pay. He threatened to sign with a team in Italy if Boston did not come up with the cash, but he got his payout. McHale played his entire thirteen-year career with the Celtics. Boston was offering $200,000 a year, but investigation showed that was a lowball offer for the third player in the draft. He believed it was ninth-pick money, so McHale resisted.

"I said to myself, 'That's not fair,'" McHale said. "'I'm just not going to do that."

A bit miffed, Celtics coach Bill Fitch, true to his often-gruff personality, said, "Let him eat spaghetti." Negotiations continued, though, and McHale ate as much spaghetti as he wished at Boston's North End, around the corner from the Boston Garden. However, McHale had come close enough to cutting a deal with Milan to fly across the Atlantic Ocean and practice with the European club.

McHale's scoring input increased every season for six consecutive years following his rookie year. For the 1986-87 season, McHale averaged a career-high 26.1 points per game and led the league in field-goal percentage at 60.4. He duplicated that feat to the decimal point the next season.

Considered one of the greatest power forwards of all, McHale averaged 20-plus points a game five times, and more than 18 points three other years. McHale was a seven-time All-Star and won All-Defensive first- or second- team honors six times. Opponents, especially shorter ones, had trouble challenging McHale on drives through the low post. His long arms provided tremendous reach to disrupt the flow of shots. He could block shots with either hand.

The Celtics viewed McHale as a cornerstone of their rebuilding plan during the early 1980s. It is little-remembered by Boston fans today, but horrifying to contemplate in terms of team history and developments, but playing out his option after his initial three-year contract, McHale nearly became a member of the New York Knicks.

This would have altered the balance of power in the NBA's Eastern Division. McHale signed an offer sheet from New York. The Celtics, with Red Auerbach playing the hard-nosed negotiator, sent three Knicks players offer sheets. In the end, the Knicks signed their players and the Celtics re-signed McHale, although for one million dollars a year, a figure that probably gave Auerbach heartburn.

The payoff was a worthy investment for both the organization and McHale, who soon after established his greatness and helped the Celtics win three NBA crowns in the 1980s.

McHale was a good locker room guy. He always wanted to have a good time and could be witty. In what has gone down in sports lore, when still a member of the Gophers' basketball team, he played the teasing straight man when Minnesota Vikings star running back Chuck Foreman entered the dressing room praising the hometown guys on a win. McHale greeted probably the most famous athlete in the city at the moment by saying, "Nice to meet you, Mr. Foreman. What do you do for a living?"

Fitch loved employing McHale as a weapon off the bench in that sixth-man job, saying he was ideal for following that Celtic tradition after Frank Ramsey and John Havlicek.

"All things considered, Kevin should go down in history as the absolutely ideal sixth man," Fitch said. "He could play any position up front. He could give you inside scoring, outside scoring. He blocked shots. That's such a luxury for a coach."

In 1981, the Celtics beat the Houston Rockets, 4-2, in the

NBA Finals. That gave McHale his first championship ring. He averaged 10 points a game that season. He was the fifth high scorer on a team loaded with firepower. Fans thought the Celtics were poised for a sustained championship run, much as they put together in the late 1950s and early 1960s. Not quite.

It took three years for Boston to get back to the Finals. The next year, 1981-82, the Celtics did have a slightly better record – 63-19 – by one game over the title season. But they were eliminated in the eastern playoff finals by Philadelphia. Injuries hurt.

"I thought we were a much better team that year than we were in 1980-81," said McHale, blaming a shoulder injury to guard Nate "Tiny" Archibald for the one-game difference in the series. "But Tiny dislocated his shoulder against Philly. That was the year we won 18 straight. We were really on a roll."

A year later McHale had his flirtation with the Knicks. Although he and Bird always respected one another all along, when sportswriters asked Bird how he felt about the likelihood of McHale departing the team Bird was his usual blunt self. "Kevin is a great player and I hope we re-sign him, but if we don't, I'm gonna knock him on his ass the first time I go up against him."

It did not come to that. McHale and Bird remained teammates and partners and although there was a coaching change, some roster shuffling, and the like, in 1984 they won their second title together. By that time, K.C. Jones, the one-time Boston backcourt star who had won eight rings as a player with the Celtics, was the head coach.

That team rolled through the regular season at a 62—20 clip, the best mark in the Eastern Conference by ten games. Boston placed six men in double figures and had depth as well as an All-Star starting lineup. The Celtics ploughed through the Washington Bullets, the Knicks and Milwaukee Bucks in the playoffs to earn their perch in the Finals against the

Los Angeles Lakers. No doubt there was an intense Celtics-Lakers rivalry, but in some ways McHale thought the analysis of it was often off-base or overly simplified with too much emphasis on Bird and Magic Johnson being the faces of their franchises.

"The Lakers was more of a media hype than anything else," McHale said. "They were so far away. The eastern cities are pretty much the same. L.A. is a whole different gig. It was Larry the brooding bad boy and the smiling Magic. And that's how the teams were perceived."

That season the Celtics were perceived as the winners.

It was during the 1984—85 season that McHale posted his single-game scoring high. Facing the Detroit Pistons on March 3, 1985, McHale pumped in 56 points. That set a franchise record. Nine days later, Bird fired in 60 points, pretty much as an anything-you-can-do, I-can-do-better retort. Bird's total is still the club mark.

McHale earned his third championship ring as a key part of the 1985-86 Celtics, the team ranked among the greatest of all-time. That club went 67—15 under Jones and some of those players wonder how they ever lost a game. The Celts topped the Houston Rockets, 4—2, in the Finals that year. McHale, who missed some games due to injury, averaged 21.3 points that regular season.

Basically, McHale was a calm guy discussing basketball between games in playoff series. In one memorable comment after being asked about home-court advantage he pretty much said what dozens of other NBA players wished they had thought to mention over the years. "What's there to worry about playing on the road?" McHale said. "I've never seen a fan come out of the stands and block a shot or make a basket."

McHale appeared in all eighty-two games in each of his first four seasons, but only once thereafter. He started having more physical ailments and he retired after the 1992-1993 season. The Celtics retired his No. 32 uniform jersey in 1994 and he went into the Hall of Fame in 1999.

Although McHale stepped off the court in 1993, he did not leave either basketball or the NBA. He promptly went to work for his home-state Minnesota Timberwolves, at first as a front-office official and broadcaster. Then he moved up to vice president of basketball operations. He became a fill-in coach for part of one season in 2005, going 19-12, then reclaimed his chair in the front office. A few years later, McHale moved back to the bench, but as the Timberwolves' fortunes failed to improve, he was fired.

McHale followed that up with five seasons coaching Houston, three full ones and two partial ones, making the playoffs in all three complete seasons.

In 971 regular-season games as a player, McHale averaged 17.9 points and 7.3 rebounds in addition to his defensive accolades. He was named one of the NBA's 50 greatest players.

Boston Celtics Franchise Stats

(As of 2021-22 season)

List Of Top Point Scorers in Team History

1. John Havlicek   26,395
2. Paul Pierce   24,021
3. Larry Bird   21,791
4. Robert Parish   18,245
5. Kevin McHale   17,335
6. Bob Cousy   16,955
7. Sam Jones   15,411
8. Bill Russell   14,522
9. Dave Cowens   13,192
10. Jo Jo White   13,188
11. Bill Sharman   12,287
12. Tom Heinsohn   12,194
13. Antoine Walker   11,386
14. Don Nelson   9,968
15. Tom Sanders   8,766

List Of Top Rebounders in Team History

1. Bill Russell   21,620
2. Robert Parish   11,051
3. Dave Cowens   10,170
4. Larry Bird   8,974
5. John Havlicek   8,007

List Of Assist Leaders in Team History

1. Bob Cousy   6,945
2. John Havlicek   6,114
3. Larry Bird   5,695
4. Rajon Rondo   4,474
5. Paul Pierce   4,305

List Of Steals Leaders in Team History*

1. Paul Pierce   1,583
2. Larry Bird   1,556
3. Rajon Rondo   990
4. Robert Parish   873
5. Antoine Walker   828

List Of Blocks Leaders in Team History*

1. Robert Parish   1,703
2. Kevin McHale   1,690
3. Larry Bird   755
4. Paul Pierce   668
5. Kendrick Perkins   646

Most Three-Pointers in Team History**

1. Paul Pierce   1,823
2. Antoine Walker   937
3. Jayson Tatum   827
4. Ray Allen   798
5. Marcus Smart   796

*Steals and blocks not always kept as official NBA statistics.
**The three-point shot did not become part of the NBA game until 1979. Boston guard Chris Ford was credited with making the first 3-pointer in league history on October 12th of that year.

Boston Celtics Individual Game Records

Most Points	Larry Bird, 60, in 1985 and Jayson Tatum, 60, in 2021.
Most Rebounds	Bill Russell, 51, in 1960.
Most Assists	Bob Cousy, 28, in 1959.
Most consecutive games played	Jo Jo White, 488, 1972–1978.
Most blocks	Kevin McHale, 9, in 1982 and 1983; Robert Parish, in 1982.
Most Steals	Larry Bird, 9, in 1985; Paul Pierce, in 1999.
Most 3-pointers	Marcus Smart, 11, 2020

Boston Celtics Players with Fifty Or More Points in a Game

Larry Bird	60	1985
Jayson Tatum	60	2021
Kevin McHale	56	1985
Jayson Tatum	54	2022
Larry Bird	53	1983
Jayson Tatum	53	2021
Isaiah Thomas	52	2016
Jayson Tatum	51	2022
Sam Jones	51	1965
Paul Pierce	50	2006
Larry Bird	50	1999
Larry Bird	50	1986
Jayson Tatum	50	2021
Jayson Tatum	50	2021
Jaylen Brown	50	2021

Boston Celtics With Highest Single Season Scoring Averages

1.	Larry Bird	29.9	1988
2.	Isaiah Thomas	28.9	2017
3.	John Havlicek	28.8	1971
4.	Larry Bird	28.7	1985
5.	Larry Bird	28.0	1987
6.	John Havlicek	27.5	1972
7.	Jayson Tatum	26.9	2021
8.	Paul Pierce	26.8	2006
9.	Jayson Tatum	26.4	2021
10.	Paul Pierce	26.1	2002
11.	Kevin McHale	26.0	1987
12.	Paul Pierce	26.0	2003

Dennis Johnson

**Y**ou didn't mess with Dennis Johnson on the court. He was unusually strong for a six-foot-four player, an extremely tough, don't-give-'em-an-inch defensive player and one of those players who exemplified the role of being a good teammate.

No hot-shot coming out of college at Pepperdine University, Johnson built himself into a second-round draft pick of the Seattle SuperSonics. He would have been seen as an unlikely character to lead Seattle to its only National Basketball Association title in 1979. Yet Johnson was the Finals Most Valuable Player and scored 32 points in the overtime clincher.

After coming to the Celtics, Johnson became a perfect backcourt complement to the All-Star frontcourt trio of Larry Bird, Kevin McHale and Robert Parish. Johnson was part of two more championship clubs with Boston, became a five-time All-Star and a six-time member of the All-Defensive Team.

The 1985—86 Celtics are regarded as a remarkable team, finishing 40—1 at home that season on the way to a title. There were four Hall-of-Famers, including Johnson, selected in 2010, and one on the bench, too.

"We were untouchable that year," Johnson said. "We were

healthy and everyone was at the top of their game. It helped having the best player in the league." The player he referred to was Bird. The men had a close bond. "Larry was a special player, one of the best ever."

Although Johnson was a three-time champion, he led as much with intangibles, defense and clutch play, rather than with big numbers. His career high scoring year of 19.2 points a game was actually recorded when Johnson played with Phoenix, not on any of the title teams.

Johnson scored the basket on one of the most famous plays in Celtics playoff history, one immortalized by broadcaster Johnny Most. The setting was the 1987 eastern playoffs versus the Detroit Pistons. Boston trailed by one point and the Pistons had the ball. Detroit star guard Isiah Thomas was making the pass-in, but Bird stole it under the hoop. Everyone thought Bird would go for the game-winner, but he spotted a streaking Johnson, who made an off-balance lay-up to win the game.

After retirement in 1990, Johnson became a scout for the Celtics and then went into coaching. He was only fifty-two when he passed away in 2007.

At Johnson's funeral, Bird praised Johnson as a player and teammate.

"He was a great basketball player, a guy that was dedicated to the game," Bird said. "It's unfortunate (Johnson's early death) because he had a lot of life left in him. He left a great legacy behind."

Bill Walton

To younger generations, Bill Walton has basically been a very tall basketball broadcaster, not a basketball player. Until chronic foot injuries marred his National Basketball Association career and cut it short, Walton was on a path to become one of the greatest centers the game had ever seen.

His time with the Celtics was short, but special, though most of his key achievements took place before he came to Boston for the 1985–86 season. The six-foot-eleven Walton was a three-time NCAA player of the year while leading UCLA to two of its many 1960s and 1970s titles. He won a Most Valuable Player award for carrying the Portland Trailblazers to an NBA crown, as well. But he could not sustain his high-level play because of repeat injuries.

Walton was both a tremendous rebounder and passer, as well as a deadly scorer. At UCLA, Walton was the cornerstone of John Wooden-coached teams that twice went 30—0 in championship seasons and he was part of the school's record eighty-eight-game winning streak. In the 1973 championship game Walton scored 44 points on twenty-one of twenty-two shooting attempts and added 13 rebounds in perhaps the greatest tournament performances ever.

He was not only an All-American but an Academic All-American three times as well. The top pick in the NBA draft,

Walton almost immediately ran into foot problems. When he was at his peak, Portland claimed a championship and he was selected for the All-Star team and named the league's defensive player of the year. But his good health did not last long.

After an interlude with the Clippers, Walton was traded to the Celtics, something he provoked. He wanted one last chance at a title. Team doctors wanted to flunk Walton on his physical, but Red Auerbach intervened.

"The Celtics are the best," Walton said. "They have the most championships. They have the most Hall-of-Famers. They have the most members of the all-time team for the NBA. They are the best."

Walton said he had to sign away his deferred compensation to the Clippers while also knowing he could never pass a real physical. He recalled doctors buzzing over the sad state of his feet on X-rays until Auerbach jumped in.

Several Celtics felt Walton would be a perfect back-up complement to the Larry Bird, Kevin McHale, Robert Parish trio and for the 1985–86 season that proved accurate. Walton was a supersub and the Celtic most relied on off the bench.

Limited to nineteen minutes a game, Walton energized the team in part-time work, averaging 7.6 points, 6.8 rebounds, and 2.3 assists. In short bursts, he was as good as ever. So were the Celtics. Under coach K.C. Jones, Boston finished 67–15 during the regular season and rolled to the NBA crown. Bird and others said Walton was a great teammate, and he was a terrific addition to the team. Walton expressed gratitude for this chance to win another title.

He did not last through another full season in good health with the Celtics and retired after the next season. Walton's ascent to television broadcasting renown was probably as much an accomplishment as his basketball performances. He overcame a life-long stuttering problem to succeed in the medium.

When retelling the tale of how he became a Celtic – and the way it played out – Walton said, "I'm the luckiest guy in the world."

Celtics-Lakers: The Second Time Around

Unlike when the Boston Celtics established their Dynasty and the Lakers were their chief foil en route to winning championships, things were different in the 1980s, more equal, very much a series rivalry. It was not preordained the Celtics would win. Jerry West would have had more fun playing, but as general manager he had a big hand in the 1980s success.

This was how the decade played out: 1980, Lakers win title over Philadelphia; 1981, Celtics win title over Houston; 1982, Lakers win title over Philadelphia; 1983, Lakers lose in Finals to Philadelphia; 1984, Celtics win title over Lakers; 1985, Lakers win title over Celtics; 1986, Celtics win title over Houston; 1987, Lakers win title over Celtics; 1988, Lakers win title over Detroit; 1989, Lakers lose title to Detroit.

So during the 1980s, the Celtics won three championships and lost in the Finals twice. The Lakers won five titles and lost in the Finals three times. Los Angeles came to be known as "The Showtime Lakers," flashy and exciting and as much celebrities in Hollywood as the actors and actresses that came to watch them play.

This renewed rivalry with the Lakers was defined by Larry Bird of the Celtics and Magjc Johnson of the Lakers. The direct rivalry between Bird and Johnson, who later became good friends, began in the 1979 NCAA championship game when Johnson's Michigan State team out-lasted Bird's Indiana State team. They both went on to the NBA and helped re-energize the pro game, as dominating players until Michael Jordan came along a few years later.

Bird once characterized the fierceness of his rivalry with Johnson this way: "When I was young, the only thing I cared about was beating my brothers. Mark and Mike were older than me and that meant they were bigger, stronger, and better — in basketball, baseball, everything. But I hadn't met Magic yet. Once I did, he was the one I had to beat. What I had with Magic went beyond brothers."

At stake against Magic Johnson was a world title.

Johnson said that when he was growing up a coach used to tell him that it was not all about talent, but hard work was critically important, too, and that somewhere out there another player was out-working him. When he first met Larry Bird, Johnson said, he knew he was the player his coach had been telling him about.

"When I go out and speak to people," Johnson said, "I tell them I wish their kids had a chance to see Larry Bird play because he did it the right way. He played a team game, but it was his will to win, his toughness, his spirit, and his knowledge of the game, that I admired the most. I'm tied to Larry — forever. That's just how it is. I can't get away from Larry. I bet he can't get away from me either."

The six-foot-nine forward Bird averaged 24.3 points, 10 rebounds, and 6.3 assists per game for the Celtics. The 6-9 guard Johnson averaged 19.5 points, 7.2 rebounds, and 11.2 assists per game for the Lakers.

While Bird and Johnson were the most prominent players on their respective teams, both squads were loaded with talent. Bird was the top dog of the Celtics during this era, but he was flanked by many other stars such as future Hall-of-Famers Kevin McHale, Robert Parish, Dennis Johnson, and if briefly, Bill Walton. Danny Ainge, who has emerged as the second most important Celtics executive behind Red Auerbach, also played for Boston then.

Hall-of-Fame center Kareem Abdul-Jabbar was the other major Lakers weapon of the era and he and Johnson were supported by James Worthy, Jamaal Wilkes, Byron Scott, Michael Cooper, Norm Nixon, A. C. Green, Mitch Kupchak, and Kurt Rambis. LA's coach for those championships was Pat Riley, although Paul Westhead won once.

While the Lakers respected the other Celtics, they despised Bird on the court, calling him "F...ing Larry Bird" because he always found a way to challenge them.

"He did everything it took to beat you," Rambis said. "That was the only important thing to Larry — beating you. And if he made you look pathetic, all the better."

Retired Boston Celtics Jersey Numbers

**B**lessed with so many great stars and Hall-of-Famers, it should not be surprising that the Boston Celtics have retired more jersey numbers by far than any other franchise in the National Basketball Association.

The Celtics have retired twenty-two numbers, about twice as many as any other pro basketball team, representing twenty-three individuals. The only other North American professional franchise to retire as many numbers is the New York Yankees of Major League Baseball. The Yankees have retired numbers for twenty-three individuals, although catchers Bill Dickey and Yogi Berra both wore No. 8. Under a Major League Baseball decree, the No. 42 is also retired across the sport to honor the contributions made by Jackie Robinson in breaking the color barrier in 1947.

The Yankees have been in business much longer than the Celtics, beginning play in 1901 as the Baltimore Orioles. These were not the same Orioles as compete in the American League these days. The team shifted to New York in 1903 and played under the nickname Highlanders until 1913. It was not until 1929 that Yankee players began wearing numbers on the backs of their uniform tops full-time.

Boston ran into a similar dilemma that confronted the Yankees with No. 8, worn by Hall-of-Famers Dickey and Berra. In the Celtics' case it was No. 18, worn by Hall-of-Famer Dave Cowens after championship-era forward Jim Loscutoff retired. The Celtics solved their conundrum by using the word "Loscy," Loscutoff's nickname, in one of the boxes instead of his original jersey number. Boston's retired numbers are displayed in the rafters of the home-court TD Garden. The banners are white with green trim and the numbers are highlighted in box shaped squares.

Boston also demonstrated great respect in paying tribute to off-court personnel, as well. The No. 1 jersey is retired to honor team founder and president Walter Brown. No. 2 is retired to honor long-time coach, general manager, and president Arnold "Red" Auerbach.

Other retired numbers:

3	Guard Dennis Johnson.
6	Center Bill Russell.
10	Guard Jo Jo White.
14	Guard Bob Cousy.
15	Forward Tommy Heinsohn.
16	Forward Tom Sanders.
17	Guard-forward John Havlicek.
18	Center Dave Cowens.
19	Forward Don Nelson.
21	Guard Bill Sharman.
22	Center Ed Macauley.
23	Forward Frank Ramsey.
24	Guard Sam Jones.
25	Guard K.C. Jones.
31	Forward Cedric Maxwell.
32	Forward Kevin McHale.
33	Forward Larry Bird.
34	Forward Paul Pierce.
35	Forward Reggie Lewis.
00	Center Robert Parish.
Loscy	Forward Jim Loscutoff.

Danny Ainge

ith the exception of Red Auerbach, Danny Ainge is the most important personnel executive in Boston Celtics history. That was after playing for the team, which then followed playing Major League Baseball and starring in basketball for Brigham Young University.

Ainge, who was born in 1959 and truly has led an amazing sports life, stepped down as the Celtics' general manager and president of basketball operations, turning the role over to coach Brad Stevens. From 2003 through the 2020—21 season, Ainge made Boston's trades and supervised their NBA draft picks.

While many athletes have great success in multiple sports in high school, Ainge basically topped them all. He was a first-team high school All-American in baseball, basketball, and football in Eugene, Oregon. That would have been sufficient achievement for many athletes, but Ainge was just getting started.

Not only did Ainge star in basketball at Brigham Young, averaging 24.4 points a game as a senior, he won the Wooden Award as the best college player. For those with long memories, Ainge also hit one of the most dramatic shots in NCAA tournament history. Time was running out in a 1981 game when Ainge took a pass and drove the length of the court to hit a lay-up that gave his Cougars a one-point win over

Notre Dame, propelling BYU into the Elite Eight. While that accomplishment lingers, right before that contest he scored 37 points to help eliminate UCLA from that tournament. Ainge wasn't even at full strength for the UCLA win, taking medication to ease the pain from back spasms.

At six-foot-four or so, Ainge had good size for a guard and the Celtics made him a second-round draft pick in 1981. By then, Ainge had already spent time in the minors and was being touted as the Toronto Blue Jays' third baseman of the future, so this represented taking a chance because most everyone believed Ainge would stick with baseball instead of ever playing professional basketball. For a moment, Ainge's selection seemed like a wasted draft pick.

By the time of the 1981 NBA draft, Ainge was in his third season with the Blue Jays. They were partial seasons, but Ainge appeared in as many as eighty-seven games one year. While he originally seemed committed to the other sport – and told basketball coaches that's how he felt – doubts began creeping in because Ainge wasn't hitting. He batted .237 as a rookie in 1979, .243 the next year, and declined to .187 in 1981. He was not making progress.

In the end, when he changed his mind about which sport to pursue, Ainge had to go to court to try to free himself from the Blue Jays. A jury ruled against him. Ultimately, the Celtics had to buy out Ainge's baseball contract so he could switch to basketball.

Starting with the fall of 1981, Ainge spent parts of fifteen seasons in the NBA, staying with the Celtics into 1989. Never a pro superstar the way he was in college, Ainge was a very good player who helped Boston win two titles, in 1984 and 1986. The 1985-86 Celtics team is regarded as one of their greatest and one of the best in NBA history. Ainge was a key contributor and he also praised how the coaching staff, with K.C. Jones the boss, and his assistants Chris Ford and Jimmy Rodgers were a perfect fit for that group.

"Sometimes it's hard to judge a coach," Ainge said. "It's the whole staff. The greatest assets K.C. had were respect from the players and his lack of ego. He would allow and encourage input from other coaches and the players. With that kind of a team, it was a great combination."

As a teammate, Ainge was somewhat of a comedian and prankster. He created some nicknames for opposing players. Probably the most famous was "Microwave" for shooting guard Vinnie Johnson because "he really heats up in a hurry." He also disparagingly called center Pervis Ellison "out of service Pervis." And he teased teammate Kevin McHale as "The Black Hole." This signified if anyone passed the ball into the low post to McHale the ball would disappear and never be passed out again because he always shot.

Ainge believed that '85- '86 definitely was a special club. "In my opinion," he said, "that was the best team ever. I've played on some good teams since, teams that went to the Finals, and they couldn't come close to that team. What I think made that team so special was that if there was an incentive to win, we'd win. There was no way anyone could beat us if we really wanted to win."

Ainge averaged 15.7 points a game during the 1987–88 season and made his only All-Star team that year. For his career, Ainge averaged 11.5 points and 4 assists a game.

As a ball-handler, Ainge was one of the Celtics players who learned to cope with whatever dead spots there might be on the old Boston Garden floor. Once, in the 1980s, Cleveland guard Ron Harper complained, "Man, my driveway is better than this."

He might have been right.

"A lot of times you're dribbling the ball up-court, the ball won't come back to you," Ainge said. "So the guys that do a lot of fancy dribbling, they never know. They go behind their back and they come up empty."

Ainge was one of those players who could irritate the opposition on defense because of his hard-nosed style. He was involved in one of the NBA's most-publicized and infamous incidents in 1983. During a playoff game against the Atlanta Hawks, Ainge and seven-foot-one Wayne "Tree" Rollins got into it.

Over the last quarter century, facts and fiction have mingled. Some say Ainge taunted Rollins by calling him a sissy and some say Rollins called Ainge a sissy. Elbows were thrown. But things did not end there. Ainge did tackle Rollins and the men began wrestling on the court. During the altercation Rollins bit one of Ainge's fingers. Ainge needed two stitches. Strangely, over the years it has been confused about who bit who. That may have been because the chewing sounded more like something Ainge would have done than Rollins.

It didn't take long for the myth to take hold that Ainge bit Rollins and fans around the league gave him grief for something he didn't do.

"The booing bothered me at first," Ainge said, "but now I just expect it. I know a lot of it comes from my personality. I've been booed in high school and college. I've just always showed a lot of emotion and played aggressively. Everywhere I go, people think I'm the dirty little guy who bit Tree Rollins' finger."

Shortly after Ainge retired as a player in 1995, his final season played with the Phoenix Suns, he was named head coach of the Suns. He coached the Suns from 1996 to 1999. Then, in 2003, with the blessing and support of the aging Red Auerbach, Ainge was hired as the executive director of the Celtics' basketball operations.

The Celtics were not winners at the time. Ainge had been a member of the last championship club in 1986. He was given the authority to revamp the roster and he did so, at times angering fans with his bold moves. However, despite acquiring the nickname "Trader Danny," Ainge built a large reservoir of goodwill when he adroitly put together the deals that brought Kevin Garnett and Ray Allen to Boston to team with Paul Pierce. That group led the team to another title in

2008 and Ainge was named the league's executive of the year.

By mixing and matching, swapping and drafting, Ainge scored points with the hiring of coach Brad Stevens, stockpiling of draft choices, and making key free agent signings. The Celtics may not yet have won another title, but they have regularly fielded strong teams contending for the best team in the East and Ainge has been creative in adding personnel when key injuries threaten the foundation.

While some fans remain bitter about Kylie Irving's two-year stint in Boston when the star seemed to turn his back on the town, taking the high road, Ainge refused to criticize Irving's actions, saying it was as much his fault that Irving did not prove to be a good fit. Ainge also brought all-stars Gordy Haywood and Kemba Walker to Boston.

"Kyrie in his first year, year-and-a-half, was terrific for us," Ainge said. "I really liked [him] and was hopeful it would be a good marriage going forward. He really wanted to go home (to the Brooklyn Nets), that's his choice, and I don't really know why he gets all the blame."

Ainge continued to add young talent to the Celtics' roster and was hungry to produce another championship. Ruminating on the challenges of doing so, Ainge brought up a point that is faced by no other pro basketball executive. The Celtics have so many retired numbers he wonders if someday a star free agent will refuse to sign with Boston because he won't be able to wear his favorite number.

"I think the number selection could be a deal," Ainge said. "It never has, but it could."

The Celtics already coped with a related uniform jersey issue once. Jim Loscutoff wore No. 18 and then the number was given to Hall-of-Famer Dave Cowens. The answer for the Boston team administration was retiring No. 18 for Cowens, but also placing Loscutoff's nickname "Loscy" on a banner above the court.

Reggie Lewis

 **L**ong-time Celtics fans will probably shake their heads upon hearing it has been more than a quarter of a century since Reggie Lewis died because he loved basketball too much. Lewis represents the greatest single tragedy in the history of the franchise, a star whose life was snuffed out too soon in a development that shocked New England and the basketball world.

A native of Baltimore, the six-foot-seven forward came out of Boston's Northeastern University, where he had been a three-time all-league player, as a first-round draft pick in 1987 and evolved into a star, being chosen for his first All-Star game in 1992. At the time he said he did not want this All-Star debut to be only a one-time thing.

Perhaps Lewis' greatest champion as a player was Hall of Fame coach Jim Calhoun. Calhoun is famed for his work building the University of Connecticut into an NCAA power. But before he supervised the Huskies' program, he coached at the lesser-known Northeastern in Boston. It was Calhoun who unearthed the diamond that was Lewis following high school. Calhoun believed Lewis was on his way to becoming a Hall-of-Famer himself when he died young.

Lewis was a member of an extraordinary Dunbar High team in Baltimore that at one point went 50—0. It was easy enough to be out-shined with that bunch that included future pros

Reggie Williams, David Wingate and Tyrone "Muggsy" Bogues.

After playing a minimum amount of time in his rookie season in Boston, Lewis worked hard on all aspects of his game and became a full-time starter for the 1988—89 season. For the next five years he averaged between 17 and 20.8 points per game for Boston, the only NBA team he suited up for.

It was stunning enough when Lewis passed out just before a playoff game in the spring of 1993, but on July 27, 1993, Lewis was playing in an off-season workout at the Celtics' practice facility at Brandeis University in suburban Waltham and abruptly seized up, collapsed to the court and subsequently died of a heart attack at age twenty-seven. Lewis had been playing ball on his own and was discovered by campus security. Two officers attempted to revive him with mouth-to-mouth resuscitation, but failed.

Doctors gave the cause of Lewis' death as hypertrophic cardiomyopathy. There were later reports that his heart may have been affected by drug use, but such contentions were never proven. Lewis was buried in an unmarked grave in a Boston cemetery.

One of the innumerable basketball people who knew Lewis and grieved for him was Red Auerbach. By 1993, Auerbach was decades removed from his coaching days and his active days in charge of Celtics personnel. But he was still the Godfather of the team.

"I was very sad and very unhappy," Auerbach said, "because I liked Reggie as a kid. Not only as a player -- he was a helluva kid."

In 1995, the Celtics retired Lewis' No. 35 jersey in his honor. At that time, former teammate Dee Brown delivered a speech about Lewis.

"I know there's not a ring of truth (about it)," Brown said of the drug abuse allegations. "I'll take to my grave (his feelings) about Reggie's character and what Reggie did as a person."

Other former teammates, Sherman Douglas and Xavier McDaniel, also participated in the ceremony.

"He literally played his heart out for the Boston Celtics,"

said Hall of Fame player Tommy Heinsohn.

The Reggie Lewis Track and Athletic Center opened in the Roxbury section of Boston honoring Lewis' memory. This was viewed as a fitting legacy by his friends and relatives, who talked of Lewis' outgoing and charitable nature and his commitment to helping young people.

"Which is one of the things I always loved so much about him," said his widow Donna Harris-Lewis, his wife of two years. "Reggie was always doing something for other people, especially young people."

Well-liked and appreciated as a player, periodically in the years following Lewis' tragic death sportswriters revisited his untimely passing, rekindling memories of the popular individual who deserved so much more from life.

One of those stories about how far Lewis had come as a player, cited his most recent five-year stretch of all-around statistics-- points, rebounds, assists, and steals -- putting him in the company of Charles Barkley, Clyde Drexler, Karl Malone, Chris Mullin, and Michael Jordan. All of those players joined the exclusive club of the Naismith Memorial Basketball Hall of Fame while Lewis never got the opportunity to extend his stellar performances long enough to be considered. One of Lewis' signature attributes was possessing long arms, often a notable advantage on defense.

Lewis came along when the Celtics' frontcourt was made up of the first Big Three, Larry Bird, Kevin McHale, and Robert Parish. As he matured, Lewis went from someone aching for playing time to someone who forced his way into the lineup by demonstrating increased skill level in all aspects of the game.

"When Reggie first came into the league," Bird said, "he really didn't know how to play the game. He shot the ball. That was about it. But he was a worker. He spent a lot of time improving his game. He loved it. You could always tell that."

One of Lewis' well-remembered showings involved blocking Jordan's shot four times in a single game. It was an event that stood out to those who witnessed it, a rarity given Jordan's talent and reputation. "His length confused me," Jordan told sports reporter Jackie McMullen 20 years after Lewis' death.

There were not many opponents who could drag such a confession out of Jordan.

In 2017, ESPN featured Lewis' high school team in one of its "30 for 30" documentaries, called "Baltimore Boys." The story of that team, which had consecutive seasons of 29—0 and 31—0 under coach Bob Wade, had already been chronicled in a book called "The Boys of Dunbar."

Bogues, an amazing player who reached the NBA despite standing just five-foot-three, said the project had been in the works for a long time and he was excited when it finally aired. "It's awesome," Bogues said. "We've been talking about this for so long and now having it come to life is great."

Williams, Lewis and Bogues were all chosen in the first round of the NBA draft, and Wingate played professionally, as well. Bogues said that Dunbar squad was probably the best high school team of all-time. He used that trio of first-round selections as a key argument. It is likely if Lewis had played out the normal span of his career, he would have ended up being the best of that quartet of schoolboy teammates.

At the least, in both big and small books and films, Lewis is being remembered.

On July 27, 2018, in response to a media inquiry, Donna Harris-Lewis released an open letter about her late husband. It was twenty-five years to the day after he collapsed on that practice court at Brandeis University.

There was both poignancy and inspiration in her words. Anyone who passes away at twenty-seven years old has been cheated in life and that was clearly true application for Reggie Lewis.

Dino Radja

The selection of Croatian Dino Radja in the second round of the 1989 National Basketball Association draft was a departure for the Boston Celtics, a signal of something new, and really a herald of what was to come in professional basketball.

Radja, a six-foot-eleven low post player was a European star in a period pre-Dream Team at the Barcelona Summer Olympics of 1992 that truly jump-started the influx of foreign players to the NBA. Radja's team, Jugoplastika Split, had just won the European Cup championship. Some European players, but not many, had competed in the NBA.

Then-Celtics general manager Jan Volk indicated this was not a casual draft pick, but one that had been sufficiently scouted. Boston felt Radja could play. However, he was under a long-term contract and was not able to immediately free himself from written obligations.

In addition, Radja had his own doubts, was not sure he was capable of NBA-caliber play despite some successful overseas examples such as Vlade Divac with the Los Angeles Lakers and Arvydas Sabonis with the Portland Trailblazers.

"They were all great, great players," Radja said. "I didn't know if I was in their class. To play in the NBA and fail, that was my biggest fear."

Simply getting Radja to Boston proved to be the Celtics' biggest problem, not that he would be a bust. Instead of trying the NBA, Radja went to Italy for three more years. He represented his country in those 1992 Olympics and had great success.

At last Radja came to the Celtics for the 1993–1994 season and fit right in. It was a good time to be a frontcourt man with experience joining the club because Reggie Lewis died from his heart condition. That first season, Radja proved he could play in the NBA, averaging 15.1 points and 7.2 rebounds per game. The best of Radja's four seasons with Boston was his last one, 1995-96, when he averaged 19.7 points and 9.8 boards a game.

Radja loved playing in Boston and when he was looking for a contract renewal, he visited with then-coach Rick Pitino, whose stint with the Celtics was pretty much his worst coaching during an otherwise Hall of Fame career. Radja said he asked Pitino whether he fit in with the new leader's plans and was assured he did. Radja said within days he was traded to the Philadelphia 76ers. He flunked a physical and didn't want to play there anyway.

He promptly abandoned the NBA and resumed his career in Europe, spending seven more years in uniform while proving he was healthy enough.

"I'm not bitter, though," Radja said. "By going back and playing seven years in Europe, I probably extended my career by two or three years because teams only play thirty-to-thirty-five games a year over there. There's much less wear and tear on a player's body."

Brian Shaw

**B**oston's No. 1 draft pick in 1988 might be the only player in franchise history who made as much of a mark in a court of law as he did on the basketball court. A six-foot-six guard who could play the point or the shooting guard position, Shaw starred for the University of California-Santa Barbara before joining the Celtics

When he inked his first contract, however, Shaw signed for only one season. His college program was not as heralded as many and it seemed as if the Celtics might not have quite trusted the goods just yet. Shaw ended up playing in all eighty-two games, as many as anyone in the league, while averaging 8.6 points a game. His 5.8-per-game assist ratio really stood out.

Things should have been fine with a mutually pleasing follow-up agreement. However, Shaw instead accepted a two-year contract from an Italian team named Il Messaggero Roma and he played for that team during the 1989–1990 season. There was only one problem -- the Celtics wanted him back and Shaw agreed to a five-year deal with Boston. Since Shaw could not compete in two places simultaneously, he had a decision to make. He told the Celtics he intended to fulfill his Italian obligations first and play another season overseas.

Management did not like that response and took Shaw to court, as in the legal kind. Shaw contended he signed with Boston without the help of an attorney and did not realize he could have become a free agent if he played his second season in Italy. The Celtics won the case and Shaw had an exceptional season for the team over the 1990-91 season, averaging 13.8 points and 7.6 assists a game.

Seventeen games into the following season, Boston traded Shaw to the Miami Heat and that was the end of his connection with the Celtics. Shaw stuck around the National Basketball Association as a player for fourteen seasons, winning three championships with the Los Angeles Lakers.

He also has been a coach in the league almost without interruption ever since. Shaw was head coach of the Denver Nuggets 2013–15. The remainder of Shaw's NBA coaching career has been as an assistant and he has won two more championships in that role, again with the Lakers.

Shaw said he learned a great deal working with former Chicago Bulls and Lakers coach Phil Jackson, who won two titles as a player and eleven as an NBA head coach.

"It's patience, and when you coach, you coach what you believe in," Shaw said. "Your philosophy and how you feel about the game."

Celtics Home Courts

From the time the Boston Celtics were founded and began playing in the NBA, their home court was the Boston Garden. The Garden was where the early Celtics competed, survived, and thrived, home of the Dynasty-era hoopsters of the 1957–1969 reign and for much longer.

The original Garden opened in 1928 and was the main indoor arena for the city until 1995. It was home to the Boston Bruins of the National Hockey League, prize fights, rock concerts, the circus, Ice Capades, professional wrestling, major indoor track meets and more.

The Boston Garden was actually designed by boxing promoter Tex Rickard and was modeled after Madison Square Garden in New York. Indeed, when the Boston version of the arena opened for business in November of 1928 it was officially referred to as Boston Madison Square Garden, though that title faded fairly quickly.

A chief distinguishing feature of the Boston Garden was its parquet floor. Instantly identifiable from a second's worth of viewing on a television set, the parquet floor was unique in appearance. It was not part of the original construction but was transferred to the larger Garden from the Boston Arena in 1952.

The design was so familiar to fans and its connection so strong to the team that even when the Garden was replaced by the new Fleet Center in 1995 (subsequently renamed the TD Garden), the parquet floor came along.

The old floor remained in use into 1999 before a new one was installed. Some parts of the old floor were incorporated into the new floor and other parts of the old floor were sold as souvenirs to fans.

Long before that, opponents of the Celtics complained that the floor was a Boston secret weapon, because it had dead spots when dribbling. Even some Celtics players conceded those dead spots existed – but they knew where they were and dribbled around them.

Sometimes, as a multi-purpose arena, the Garden's playing surface could be turned over quickly. There might be a Celtics game in the afternoon and the Bruins might take to the ice three hours after it concluded.

The changeover by teams of laborers was impressive. Those double-headers may be rarer two decades into the twenty-first century, but they still take place, usually on Saturdays. Next thing you knew, the surface was switched back for another Celtics game.

"The parquet floor changes after every Bruins game," said Celtics Hall of Fame forward Kevin McHale, who apparently could not keep up with the temporary alterations. "The dead spots aren't in the same places. There's no meter registering the amount of torque on each bolt. The Bull Gang just screws 'em in."

Many opponents regularly griped about playing at the Garden as it aged. There were allegations they spotted large rats roaming the hallways. There were charges that the shower water in the visiting locker room was always too cold. There were further charges there was no air conditioning on the hottest days of the year during the June playoffs. These were all supposed to be part of a Red Auerbach conspiracy to put opponents at a disadvantage. It was true that by the end of its lifespan, the Garden was in need of considerable sprucing up. Once, long after he retired, Hall of Fame center Bill Russell said, "Between you and me, it was a dump."

Still, there was a home-court advantage with the Celtics aware of the flaws. But the biggest disadvantage foes had when they came to town was playing the Celtics. The Celtics were so good for so long, they dominated at home. As the Celtics won and won, the phrase "Celtics Mystique" was applied to the team. Part of it stemmed from the oddities of the Boston Garden. John Havlicek said though, the players did not really respond to any of the physical deformities. They were part of the landscape and not always helpful.

"Red's the one who created the mystique," said Havlicek. "It was always the result of some shenanigan. We didn't know where the dead spots were on the floor. Meanwhile, we had cold showers, too."

Among the famous musicians who played the Garden were The Beatles, the Rolling Stones, The Who, Led Zeppelin, and the Grateful Dead. John F. Kennedy spoke at a memorable political rally when he was campaigning for the presidency in 1960. The Bruins clinched two Stanley Cup championships in the Garden in 1939 and 1970. Hulk Hogan and Andre the Giant were among the pro wrestlers who grappled there. Billy Graham even conducted a religious meeting in the building. Still, no one really defined the Boston Garden the way long-time radio broadcaster Johnny Most did with his raspy voice. Most opened his game talk by reminding listeners he was "high above courtside at the Boston Garden." They knew exactly where his vantage point was if they had ever been to a game and his call brought them. Until 1968, a capacity crowd at Boston Garden for Celtics games was 13,909. Some seats were added after that. First as the FleetCenter, beginning in 1995, and then as the TD Garden, starting in 2005, capacity was much larger. The building now seats 18,624 people.

Some Celtics liked the Garden more than others. Larry Bird, the icon of the 1980s, was a small-town guy from Indiana where basketball is king. He spent his college career with

Indiana State, a school which did not play many games in super-large venues.

"I'd never seen any arenas, so I really didn't know," Bird said of his first impression of the Garden with no other NBA buildings to compare it against. "I thought it was pretty neat that the railroad station was below (North Station) and the gym was up above. In high school, there was a place we played where we had to walk these stairs, and I thought that was so neat. We had to walk up these little-bitty staircases and duck going up there, and they filled it up with about three thousand people, and I thought it was unbelievable. So, I liked that about the Garden. And you can see good in there. I can tell right away when I walk in a gym if the lighting is good."

The final Celtics game played in the original Boston Garden took place on April 21, 1995. The official game programs sold were numbered and featured a photograph of Red Auerbach on the cover holding one of his trademark cigars. In the background of the picture were the rows of Celtics white and green championship banners.

At halftime of the game between the Celtics and New York Knicks, two dozen Celtics honored figures of the past showed up to pay homage to the old building's last stand as a basketball arena. Coincidentally, the Knicks were then coached by Pat Riley, one of the lightning-rod foes of many major showdowns. "I became seriously paranoid about this place," Riley said.

The Celtics were not particularly good that season, finishing 35-47 under coach Chris Ford. They lost the milestone game, 99-92, to New York. Guards Dee Brown and Sherman Douglas, with 22 points apiece, were Boston's high scorers that day.

It was not the best of times for the franchise, so the shuttering of the iconic Boston Garden when it occurred did not coincide with a fresh championship. But the nostalgia was thick as the Celtics walked off the court for the last time in the famous building that was the location of so many great basketball and sports moments.

Kevin Gamble

ll of Kevin Gamble's best seasons in the National Basketball Association took place while he was affiliated with the Boston Celtics. A six-foot-five player, who played forward and guard, the Celtics took a gamble on Gamble when he was playing in the Continental Basketball Association.

Gamble started his college career at small-school Lincoln College in Illinois, but transferred to the University of Iowa for his final two seasons and became a member of great Hawkeye teams. That exposure got him drafted in the third round (when there still was a third round) by the Portland Trailblazers in 1987, but Portland ditched him after short-minute appearances in just nine games.

Gamble honed his game playing for the Quad Cities Thunder. "I just kept plugging away," he said.

As a guy whose first college playing time was at a small school, who only started one year at a major college, been drafted in a lower round, and then cut. Gamble understood he had to keep pushing and hustling to get a second chance.

"There's a lot to be said for perseverance and following your dream," Gamble said. "If you're a guy on the fringe, you've got to be willing to do whatever it takes to give yourself a chance."

Gamble was averaging around 21 points a game late in 1988 in the Continental Basketball Association when Larry

Bird got hurt and the Celtics went shopping for help. Then guard Dennis Johnson got hurt. The more injuries the Celtics incurred, the more playing time Gamble got.

Gamble spent the rest of that year and the next season as a bench player, but he kept improving and in the 1990—91 season Gamble averaged 15.6 points a game. Gamble shot 58.7 percent from the field that year. The scoring average was his career high, but Gamble averaged in double figures for the Celtics three more times before he turned to the Miami Heat as a free agent in 1994.

He also suited up for other NBA teams for short stints, but Gamble's time spent in Boston was the highlight of his playing career. "I'll always be a Boston Celtic," Gamble said. "There were so many great times."

After he finished playing, Gamble, who was born in Springfield, Illinois, returned home when the University of Illinois-Springfield started an NAIA basketball program. Gamble nurtured the program into a success, winning twenty or more games four times before the school moved to NCAA Division II for the 2009—10 season. Gamble then moved on to other schools in administration or as an assistant coach, primarily Western Michigan.

In 2018, Gamble returned to the NBA as an advance scout for the Toronto Raptors.

Rick Fox

n many ways, it would be logical to state that Rick Fox has led a dream life. The six-foot-seven Fox played college basketball for North Carolina, played his entire National Basketball Association career, 930 regular-season games worth, with the Boston Celtics and the Los Angeles Lakers, became a professional actor, and married a Miss America.

Fox played for the Celtics between 1991 and 1997 and all of his best pro seasons came while wearing green and white. Fox's highest-scoring campaign was the 1996-97 season when he averaged 15.4 points a game.

Fox, born in Toronto, was of Canadian-Bahamian origin. He played some high school ball in the Bahamas, but also two years in Warsaw, Indiana, getting a real taste of the American game. However, he was not allowed to play his senior year because Indiana high school authorities ruled he was out of eligibility. That did not prevent him from signing with the Tar Heels. While in Chapel Hill, Fox twice earned All-Atlantic Coast honors. The Celtics made him a No. 1 draft pick.

Boston released Fox when he was only twenty-eight, putting him on waivers because of health issues. It was thought he was going to retire, but Fox kept on playing, shifting to the Lakers. In seven additional seasons with Los Angeles, Fox never matched his best performances with Boston. But he was a member of three NBA title teams. When he was thirty-five, L.A. traded him back to Boston, but fresh rounds of injuries led him to true retirement rather than reporting.

"I gave it the effort to get my body back into the condition it needed to be [in] to play at this level," Fox said. "Age crept up. I thought it was time to go off into the sunset."

Access to Hollywood helped jump-star Fox's acting career. He made his first television appearance in 2005, was on the HBO show "Oz," and in recent years he appeared in the Showtime show "Shameless" and the OWN show "Greenleaf." He also was a celebrity entry on "Dancing with the Stars."

In 1999, Fox married former Miss America and actress and singer Vanessa Williams. They both appeared in the show "Ugly Betty." The couple divorced in 2004.

A few years ago, Fox attempted to return to basketball when he applied for the job as head coach of the New York Knicks.

Antoine Walker

**F**ormer Kentucky star Antoine Walker was one of those Celtics players who emerged as a key factor during the dark days when Boston was not contending for a championship and merely hoped to reach the playoffs. Walker was the team's No. 1 draft pick in 1996 and his six-foot-nine, 265-pound stature allowed him to be a regular up front. Less likely for a man of his size at the time was Walker's ability to shoot the 3-pointer.

Walker came out of Kentucky after two years and with an NCAA title on his resume. He made a splash with the Celtics right away and was named to the league's All-Rookie Team for 1997. He played in all 82 games that year, averaging 17.5 points, 9.0 rebounds, and 3.2 assists a game. He was a handful to cover for opponents.

Five times with the Celtics in his career-opening seven seasons, Walker averaged at least 20 points a game with a high of 23.4 in the 2000—01 season. Walker also played for Dallas, Miami and Minnesota in twelve seasons, ending in 2006—07. Along the way he returned to Boston for part of one season and earned a championship ring with the Miami Heat. Walker was selected for three NBA All-Star teams.

After the Celtics' poor records during Walker's earliest years with the team, Boston improved and he helped the squad advance in the playoffs in two seasons, making major contributions, including scoring at a 22.1 clip in sixteen post-season games in 2002. The Celtics won two playoff series before losing to New Jersey in the Eastern Conference finals.

Alas, away from the court, Walker ran into various legal troubles. He was stopped for drunken driving, was charged with writing bad checks to cover gambling losses at Las Vegas casinos, and although he earned one hundred and eight million dollars from NBA salaries, he later declared bankruptcy because he was millions of dollars in debt. In-between, Walker was twice robbed, once in his own home.

With his troubles apparently behind him, Walker has worked as a basketball broadcaster since 2010. He turned forty-three in 2019, after making a hoops comeback with the Idaho Stampede in the NBA Development League.

As a teenager at Kentucky, Walker became friends with teammates Tony Delk and Walter McCarty. The trio also overlapped with the Celtics.

"Tony and Walt were great teammates and guys that I looked up to when I came to school," Walker said. "They were two years ahead of me, so they were elder statesmen on the team. They welcomed me with open arms and really embraced me. I became very close to Tony and Walt."

Delk played with eight NBA teams, including Boston for two years, then finished his active days in Europe. He also worked as an assistant coach for Kentucky and New Mexico State. McCarty spent seven-and-a-half seasons with the Celtics and later coached Evansville University in his Indiana hometown.

At the start of the 2019—20 season, Walker expressed pleasure that a new star for the Celtics, guard Kemba Walker, was going to be wearing his own old No. 8 uniform, even though others have worn it in-between.

"But to see it on a guy like Kemba Walker, who actually has the last name I've got, he kind of made people remember me in Boston," Antoine Walker said. "And I think that's the great thing about it."

Dee Brown

uring a thirteen-season National Basketball Association career, Dee Brown's play gave him one of the most endearing of nicknames: Dee-lightful. It seemed almost certain, give his birth name of Dee Covan, somewhere along the line in the sport someone would dream up a substitute

The six-foot-one, 160-pound Brown was not the most physical of guards, but throughout his eight seasons with the Celtcs at the beginning of his career he was always one of the team's key players. His best seasons were 1993—94 and 1994—95 when he averaged 15.5 and 15.6 points a game. His best assists season, Brown handed out 5.8 a game.

Brown was a No. 1 draft pick of the Celtics out of Jacksonville University in 1990 and always played point guard. He impressed Boston from the start, playing eighty-two games as a rookie and being chosen for the NBA's All-Rookie Team. One of Brown's career highlights — one that surprised fans — was his victory in the 1991 All-Star game Slam Dunk Contest. He had no slam-dunking reputation at the time and was a smaller player who did most of his work on the perimeter.

Late in the competition, Brown performed a dunk — left-handed with his right covering his eyes — that stunned fans and allowed him to best Shawn Kemp, a much-stronger and taller (six-foot-ten) forward for Seattle.

The sheer act of performing a slam dunk in basketball is somewhat routine. Some players make an art of it. Others only occasionally employ the weapon as one of opportunity. High schoolers either fool around with them in practice or are even accomplished enough to use the shot at will. Style points under pressure is another thing altogether.

"A lot of guys can dunk," Brown said. "Very few leave their mark."

There is no question that among basketball fans, Brown's dunk is still well-remembered. "Shawn Kemp just had an unbelievable dunk where he took off from almost the free-throw line," Brown said. "His foot almost touched his back. I was thinking, 'I got to do something special. I got to do a signature dunk that people remember me for twenty-five years later.'"

He did.

Brown played for the Celtics during what was a down period for them and was not part of any Boston championship team despite his personal excellence on the court and popularity with fans. Serving as a team captain showed the esteem in which he was held. He later finished his career with the Toronto Raptors and the Orlando Magic, appearing in just seven games in each of his two partial seasons with Orlando.

After retiring as a player in 2000, Brown went into coaching. He was able to snag head coaching jobs in the Women's NBA with the Orlando Miracle and the San Antonio Silver Stars. He became a head coach in the NBA Development League and then a director of player operations. Moving along, Brown worked as an assistant coach for the Detroit Pistons and the Sacramento Kings and then joined the Los Angeles Clippers.

Most recently, Brown was working as a general manager for the Clippers' NBA G League team, the Agua Caliente Clippers.

Winning It All In 2008

**O**lder generation Boston Celtics fans were spoiled. Anyone who grew up with the Dynasty Celtics from 1957 to 1969 developed a sense of entitlement. The championships just kept on coming. It was difficult not to think of the National Basketball Association victories almost as a sense of birthright. Everyone knew the run had to end someday, and, of course, it did.

The Celtics then became like any other franchise, going through the steps of rebuilding and winning some titles in the 1970s and 1980s. Then Boston became too much like other clubs. The drought between championships dragged on and on, from 1986 to 2008.

Drafting, trading and signing, the Celtics added new faces for the 2007—08 season. Much was due to the acumen and cleverness of general manager Danny Ainge. The Celtics already had All-Star Paul Pierce on board. Trades brought seven-foot power forward Kevin Garnett from the Minnesota Timberwolves and guard Ray Allen from the Seattle SuperSonics. This trio packed the type of firepower that made an instant impact. Ainge also knew that as great as Allen and Garnett were they were especially hungry to win a championship, take home a ring and add to their legacies. They did not want to spend their entire NBA careers without the glorious feeling of at least one season winning it all and checking off that box on their resumes.

"In my twelfth year I paired up with a couple of Hall-of-Famers in Paul Pierce and Kevin Garnett," Allen said of winning the crown together. "Never in my wildest dreams could I have imagined that I'd end up on that stage."

Pierce was a building-blocks player, but needed help for the Celtics to take a step up. He stood at six-foot-seven and weighed 235 pounds and could score with a startling array of shots. Over 1,343 regular-season games, Pierce, who played nineteen professional seasons (fifteen of them with Boston) averaged 19.7 points a game. He averaged more than 20 points in a season eight times for the Celtics, some of those being way over 20, five of them at 25 points per game or higher. He was a strong rebounder, with a career mark of 5.6 a game, plus he passed off for 3.5 assists a game.

Ainge did not want to squander Pierce's Boston career and he pulled off the magic trick of trades to find complementary stars. That season, the Celtics went 66—16 during the regular season, a spectacular turnaround that marked a 42-game improvement in victories from the 2006—07 season.

In the playoffs, the Celtics took out the Atlanta Hawks, Cleveland Cavaliers and Detroit Pistons before (appropriately) once again facing the Los Angeles Lakers in the Finals. It was a six-game series and the last game was a coronation more than a contest, Boston crushing the Lakers, 131—92. Fittingly, Allen and Garnett scored 26 points apiece in the deciding game, and Pierce 17. Pierce won the Finals Most Valuable Player award.

The players, from those principals to coach Doc Rivers, and players like Kendrick Perkins, Rajon Rondo (who had 21 points in the final game), Eddie House, James Posey, Glen "Big Baby" Davis, Tony Allen, and P.J. Brown cherished the title, as did Boston fans, so hungry to have their team back on top again.

Boston won the Atlantic Division and the Eastern Division

and improved from 24-58 the year before, the most dramatic one-year turnaround in league history. The swiftness of the rise surprised most.

Garnett came of age during a period when the NBA allowed players to jump straight from high school to the pros. He ended up playing twenty-one seasons, won a Most Valuable Player and Defensive Player of the Year award, and was a fifteen-time All-Star selection. Garnett played with fire and in many ways was the spiritual heart of the team. Garnett, a twelve-time all-defensive team selection, played the best defense in the frontcourt that anyone in Boston had seen since Bill Russell retired.

Ainge had been trying to pry Garnett away from Minnesota for some time. Pierce, the team captain, was in the loop, but pessimistic about it happening. During that time period, stars with leverage were avoiding the Celtics. "I didn't want to get my hopes up," Pierce said. "I've been hearing that kind of talk for all these years. We couldn't even get a C level player to come. How are we going to get an A type player like KG?"

Boston and Ainge were desperate to obtain Garnett and Ainge never gave up. So the team traded five players, two draft picks, and some cash to Minnesota. Despite that extraordinarily high price, Garnett proved worth it.

Allen, one of the best three-point shooters in league history, Pierce, and Garnett, formed a Big Three trio of merged talents that turned out to be unbeatable together. As each of the three stars became eligible, they were elected into the Naismith Memorial Basketball Hall of Fame.

Ainge explained why Garnett was the linchpin of it all. "I watched that guy play so much over the years that there wasn't any doubt in my mind that he would fit in with Paul and Ray," Ainge said. "Or that he would bring all that energy and emotion."

When the Finals were underway – and the Celtics were involved for the first time in his career – Pierce said he was a little bit nervous, especially when some of the games were being played in his hometown of Los Angeles.

"I was probably a little more anxious than normal," Pierce said, "being that I'm at home in front of more family and more friends. But I've got to block that out and go out there and leave it on the court. I've done that in the past. I've been here and played well despite having family and friends. It's time for me to do it again."

Garnett, whose nickname was "Big Ticket," played six seasons with the Celtics before wrapping up his career in 2016 with another stop in Minnesota. He led the league in rebounding four times and at a percentage of .497, made about half of his shots. For his career, Garnett averaged 17.8 points, 10 rebounds and 3.7 assists. In 2019, Garnett appeared in the movie "Uncut Gems." He played himself, but in a fictional role.

The six-foot-five Allen, who had played near Boston in college at the University of Connecticut (which later retired his number 34), spent eighteen years in the NBA, five of them with the Celtics, and averaged just shy of 19 points a game for his career. He retired in 2014 as the league record-holder for most three-point shots, but has been surpassed by the Golden State Warriors' Stephen Curry. Although the teaming of Allen with Pierce and Garnett to capture that 2008 title was a special moment, Allen won an additional championship with the Miami Heat in 2013.

Probably no one was happier or more satisfied than Pierce, who was in his 10th season wearing the green.

"You know, I'm not living under the shadows of the other greats now," said Pierce, who had spent his entire career to that point playing his home games under the banners announcing retired jersey numbers and the seasons of past titles. "I'm able to make my own history with my own time here. If I was going to be one of the best Celtics ever to play, I had to put up a banner."

He did so, with a little help from his friends.

There was one bizarre and scary incident attached to Pierce's career while playing in Boston. In 2000, not long before the beginning of the season, he was out on the town at a nightclub when attacked. Pierce was hit over the head with a bottle and stabbed eleven times. Teammate Tony Battie, and Battie's brother, rushed him to the hospital. Despite the initial impact, the fright, and undergoing lung surgery, Pierce played in all eighty-two of the Celtics' games the next season.

However, for some time afterwards, Pierce said he coped with paranoia and depression and tried to avoid crowds. He said he was able to free his mind from those worries by concentrating on basketball.

Pierce was more closely linked to the Celtics over the long-term than Garnett or Allen. Pierce, who attended Kansas, and who sported the nickname "The Truth," spent nineteen years in the NBA, all but the last few in Boston. After retirement he did some broadcasting work for ESPN. Star center Shaquille O'Neal anointed Pierce with the nickname after Pierce lit up Shaq's team for 42 points one night.

Pierce averaged more than 20 points in a season eight times for the Celtics. In 2005-06 he led the league at 26.8 points a game. At the end of the title run, Pierce was chosen the MVP of the Finals.

In February of 2018, the Celtics retired Pierce's No. 34 uniform number in a ceremony at the TD Garden. Fans shouted out thank-you, and Pierce teared up. He also raised the 2008 championship trophy into the air as part of the event. Pierce, Allen, and Garnett were all bound for the Hall of Fame (Allen was voted into the Hall in 2018). Of the trio, Pierce was always going to be the most closely identified with the Celtics because of his longevity.

"When you're forever with the Celtics, you're forever," Pierce said.

Rajon Rondo

Possessor of a euphonious name that was never confused with any other player's, guard Rajon Rondo was a terrific passer and playmaker for the Celtics when the club won the 2008 National Basketball Association title and continued his career elsewhere after concluding his days in Boston.

Rondo broke into the NBA in 2006 after playing for the University of Kentucky (just two seasons before coming out) and the six-foot-one ball-handler made his presence felt quickly. Three times, Rondo led the NBA in assists, all three of those seasons topping 11 per game. Also a double-figure scorer throughout his career, Rondo led the league in steals one season.

Rondo played his first eight-plus seasons with the Celtics and was a core member of first-rate teams. The Big Three of Kevin Garnett, Paul Pierce, and Ray Allen depended on Rondo to get them the ball and Rondo made it easier for those guys to finish at the basket with his sharp passes. His excellence running the offense made him a four-time All-Star.

"I'm a point guard, so I want to see everybody else score and be happy," Rondo said once. "I don't necessarily need to score at all. I could be happy with zero points as long as it was a team game and everybody contributed."

As that steals title indicated, Rondo, who has long arms, was a superb defender, and four times was recognized as a member of the league's All-Defensive Team.

The Celtics actually identified Rondo's potential long before most colleges and pro teams and watched his progression from afar. Rondo said he was barely a top-200 high school prospect before taking an extra year at Oak Hill Academy, where he said he improved to top ten and he also changed his focus from shooting guard to point guard.

Rondo was aflame during the 2007–08 championship run. Until then he had been challenged for playing time by other point guards, Delonte West and Sebastian Telfair. The team traded both away and handed the starting job to Rondo, a very swift player who could dribble past many defenders and duck under big men. He scored 10.6 points a game that season and averaged 5.1 assists. Rondo worked hard in the off-season to record those numbers. He knew his shooting had to improve so in his practices he took up to five hundred outside shots a day.

The season was a coming-out party for Rondo and general manager Danny Ainge seemed to truly comprehend the difficulties the young player endured and conquered.

"I don't think anyone understands the pressure of being a twenty-two-year-old kid like Rajon who has no real basketball pedigree," Ainge said. "I mean, he's not Magic Johnson. He's not Chris Paul. To have been the whipping boy of the veteran players and the coaches, and to have all that pressure because opposing teams aren't guarding him, and commentators are all talking about him being the supposed weak link. I was just so happy for him. And when I went over to the bench to congratulate him, I saw tears coming out of his eyes and rolling down his cheeks. I couldn't have been prouder of him in that moment. It was like one of my own children had done some miraculous thing."

Rondo had very much begun to grow up in the game when the Celtics needed him most. It was a special team year, though Rondo's individual numbers improved from there. He began scoring, stealing, and creating brilliant plays more. His assist totals skyrocketed.

It might be that at the beginning of his career Rondo's confidence out-stripped his performance, but it did not take long to catch up once he was given the keys to the car, the freedom to run the offense. He was definitely not a weak link, but became an All-Star.

When Ainge mentioned pedigree, it might well have been because Rondo was a latecomer to basketball. A good athlete, he enjoyed playing football more than hoops and said he didn't even start playing at all until he was at least ten years old. Certainly, that did not make him over the hill, but it wasn't as if he had stars in his eyes for the game. What he realized was that since he was topping out at six-foot-one, he did not fit the prototype of a National Football League quarterback, often standing six-foot-five. Not that six-foot-one guards were heavily sought-after, either, as point guards kept growing taller and defying previous stereotypes.

Rondo did not know the Celtics began eyeing him before he started college play, when he spent a post-high school year at the famous Oak Hill Academy, a breeding ground for star college stars and future pro players. At Kentucky, he did not get along well with Wildcats coach Tubby Smith and that affected his on-court performance. That could have doomed his initial pro prospects.

The Celtics did not obtain Rondo in the 2006 NBA draft. It is typically forgotten he was selected by the Phoenix Suns late in the first round. However, Ainge did not give up on Rondo. Instead of drafting him, he traded for him as part of a three-way deal also involving the Cleveland Cavaliers.

The Celtics also reached the 2010 Finals with Rondo as point guard, too. He averaged 13.7 points and 9.8 assists that year and he set a single-season Boston record of 794 assists. While Rondo was a major contributor, when basketball people talk about the 2008 title team they give the most credit for the Celtics' success to the Big Three (the second Big Three in franchise history) of Kevin Garnett, Paul Pierce and Ray Allen.

In a 2018 book featuring Allen's basketball life, he indicated there were some personality problems within the locker room. He wrote that in 2011 Rondo claimed, "I carried all of you to the championship in 2008" and players responded by saying together, "You what?"

The 2008 championship win was Boston's first in twenty-two years and was very satisfying, but the team could not repeat it.

Rondo spent the first eight-and-a-half years of his NBA career with the Celtics and ranks highly on some club all-time lists. He was traded to the Dallas Mavericks in the middle of the 2014-15 season, and although that did not work out particularly well, the next year he joined the Sacramento Kings back in top form, leading the league in assists with an 11.7 mark, equaling the best of his career.

The point guard still had it while bouncing from team to team for a few years, still collecting large amounts of assists. While with the New Orleans Pelicans in 2018, Rondo set a team record for most assists in a playoff game with 21. More than a decade into his career, Rondo turned up with the Los Angeles Lakers, and often was starting games in his thirties alongside LeBron James, also an extremely proficient passer.

"I'm always going to play my game," Rondo said. "I think me at point is a pretty good (option)."

It was rarely said otherwise by any team Rondo represented.

In his second season with the Lakers -- Boston's long-time rival -- during the 2019-20 season as he approached his thirty-fourth birthday, Rondo harbored at least one more major goal to accomplish before retirement. He announced he wanted to become the first player in NBA history to capture a title with both the Celtics and the Lakers.

As the season began, the Celtics owned seventeen championships and the Los Angeles Lakers owned sixteen.

"I need another ring," Rondo. "It's simple. I want to be the first to win for the two most historic franchises that's ever put a basketball to use. So I got one in Boston and I'd love to get one with this organization."

That worked out for him. During the drawn-out, partially-in-the-bubble NBA season of 2019-2020 due to the coronavirus pandemic, the Lakers won the crown, and Rondo received another ring.

However, while the achievement was noteworthy, and rare, it was not unique. Hall-of Famer Clyde Lovellette won two titles with the Celtics in 1963 and 1964 as a back-up. But he also was a member of the Minneapolis Lakers, the NBA's first dominant team, as a rookie in the 1953—54 season. That team won it all in pre-Los Angeles days.

Celtics guard Bill Sharman won several titles with Boston and later coached the Lakers to an NBA championship, an accomplishment that played a role in Sharman being inducted into the Naismith Memorial Basketball Hall of Fame as both a player and a coach.

When Rondo made his first appearance playing in Boston as a member of the Lakers, he won the game for his new team, 129–128, with a twenty-foot jump shot at the buzzer.

Celtics Major Award Winners

Most Valuable Player

(The Most Valuable Player award in the National Basketball Association was first presented at the end of the 1955–1956 season.)

1956–1957	Bob Cousy
1957–1958	Bill Russell
1960–1961	Bill Russell
1961–1962	Bill Russell
1962–1963	Bill Russell
1964–1965	Bill Russell
1972–1973	Dave Cowens
1983–1984	Larry Bird
1984–1985	Larry Bird
1985–1986	Larry Bird

Rookie of the Year

(The Rookie of the Year award in the National Basketball Association was first presented after the 1952–1953 season).

1956–1957	Tommy Heinsohn
1970–1971	Dave Cowens (shared)
1979–1980	Larry Bird

Sixth-Man of the Year

(The Boston Celtics were credited with creating the sixth-man through the use of Frank Ramsey and then John Havlicek, but the National Basketball Association did not formally present a Sixth Man Award until after the 1982–1983 season.)

1983–1984	Kevin McHale
1984–1985	Kevin McHale
1985–1986	Bill Walton

Defensive Player of the Year

(Celtics center Bill Russell essentially re-invented defense in the National Basketball Association, but a Defensive Player of the Year was not chosen until after the 1982–1983 season, long after he retired.)

| 2007–2008 | Kevin Garnett |
| 2021–22 | Marcus Smart |

Coach of the Year

(The first National Basketball Association Coach of the Year award was handed out following the 1962–1963 season.)

1964–1965	Red Auerbach
1972–1973	Tom Heinsohn
1979–1980	Bill Fitch

Executive of the Year

(Executive of the Year joined the list of National Basketball Association post-season honors following the 1972–1973 season).

| 1979–1980 | Red Auerbach |
| 2007–2008 | Danny Ainge |

League Rebounding Champions

(Rebounds were not counted as an official statistic by the National Basketball Association until after the 1950–1951 season).

1957–1958	Bill Russell
1958–1959	Bill Russell
1963–1964	Bill Russell
1964–1965	Bill Russell

League Assists Champions

1952–1953	Bob Cousy
1953–1954	Bob Cousy
1954–1955	Bob Cousy
1955–1956	Bob Cousy
1956–1957	Bob Cousy
1957–1958	Bob Cousy
1958–1959	Bob Cousy
1959–1960	Bob Cousy
2011–2012	Rajon Rondo
2012–2013	Rajon Rondo

League Steals Champions

(The steals category was introduced by the National Basketball Association after the 1973–1974 season).

2009–2010	Rajon Rondo

All-Star Game Most Valuable Players

1951	Ed Macauley
1954	Bob Cousy
1955	Bill Sharman
1957	Bob Cousy
1963	Bill Russell
1973	Dave Cowens
1981	Nate "Tiny" Archibald
1982	Larry Bird

All-NBA Recognition

FIRST TEAM

1950–1951	Ed Macauley
1951–1952	Ed Macauley
1951–1952	Bob Cousy
1952–1953	Ed Macauley
1952–1953	Bob Cousy
1953–1954	Bob Cousy
1954–1955	Bob Cousy
1955–1956	Bob Cousy
1955–1956	Bill Sharman
1956–1957	Bob Cousy
1956–1957	Bill Sharman
1957–1958	Bob Cousy
1957–1958	Bill Sharman
1958–1959	Bob Cousy
1958–1959	Bill Sharman
1958–1959	Bill Russell
1959–1960	Bob Cousy
1960–1961	Bob Cousy
1962–1963	Bill Russell
1964–1965	Bill Russell
1970–1971	John Havlicek

1971–1972	John Havlicek
1972–1973	John Havlicek
1973–1974	John Havlicek
1979–1980	Larry Bird
1980–1981	Larry Bird
1981–1982	Larry Bird
1982–1983	Larry Bird
1983–1984	Larry Bird
1984–1985	Larry Bird
1985–1986	Larry Bird
1986–1987	Larry Bird
1986–1987	Kevin McHale
1987–1988	Larry Bird
2007–2008	Kevin Garnett
2021–2022	Jayson Tatum

Isaiah Thomas

ust when it seemed guard Isaiah Thomas would be a long-time star for the Celtics, he turned into a shooting star, so to speak, a bright light in the night sky who disappeared quickly. At times, Thomas loomed as potentially the greatest scorer in Boston basketball history, then he was injured and was gone.

A three-time Pac-10 All-Conference choice for the University of Washington, the left-handed jump shooter passed through Phoenix and Sacramento before being traded to Boston. By then the under-sized, five-foot-nine whiz was a 20-point-per-game man and he just improved from there.

Thomas played twenty-one games for Boston in the 2014-15 season, but when he got the chance to play all eighty-two games the next year, Thomas became a fan favorite and was one of the most important members of the Celtics. He averaged 22.2 points and 6.2 assists a game. He was named to the All-Star team for the first time and was a thrill-a-minute player as the on-court leader. A year later during the 2016-17 season, Thomas was again the focus of the offense, the man who made things happen. Thomas scored 28.9 points a game while his free-shooting improved to 90.9 percent.

Highly regarded anyway, Thomas gained not only the applause of Boston fans, but also their sympathy during the playoffs in 2017. As the Celtics eliminated the Chicago Bulls in a series, Thomas learned his younger sister had been killed in an automobile accident. He flew home for the funeral and returned to play in the next round immediately afterwards.

Thomas' hoops heroics, including a 29-point, 12-assist performance in Game Seven of the next round to defeat Washington sent the Celtics into the Eastern Conference finals against Cleveland. However, two games into that series, Thomas incurred a hip injury and was sidelined.

In a stunning off-season trade while he was recuperating, Thomas became part of a deal with Cleveland when Boston acquired All-Star Kylie Irving. Thomas' surprising departure from Boston was complicated by this new injury problem. While still in the league, he has bounced around to other teams, not quite regaining the status he reached with the Celtics.

Much later, Thomas admitted he was hurt and disappointed by being traded after he had given his heart to the Celtics and played through hardship.

"After everything I went through," he said peppering his comment with an expletive. "You're not supposed to do that."

When Thomas returned to Boston as a visiting player, the fans did not forget what he had done for the Celtics. He was welcomed like royalty, cheered mightily.

"That was a special moment, for real," Thomas said of returning for a game with the Denver Nuggets. "The love they showed me, you would have thought I won a championship and was there ten years-plus. I was only there almost three years."

Brad Stevens

The Celtics recruited Brad Stevens as a head coach because of his brilliant success at Butler University, his creative approach to the sport, and because he possessed both a strategically wise mind and also had many years ahead of him as a coach

They needed a coach who could nurture a rebuilding franchise starting in 2013. Stevens, whose Butler teams regularly made waves in the NCAA tournament, led the Celtics from the bench through the end of the 2020-21 season, reaching the playoffs in all but his first season. Then he moved to the front office, replacing the retiring Danny Ainge.

It was an abrupt transition for Stevens between NCAA Division I and professional ball, but he seemed to ease into it quickly.

"The schedule is so much more difficult during the year," Stevens said of the longer NBA season. "You don't get to practice hardly at all. The travel is real. My first year, in the middle of March, it hit me like a ton of bricks and we still had a month left."

College games are scheduled for forty minutes with two halves of twenty minutes each. NBA games are four quarters, twelve minutes each, for forty-eight minutes total. There are eighty-two regular-season games scheduled, plus playoffs, compared to thirty-something if a college team advances to the NCAA tournament and competes in a pre-season tournament.

"It's very hard on the body," Stevens said, "but the body is only a small part of it. I mean, with all the scrutiny these guys play under and all the praise and all the distractions, I just think they are amazing to be able to tune it out."

Stevens is an Indiana guy. He played guard for small-school Depauw University. As head man at Butler, he guided his teams to a 139-40 record, four league titles and twice took the Bulldogs to the title game of the NCAA championships. Given that he was just thirty-three years old when he led Butler to the first Final Four, he seemed to be on everyone's radar screen as the hot young coach, though he kept turning down offers from bigger schools.

Butler was playing in the comparatively unheralded Horizon League at the time, not the Big East as the Bulldogs do now. To the world at-large, that made them perennial underdogs in the NCAA tournament. Sometimes just one good run during March Madness makes a coach the flavor of the month to other schools seeking to import a magic touch. Stevens twice took his club within one game of the title, so that proved what he was doing was no fluke and made him an even hotter commodity.

It did not hurt any that Butler seemed to be a storybook come to life, following in the footsteps of the popular 1986 basketball movie "Hoosiers" that in fiction tracked the true story of tiny Milan, Indiana winning the state championship by upsetting much bigger schools in 1954. Butler was routinely called "real-life Hoosiers" and compared to fictional Hickory in the Hollywood tale. It was a feel-good genuine story translated from the past to the screen to real life all over again.

Stevens and his players were amused by the never-ending comparisons, but didn't let it get in the way of taking care of business.

It's not clear how many genuine offers Stevens received to take his coaching prowess elsewhere, but he turned down any and all colleges. It was not until Celtics boss Danny Ainge approached and offered a six-year deal to coach that Stevens bit. The temptation, challenge, and money offered were too strong to say no. He was well aware of Celtics history and was appreciative of being placed in charge of what is a public trust of sorts in Boston.

In those early days, Stevens reached out to Celtics legends like Bob Cousy, John Havlicek, and Tom Heinsohn so they understood him, did not look at him as an interloper, and so he could learn a little bit about Celtic Mystique.

"It was important to me to take the time to learn what Celtics pride meant to them," Stevens said.

As a rookie pro coach Stevens was thirty-seven and he inherited a team that was in need of many repairs. The Celtics finished 25-57 for the 2013-14 season. The next year Boston went 40-42 and even though the team went 0-4 in a first-round series, they did reach the playoffs. Since then, the Celtics have been winners every year.

Stevens did not appear much-changed coaching in the pro ranks. He didn't look much older and retained his typical calm. He regularly paced the sideline and when he paused, he typically folded his arms to survey the action.

"He's not a yelling coach," said forward Gordy Hayward, who rejoined Stevens in Boston temporarily after playing for him at Butler. "It's more difficult. In college, you play two games a week. In the NBA, you play a game every other day."

It is also true that not every star college coach has been able to duplicate the same kind of success in the pros. Certainly, Stevens adapted to the rhythm of the pro game. But he also recognizes he coaches in a special place, that he is representing the Boston Celtics when he takes the court to lead the team. It reads either "Boston" or "Celtics" on the front of the jerseys.

"I think the only thing that goes through your mind is just the responsibility of having your team playing the right way, playing hard and together," Stevens said of going into games. "You know, the results are what they are. You're coaching the Celtics. You're coaching in Boston, you know. There have been so many championships, and even in this generation with the Patriots winning six (Super Bowls), the Red Sox doing what they've done in the last years. The Bruins won one in the last ten years. We won one in the last ten years. It's a pretty special place to get a chance to coach and play."

Stevens wants to put his own stamp on Celtics history with his own team, to add another banner to the Garden rafters signifying a championship.

"Oh, of course," he said. "I mean, that's why we all do what we do. At the end of the day, my goal is just to put our signature on it and do as well as we can and then let the chips fall where they may."

Top Boston Celtics Coaches

1. Red Auerbach

Auerbach was coach for nine Celtics NBA titles and had one of the best records in the history of the league. Auerbach won 938 games and lost 479 in the regular season for a 66.2 winning percentage. A master psychologist, Auerbach sought every edge he could obtain when his teams took the floor. He was a strong proponent of the fast break when the league moved at a slower pace and did not hesitate to play five African Americans at one time during an era when the United States was struggling with civil rights. His insight and reading of talent allowed the Celtics to make key draft picks when they were needed and he regularly fleeced foes by making savvy trades

2. Tommy Heinsohn

It is difficult to separate Heinsohn as coach from Russell and K.C. Jones as coach. The former teammates represented in-house hires by Auerbach in his role as general manager. Heinsohn, Russell, and Jones, each won two championships at the helm, but Heinsohn spent longer in the job and also probably faced a more challenging task of rebuilding. Heinsohn's career record was 427-263 and his 1972-73 team finished an NBA-best 68-14. Heinsohn was awarded Coach-of-the-Year that season.

3. Bill Russell

Russell, the six-foot-nine center who revolutionized NBA defense, was Auerbach's hand-picked successor when the boss moved upstairs to the front office. Auerbach understood Russell's nature and believed he would have trouble taking orders from any fresh coach. With himself still in the starting lineup, the Celtics won two additional crowns in Russell's three seasons as coach. Selecting Russell as head coach was a barrier-breaking move as well. Russell was the first African-American coach in the NBA and the first modern-era African-American coach among North America's four professional sports leagues. Russell also became the first Black of a North American professional sports team in nearly a half-century. Fritz Pollard, who coached the Akron Pros in the National Football League in 1921 and was a member of the Pro Football Hall of Fame, is also one of the first two Black players to compere in the National Football League.

4. K.C. Jones

Jones was another member of the family from the dynasty era of the late 1950s and 1960s to ascend to the head coaching job for his old team. Under Jones' tutelage, the Celtics won two titles in the 1980s. That included the 1986 title. Some call that Larry Bird-led club the greatest team in NBA history. Jones' Celtics coaching mark of 308-102 gave him a 75.1 percent winning percentage.

5. Bill Fitch

Fitch was a fix-it man. He was often hired to transform losing squads into playoff contenders during his twenty-five seasons as an NBA coach. His high point was being the head man when the Celtics won the 1981 championship. A two-time winner of the NBA's coach-of-the-year award, Fitch was voted into the Naismith Memorial Basketball Hall of Fame as an eighty-seven-year-old in 2019. However, in September, at the time of his enshrinement in Springfield, Massachusetts, Fitch was in ill health and unable to attend.

6. Glenn "Doc" Rivers

Rivers came out of Marquette and played in the NBA from 1983 to 1996. His first head coaching job in the league was with the Orlando Magic between 1999 and 2003 and he joined the Celtics in 2004. Rivers, who excelled on defense as a player, guided the Celtics to the 2008 title, naturally enough out-lasting the Lakers. That was Boston's most recent crown, the one where Kevin Garnett, Ray Allen and Paul Pierce constituted a second Big Three for the Celtics.

7. Brad Stevens

Stevens not only never played in the NBA, he only played small-college basketball. However, he performed near-miracles -- or at least they were perceived that way at the time -- by leading comparatively unheralded Butler University to the NCAA championship game twice. Stevens was in huge demand across the country to lead many of the most storied college programs. Instead, pursued by Celtics executive Danny Ainge to preside over a rebuilding job, he leapt straight to the pros in 2013.

Kemba Walker

nce a star at nearby University of Connecticut, leading the Huskies to an NCAA championship, it was a logical move for Kemba Walker to sign with the Boston Celtics before the 2019-20 season.

It was a sign-and-trade deal that sent Boston guard Terry Rozier to Charlotte and Walker to Boston where he could make much more money and get a fresh start with a club that was closer to winning a championship than Charlotte. The six-foot guard spent the first eight years of his National Basketball Association career with Charlotte, several times averaging more than 20 points a game, and was wildly popular there.

The Celtics needed Walker when he was ready to make a change. They had just lost Kylie Irving through free agency when he signed with the Brooklyn Nets. Irving was a take-charge star and his departure created the need for a player of Walker's talent, but had not proved to be a great fit with Boston.

Walker signed a four-year, $141,000,000 contract with the Celtics and was plugged directly into Irving's spot. While Irving was a valuable component of the team for two seasons, there was always the underlying feeling he did not feel a long-time allegiance to Boston and was never really happy with the franchise. When he got the chance, he bolted.

The signing of Walker was a perfect substitute. There was no real mystery why Walker went with Boston -- and yes, history had something to do with it.

"They've been winning for years," Walker said. "You see all the banners upstairs and in the arena. It's a winning organization and I want to win. That's what I'm about throughout my basketball career. As a pro, I haven't won consistently and I just want to get a taste of that. And I thought this was the best place for me to do that."

Early on with his new team, Walker was averaging 22.6 points a game accompanied by averages of 4.9 rebounds and 4.8 assists. It seemed obvious Walker was the Celtics' newest star.

However, after twelve minutes of playing time in Boston's fifteenth game of the season against the Denver Nuggets, Walker crashed into teammate Semi Ojeleye, bending his neck back as he jammed his head. He was taken from the court on a stretcher with a possible concussion, though not one likely to produce long-term damage. To Walker's and the team's relief, the diagnosis was a neck sprain instead. He missed just one game and returned to the lineup five days after the injury with a 39-point performance in a win over the Brooklyn Nets. Despite healing, Walker's stardom in Boston and good health, did not last long and he moved on from the Celtics.

Marcus Smart

enacity. That is probably the best brief way to describe what guard Marcus Smart brings to the court. A relentless defensive player, the six-foot-four Smart throws opponents off their games.

On offense, while not the purest of players, he has constantly improved from his rookie year, bringing new range to his jump shot and broadening his vision on the court. In other words, he grew on the job after coming out of Oklahoma State to join the Celtics for the 2014-15 season.

More than anything else, no matter how he is used, as a fill-in off the bench, or as a starter, Smart lives up to his last name because that's the way he plays the game. While Smart may not be an A-1 superstar, he is the type of player every good team needs to be successful. Historically, Smart could have been a Celtic in any era. In 2021-22, Smart became a rare guard recognized as Defensive Player of the Year.

Smart was in no way a big threat in his first Boston seasons, but through hard work and repetition he has improved his three-point and mid-range shooting. His shooting percentage was regularly under 40 percent. About four seasons ago, Smart's hard work began making himself a more dangerous offensive threat.

From Flower Mound, Texas, Smart was a McDonald's All-American in high school. At Oklahoma State, Smart showed off his all-around talents as a scorer, passer, and disproportionately good rebounder for his size. He won a

Big Twelve Player of the Year award and twice received All-American recognition. Smart was Boston's first-round draft pick in 2014. Although he also spent some time with the Maine Claws during his first season, Smart was a second-team National Basketball Association All-Rookie Team selection and has improved from there.

Showing their faith in Smart's steady play and importance to the team, Boston signed him to a new four-year contract in 2018. Mostly a 10-points-per-game scorer, at the end of the 2018-19 season Smart was voted onto the NBA's All-Defensive squad, which showed that foes were paying attention to his real talents.

Smart's defensive prowess earns him his loudest raves. Speculation began mounting that one day he might earn Defensive Player of the Year honors. Sure enough, at the end of the 2021-22 season, that forecast came true. For quite some time this has been a reward almost solely for big men in the league. Fooling experts, Smart has even covered players many inches taller than he is. Basically, when Smart is deployed on stars they shoot lower percentages from the field and have many of their offensive weapons neutralized.

"Smart's been an animal this year," said teammate Jaylen Brown early in the 2019-20 season.

There was no doubt that during his sixth year in the league, Smart was reveling in his growing reputation as a shut-down defensive force.

"The way I think, it's like we're in the jungle," Smart said. "When a lion is ready to own his territory or take over his territory, he comes right at you full-throttle, and nine times out of 10 you don't escape those attacks. With me, it's that mentality, that when it's time for me to own my territory, it's time to take over somebody else's territory, I pounce and I attack, and there's no looking back on that."

That's bringing a loud roar to the role. He progressed during the early years of his pro career until receiving all-league defensive recognition at the end of the 2018-19 season.

It was widespread admission of what those close observers had long been aware of -- it was hard to score on Marcus Smart.

Smart is the kind of player who seems to have been born with the instinct to dive for a loose ball. Some players are instructed to and for others it seems to come naturally. Smart is the kind of player who it seems it may never not have occurred to pounce on a bouncing ball. At the start of the 2019-20 season, USA Today referred to Smart as a maniac on defense -- and that was a compliment.

Basketball people have always praised Smart for the determination he brings to the court. Travis Ford, his college coach at Oklahoma State, said that has been Smart's way for years, so it is no surprise the same mindset transferred to the NBA. "There's never a player that can play like that for eighty-two games, that's built for that mentality and (physicality) as Marcus Smart," Ford said.

One Boston ex-teammate, Jae Crowder, later with the Utah Jazz, used the cliche that Smart is someone another player would be willing to go to war with. Maybe that's because it always seems Smart is going to war to defeat the opponent.

If any more vivid proof would be necessary than watching games, Smart himself pretty much admits he is a football player in a basketball player's body. Once upon a time, coaches used to teach the sport by saying, "Basketball is a non-contact sport." That phrase seems to have disappeared from the instruction manual.

Telling it like it really is in the sport these days, Smart says, "I thrive on contact. Contact is in my nature."

That doesn't mean he clotheslines offensive players, but he doesn't back off, tries to never yield an inch. Carrying 220 pounds on his frame makes him more resemble a linebacker than a hoops guard. The reality is, before he grew into his current NBA self, Smart might seek out a little bit too much contact and he might mouth off too often letting go of his temper. As he was going on twenty-six, it was likely Smart was at his peak, knowing when to hold 'em and knowing when to fold 'em in terms of taking defense to the edge of an official's whistle.

Smart has announced he knows who he is and that he was not about to change for anybody. But a player who already was smart about the sport made himself smarter. He admitted he was not going to duck a challenge, but he was wiser about picking his fights. The key aspect of that was fouling less so he could be on the court when needed.

When Smart says, "It's about winning," he is merely annunciating what anyone who has been around him knows is spelled out in his body language.

Whether it has anything to do with Smart's constant hustle or not, he often seems to be incurring problematic injuries that slow him down. But he also shrugs them off and returns better. His rookie year Smart suffered a sprained ankle. During the 2019-20 season Smart dealt with niggling injuries to a hip, ankle, and finger. Then he had an abdominal injury and subsequently missed several games with a double eye infection during the second half of December. It was like being a football player under constant siege from hard hits.

The eye injuries, stemming from viral conjunctivitis, were both bothersome and almost an insult.

"So it was painful, it was burning," he said as he was about to miss his seventh game in a row. "It was really hard. I couldn't see. I had outdoor sunglasses everywhere. Even in the dark I was wearing sunglasses. It was that bad. Just every morning I would wake up just having sticky discharge coming out of my eyes, sealing my eyes shut. It was really just gross."

This was not your commonplace athletic injury, sprained ankle, or torn knee ligaments. Above all, Smart needed patience before returning to the lineup and that is often something in very short supply for sports figures when their season seems to be passing them by.

"I actually have a picture that I showed the guys," Smart said. "It was pretty gross. I was bleeding tears every time they (doctors) did it (did a procedure), for like a day. They did that for about four days straight. It felt like they were putting needles in my eyes."

Smart said that not only did he hope to never go through such an ordeal again, he wouldn't wish this infection on anyone.

He ended up missing eight games. The Celtics miss Smart when he is sidelined. He plays for a team that appreciates his particular set of skills and pays him well for it, evidence being a four-year, $52,000,000 contract extension five seasons into his pro career.

"He's doing it at an even higher level," said Brad Stevens, Smart's coach for most of his pro career. "When he's on the court, people play better."

When a coach says that about you, you know your team appreciates you.

Al Horford

A six-foot-nine, 240-pound pivotman, Al Horford joined the Celtics for four years after becoming a free agent in 2016 and leaving his original team, the Atlanta Hawks. He left the Celtics briefly for a year, but then came right back for the 2021-22 edition. A second-generation NBA player, the son of Tito Harford, was more grounded than his father and was a key piece in Boston playoff runs during his stay with the Celtics.

The native of the Dominican Republic was a five-time All-Star. One reason he joined the Celtics was the reputation of the franchise. Even so, Horford took time to digest the Boston basketball atmosphere, the display of retired numbers, and championship flags that greeted him for every home game -- even when he was representing the Atlanta Hawks.

"I was pretty amazed by it," Horford said. "When I first got here, my rookie year, the first time, I was in awe. I really couldn't believe all those banners. That's one thing. Year after year I kept coming here, seeing all along how much passion the people here have."

Originally, those were a couple-times-a-year stops with the Hawks. When he became a Celtic, Horford said the emotion was a daily thing.

"The people here, I mean, I feed off that," Horford said.

Horford, who averaged in double figures for fifteen NBA seasons in a row, was a star on the University of Florida teams that won two NCAA titles in a row in the 2000s. For just about any player, he said, it is an adjustment from college, where time is spent attending classes and the season is much shorter, to the pros, where the entire job is to get ready for games.

"You have a lot more time," Horford said. "Here you prepare much more. You have a lot of games. You're watching a lot of film. Then you spend a lot of time getting treatment[s]. You have much more time to work on your game."

Horford said playing for Celtics coach Brad Stevens, known as a cerebral thinker about the sport, was a good experience.

"Playing for a coach like Coach Stevens, he really challenges you to think the game," Horford said. "That's been very good for me. I've learned a lot."

Gordon Hayward

here was a strong chance that if forward Gordon Hayward could stay in one piece, he would become a serious star for the Boston Celtics. Drafted by the Utah Jazz on potential shortly after the six-foot-eight forward's last-gasp, long-range shot came within a few inches of giving Cinderella Butler an NCAA championship over Duke, Hayward had matured into stardom in Utah.

When he made the tough choice to leave Utah behind, Hayward crafted a goodbye piece for the online organization The Players Tribune, formed by former New York Yankees star Derek Jeter as a voice for professional athletes.

"Thank you, Utah," Hayward wrote on July 4, 2017. "This has been the toughest decision that I've ever had to make in my life. This weekend has probably been the longest weekend of my life. And today, well, today has definitely been one of the craziest days of my life."

Hayward wrote of being wooed by the Jazz to stay and Boston and the Miami Heat to change allegiances.

"My meetings with all three teams during this process -- Miami, Boston and Utah -- were just unbelievable," he said. "They couldn't have been more impressive. Each meeting left me convinced that the team I'd just met with was the right fit."

It was an intriguing glimpse into free-agent pressure and the lures of being offered riches and making a huge workplace shift.

"This was a life-changing decision for me and my family, and something we took really seriously," Hayward said. "And from the very start of this process, one thing stood out as important: I knew that I wanted the fans and the organizations to hear my decision directly from me."

And that was the public forum Hayward employed to tell Jazz fans that after seven seasons he was departing and to inform Boston fans he was coming.

Hayward, who was going to obtain a lucrative, long-term contract from any of his suitors, in the end seemed to believe he had the best opportunity to win an NBA crown with Boston.

"The feeling of putting on a Boston Celtics uniform and competing for a title out-weighed everything," Hayward said.

When he became a free agent, Hayward took a rich deal from the Boston Celtics to reunite with his college coach Brad Stevens in pursuit of an NBA championship. There was obvious good feeling engendered at Butler or Hayward would not have signed on for more time under Stevens' tutelage. How much of a selling point was this? Not easy to tell. But Stevens' presence had to be in the plus column.

It seemed to be a nice match. Yet almost immediately, just minutes into his first game wearing green, Hayward suffered a horrendous injury, stifling any ambitions for the player and the team in stunning fashion. As he lay on the court, unable to rise, he said his mother was crying and that affected him more than anything else.

The entirety of Hayward's 2017–18 with the Celtics consisted of five minutes of playing time and uncounted hundreds of hours of rehabilitation time. His terrible injuries were a broken tibia and dislocated ankle. This was a terribly frustrating period for Hayward, the team and the fans. Occasionally, a rumor would flare up that Hayward would make it back into action before the end of the season, but that was never a realistic analysis. Once in a while a genuine update of Hayward's condition and progress was issued by him or the team.

"There's no reason to sulk and wallow in self-pity," Hayward declared, which may have been true, but a challenging mindset to adopt. I'm gonna come back better than that and I firmly believe that."

Everyone in basketball wanted that pronouncement to come true, but there was an undercurrent of either doubt or wonder. Hayward did return for the 2018-19 season, but Stevens and the Celtics were careful with his minutes. During that next season, though Hayward participated in seventy-two games, he averaged only 11.5 points a game. That was not better than ever.

While he became quite weary of discussing the old injury, Hayward still soaked his foot and ankle in a bucket of ice and freezing water in the Celtics locker room after games. He was able to play, but was not back at 100 percent in his court movements.

By then twenty-eight years old, married and with children, Hayward was a seasoned pro who could offer perspective on the differences between the pro and college games.

"The shot clock makes a huge difference," Hayward said. "There are different NBA rules for defense. In college, you only have four years separating people on the team. In the pros there are guys who are married with kids."

In college, it seemed, if a team built a substantial lead, the game was over. In the pros, the players are so good and can get so sizzling hot, they can make up any deficit.

"Twenty points is nothing," Hayward said.

Hayward said he has played so much basketball since his near-miss Butler shot that he doesn't think about it unless someone else brings it up. He is aware that he is part of a memorable Bulldog team and his name comes up whenever the NCAAs gear up in March.

"I think about it when tournament time comes around," he said.

Hayward was a latecomer to basketball, interested more in soccer and rugby, even growing up in Indiana, the hotbed of hoops, until he was sixteen. The first NBA teams he became aware of were the Los Angeles Lakers, the San Antonio Spurs, and the Boston Celtics.

Still hoping to be part of a single NBA champion, Hayward said looking at the rafters in the TD Garden each game and seeing the green and white championship banners stretched from one side of the court to the other signifying Boston's past success, it reminds players of this franchise's history.

"Definitely, it's always humbling," Hayward said.

When the 2019-2020 season began, Hayward was on display as his old self, the All-Star self, fully recovered from the nasty injury of two seasons earlier. He started on fire, averaging 18.9 points a game, passing slickly and rebounding like a demon.

This was the Hayward Boston signed and had been waiting to see on a nightly basis. It was reassuring to Hayward, as well, that the awful injury of two seasons prior was not career-threatening.

Very early in that season, Hayward scored 39 points against the Cleveland Cavaliers, hitting 17 of his 19 field-goal attempts and all 16 of his free throws. Some proclaimed it the greatest game of his career. Others said it illustrated that the real Gordy Hayward was back in business.

Then, in the eighth game, Hayward was waylaid by another fluke injury after bumping into the Spurs' LaMarcus Alridge. He broke his left, non-shooting hand and underwent surgery. This setback was due to cost him six more unwanted weeks on the bench.

"Certainly, on the play, I didn't know exactly what happened," Hayward said. "But I heard it and felt it, and knew something immediately was wrong."

Compared to the previous injury, "It was a drop in the

bucket, for sure," he said.

Then he got hurt again, this time a foot injury, that he attributed to an off-shoot of his major foot problem of two years earlier. He took three cortisone shots to aide a nerve problem. Still, he returned to action for the Celtics' Christmas day game versus the Toronto Raptors after sitting out a few more games. He played twenty-six minutes, scored 14 points, and grabbed six rebounds, once again showing off the sound body the Celtics would need if they wished to contend for another title.

"It's still a little sore, but it's playable," Hayward said.

Still playable is how the Celtics wanted to view Hayward. Then the season was halted because of the COVID-19 pandemic and Hayward missed the early rounds of the playoffs when play did resume.

Perhaps stunning the Boston fan base, during the off-season Hayward opted out of his Celtics deal and became a free agent, signing a three-year $120,000,000 contract with the Charlotte Hornets. Hayward's injury-marred stay with Boston was over, filled with a promise not quite fulfilled. Then Hayward got injured still again, missing a large chunk of Charlotte's season.

Tacko Fall

**F**rom Gulliver to Wilt Chamberlain, giants have always fascinated the masses. It has always been true that tall players draw special attention in the National Basketball Association, the sport most in tune with height.

For the 2019-2020 season, the Boston Celtics added the tallest player in team history when Tacko Fall, nearly seven-foot-six, joined up. The 310-pound center from Senegal, who appeared much thinner than his listed weight, was a project, a player with innate skills and potential, but still in need of development as he traveled back and forth from Boston to the team's Maine Claws in the NBA G League.

At the time, Fall was the tallest player affiliated with an NBA team, and one of the tallest in league history, along with such former bigs as Manute Bol, Chuck Nevitt, and Gheorghe Muresean.

Lengthy, long-armed, with large hands, Fall had the makings of a great defender and notable space-eater in the lane as he absorbed the nuances of the game in the best basketball league in the world at twenty-three.

Fall played college ball at the University of Central Florida, where over three seasons he averaged 10.1 points a game and majored in computer science. Fall's full given name is Elhadji Tacko Sereigne Diop Fall, bestowed on him at birth in Dakar. He moved to the United States when he was sixteen and his main sport was soccer, making him a latecomer to hoops.

His standing reach is ten feet, two inches, meaning being on tiptoes he can practically dunk. His wingspan is pterodactyl length.

Friendly and out-going, Fall graciously signs autographs and poses for photographs with fans and ignores the types of teasing all tall people run across in American society, being asked the time-worn comment, "How is the weather up there?" many times.

He said it has always been this way, since he was a youth in Senegal. He was basically stoical from the start, letting remarks roll over his long back. "As a kid," he said, "these are things you go through. These are the things that make or break you.

Fall stands out in many ways, including being a devout Muslim who wore No. 99 on his Celtics uniform before signing with the Cleveland Cavaliers in hopes of bettering his status. Boston general manager Brad Stevens, who coached Fall in his brief Celtics stints, liked him. "He's not just tall," Stevens said. "He's someone who cares about the community, who cares about the team. His energy is contagious. I hope people appreciate there's more to him than his size."

Fall seemed to form an instant love affair with Boston fans. He was moved back and forth between Boston's G League team, but when he was up with Boston from the minors, and the team was at home, and fans began chanting his name, urging Stevens to insert Fall into the game. Fall scored a quick five points in one of those games, perhaps offering a glimpse of a golden future.

Shortly before Christmas, and as a signal of his expanding celebrityhood, Fall acted as a guest conductor for the Boston Pops Orchestra. Fall appeared wearing a tuxedo (the first one he adorned in his life, he said) and spectators gave him a huge ovation at famed Symphony Hall. He conducted the playing of "Sleigh Ride."

The Bubble

**T**he 2019–2020 NBA season was the weirdest in league history. Just like much of America, and the world, basketball play halted in March because of the COVID-19 pandemic.

The regular season had not concluded. While the season was suspended, the United States was challenged by massive internal dissent over the Black Lives Matter movement.

Protests erupted across the country in response to unarmed Black men being killed by police officials. The NBA was in the forefront of North American professional sports leagues in demanding justice for Black Americans.

One individual emerged from the Celtics with a strong and visible voice in the midst of the controversial period. That person was Jaylen Brown. He participated in rallies and demonstrations in different cities and became a noted leader among professional athletes in support of racial justice.

Brown was an advocate of the late Civil Rights leader John Lewis and quoted the former Congressman. "It's a struggle of a lifetime. So don't be afraid to be loud, to make noise, and to get in good trouble, or unnecessary trouble."

The Celtics nearly made another run to a championship inside the cocoon of Disney World, falling one step short of the finals during the playoffs.

Boston Celtics Championships

**W**inning seventeen NBA champion-ships has given the Boston Celtics the record for the most titles, but now the Lakers, who began their winning habits in Minneapolis before moving to Los Angeles, have tied them.

The Boston franchise was founded in 1946 as one of the original teams in a fledgling league, but did not win a championship until the 1956–57 season. That season, the Celtics roster included rookie center Bill Russell, and rookie forward Tommy Heinsohn, both Hall-of-Famers. Russell joined the team late because of his participation for the United States in the Summer Olympics in Australia.

Russell's arrival announced the start of a Boston dynasty. With the over six-foot-nine Russell in the middle, the Celtics won eleven championships in the next thirteen seasons. Between 1959 and 1966, the Celtics won eight straight world titles.

This was the most remarkable stretch in professional basketball history. Boston also won two titles in the 1970s with rebuilt, post-Russell teams featuring center Dave Cowens and guard John Havlicek. The club captured three championships in the 1980s, the Larry Bird Era. The most recent title came in 2008 with Paul Pierce, Kevin Garnett and Ray Allen the keys.

The Celtics also lost in the championship round in 1958 to the St. Louis Hawks, in 1985 to the Lakers, in 1987 to the Lakers, and in 2010 to the Lakers.

In addition to those world crowns, the Celtics have won twenty-one conference titles (the most recent in 2010) and twenty-two division titles (the most recent in 2017).

When the league first conducted championship playoffs, the last series was referred to as the NBA Finals Trophy. Starting in 1964, the winner's trophy was named after Celtics founder Walter Brown. Beginning twenty years later, the prize's name was changed to the Larry O'Brien Trophy, a past commissioner.

As of 2022, over the decades, the Celtics have qualified for the playoffs fifty-nine times.

List of Boston Celtics NBA Titles and Championship

Series Opponents

1957 (St. Louis Hawks)*

1959 (Minneapolis Lakers)**

1960 (St. Louis Hawks)

1961 (St. Louis Hawks)

1962 (Los Angeles Lakers)

1963 (Los Angeles Lakers)

1964 (San Francisco Warriors)

1965 (Los Angeles Lakers)

1966 (Los Angeles Lakers)

1968 (Los Angeles Lakers)

1969 (Los Angeles Lakers)

1974 (Milwaukee Bucks)

1976 (Phoenix Suns)

1981 (Houston Rockets)

1984 (Los Angeles Lakers)

1986 (Houston Rockets)

2008 (Los Angeles Lakers)

*Later became Atlanta Hawks
**Became Los Angeles Lakers

Jayson Tatum, Jaylen Brown, and the Celtics Today

**A** wise draft pick by general manager Danny Ainge, forward Jayson Tatum was a coming star soon after joining the Boston Celtics. A rookie in the 2017–2018 season, Tatum was just nineteen for his National Basketball Association breakthrough after a single season at Duke. The third pick in the first round, Boston felt he was a future All-Star and gave him plenty of playing time right away.

Tatum, born in 1998, was an acclaimed high school star who during an earlier era may well have turned pro without enrolling in any college. His stay with Duke was fruitful, but brief. There was plenty of recruitment competition for Tatum from Kentucky and North Carolina, as well as St. Louis University. His father went to school there and the Billikens were located near his Missouri home. Although Tatum did excel during his short stay at Duke, there was some worry when an injured foot kept him out of eight games. However, he was chosen to the All-Atlantic Coast Conference third team anyway.

The Celtics seemed to be stronger believers in Tatum, especially general manager Danny Ainge, than other teams. Tatum instantly showed off his potential in the NBA's summer league with an average of 15.7 points in his second season. Then he got better, raising his status around the league to the point that by 2021-22, he was one of the five best players in the league. Over his next three seasons, Tatum averaged between 23 and more than 26 points a year.

He emerged as the Celtics's go-to offensive force who could carry the team. In one game, he scored a franchise-equaling 60 points in a game and by the end of the 2021–22 regular-season campaign, Tatum had registered six games of 50 points or more, more than anyone else who ever suited up for Boston.

The six-foot-eight Tatum averaged 13.9 points a game in his first season, 15.7 in his second, and was closing in on 20 points per game in his third season even before his twenty-second birthday. He was a guy who hit about 84 percent of his free throws and whose rebounding was on a steady upward swing. In 2019, he won the Skills Challenge during the All-Star weekend.

Ainge believed in Tatum from the start, trading up in the draft to obtain him and his judgment was quickly vindicated. The son of a coach, Tatum grew up in St. Louis and is a religious individual who often cites his beliefs as a reason for his success.

Tatum knew enough basketball history to be impressed with his selection by the Celtics, the franchise's reverence for its past, and the way the team displays information about its past successes. Tatum, like other players, was wowed when he first glimpsed the famed banners overhead at the TD Garden.

"This is really a special place," Tatum said, "and it has a lot of history. A lot of players came before me."

Tatum said the best year of his life was the season he spent at Duke. But Tatum also said it is his dream to be part of another Celtics National Basketball Association champion.

"That is what is my motivation," Tatum said. "One day I'm going to help play for a championship. Unfortunately, I haven't yet. That's the goal. It is."

There is little doubt, and much evidence, that Tatum is improving all the time. Three seasons into his career he became a much larger presence for the Celtics on offense. Near the end of 2019, Tatum threw down a career-high 39 points against the Charlotte Hornets and he has just kept getting better from there. He also had double-figure rebounds.

"I just try to stay aggressive, no matter what," Tatum said after that game.

A lot more attention was being paid to Tatum's increasing maturity on and off the court. There have been myriad stories over the years about how highly paid athletes, even those who make millions of dollars in salaries, waste their money, blow through it all and end up penniless. Tatum's approach seems diametrically opposed. His 2019-20 payroll claim on the Celtics of $7.83 million was going directly into the bank, just as all his paychecks from his first two seasons did.

Tatum is a popular enough player that he is being rewarded with endorsement cash from such organizations as Gatorade, an outfit called Imo's Pizza, and another named Honey Dew Donuts, and makes enough from those deals to live on. Tatum may not have graduated from Duke, but he obviously has some kind of good business education and knowledge working for him.

"All the money I get from the Celtics, I put it in a savings account," Tatum said. "Tomorrow is not promised. You're not promised the next contract. You want to save all the money you can."

Tatum said he did not grow up well off, and that influenced his thinking. He did buy himself and his mother their favorite vehicles, and said he likes nice clothes, characterizing those purchases as splurges. His mother offered sound advice when he first began making money and still does.

Jaylen Brown and Jayson Tatum are not the same guy. They are starting lineup partners for the current Celtics, are only an inch apart in height (Brown is six-foot-seven) and they were both first-round draft picks taken a year apart, Brown in 2016. He is two years older than Tatum. But on any given game night they can take turns exploding.

Brown attended the University of California at Berkeley and earned Pac-12 All-Star honors. There, he was an all-around scorer, rebounder, and assist player. As was Tatum, he was the third player taken in the draft by Boston and also immediately impressed the team with sterling NBA summer league play.

After playing only seventeen minutes a game as a rookie, Brown emerged in his sophomore season to average 14.5 points a game. Brown did even better in the 2018 playoffs, averaging 18 points a game. After his initial three-year contract ran out, Brown re-upped with Boston with a $115,000,000 deal that keeps him with the team through the 2023-24 season.

On Christmas Day, 2019, the Celtics met the defending champion Toronto Raptors as part of an expanding NBA television tradition. Not long ago the NBA tested the viewership on the holiday with a single game. By 2019, it was scheduling five, crossing the nation's time zones as the day progressed. The Celtics were in the first game of the day and Brown was excited to be part of it.

"I always loved watching LeBron (James) and Kobe (Bryant) play on Christmas," Brown said a couple of days before the Celtics competed on national television on the holiday. "I remember being at my grandma's house and when the game ended my cousins and I would shovel the snow out of the driveway and re-enact all the best moves from the game."

It's not exactly clear from that particular message where Brown encountered the snow since he was a high school star in Georgia and a college star in California, but he didn't need his snow shovel in 2019, even though the Celtics game was played in Canada.

Demonstrating his enthusiasm for the circumstances, Brown turned in one of the greatest games of his pro career with 30 points as Boston easily handled Toronto, 118-102. Brown made ten of thirteen shots from the field to give the Celtics their first victory in Toronto since 2015.

"It was good to get a win here on Christmas," Brown said. "I've never won here, period. So it was great to just get one."

A few days later, Brown equaled his career high with 34 points and Tatum had 30 against the Cleveland Cavaliers, as the two began gaining league-wide notoriety for their growing number of star turns.

"Yeah, you see progression from both of those guys and they're going to continue to get better because they're so young and hungry to get better," said Cavalier forward Kevin Love.

Brown and Tatum seemed to be sensing they were on the cusp of something special playing together, as well. "I think that both of us together, it's hard to scheme and stop us both," Brown said. "Days like today they couldn't stop either of us."

Brown has continued to improve, averaging a career-best 24.7 points per game despite missing some time with health issues. Brown and Tatum have matured into one of the deadliest duos in the league; they are players who can lift the Celtics with key rallies.

This became increasingly evident during the second half of the 2021-22 season. After Danny Ainge retired as general manager and Brad Stevens was elevated into his spot, the Celtics needed a new coach. They hired Ime Udoka, previously an assistant with the Brooklyn Nets, the team Boston eliminated in a first-round 4-0 sweep in the Eastern Division playoffs.

It took some time for Boston to jell under Udoka, but after a slow start to the season, they closed with a rush, posting the NBA's best record from January on and becoming the best offensive and defensive team in the league. That made them a dangerous squad to face in the playoffs.

"The playoffs bring the best out of people," said Tatum, who scored at the buzzer to top Brooklyn in one game.

The playoffs in the spring of 2022 did bring out the best in the Boston Celtics as a whole, and Tatum and Brown, who truly emerged as a duo of threats as the Celtics chased what would be a record 18th NBA crown.

For the first time in 12 years, Boston reached the league's finals, the Celtics working their way through a minefield of opponents to capture the Eastern Conference championship and earn a place in the culminating round against the Golden State Warriors.

Although it took a few months for the Celtics to adjust to new coach Udoka, as each series unfolded the team demonstrated fresh maturity. The club finished the regular season with a 51-31 mark after standing at 25-25 at one point.

Stevens, in his GM role, made a key pickup in guard Derrick White and Udoka blended the pieces well. Besides Tatum and Brown's one-two All-Star punch, guard Marcus Smart, center Robert Williams III, forward Al Horford and forward Grant Williams were major contributors and second-year guard Payton Pritchard became a critical component off the bench.

Tatum averaged 26.9 points a game for the regular season and upgraded his court vision, feeding others. Brown averaged 23.6 points a game and could explode when needed. Boston played the toughest team defense in the league.

It was believed the Celtics could be in jeopardy during their first-round playoff series, yet Boston blitzed the Brooklyn Nets, winning four straight games. They battled and overcame defending league champs Milwaukee in seven games, eliminating the Bucks. Tatum pumped in 46 points in Game Six. That was a Finals-worthy series itself, but only earned Boston a next-round showdown with the rugged Miami Heat. The Celtics were extended to seven games in that series, as well.

This was no easy path to the Finals. Golden State, featuring guard Stephen Curry, the NBA's all-time greatest three-point shooter and foul shooter, provided a dangerous matchup. This was another fiercely contested series. It was 2-2 in games before the Warriors moved away, capturing two straight to win their fourth championship in eight years. Curry was an offensive force, scoring 34 points in the clincher after a stirring, 43-point game in the fourth game, turning the series Golden State's way.

"I know that obviously it was a game we felt like we could have won," said Brown, who scored 34 points in the 103-90 last loss. "It stings that we kind of didn't play to our potential. But it is what it is. You've got to learn from it and move on. As tough as it is, it's been a great year, been a great journey. It just wasn't our time."

Tatum was equally philosophical after the defeat.

"This is tough," said Tatum, who averaged 25.6 points in the playoffs, "getting to this point and not accomplishing what we wanted to. It hurts."

The Celtics came close in 2022, but seizing another title was put on hold for the NBA's proud franchise. Yet the playoff run may have provided a glimpse of the future, of a team on the cusp of greatness.

SOURCES

BOOKS

Hubbard, D. (2017). *100 Things Celtics Fans Should Know & Do Before They Die.* Chicago: Triumph Books.

Bjarkman, P. (1999). *Boston Celtics Encyclopedia.* Sports Publishing LLC.

McClellan, M. (2018). *Boston Celtics: Larry Bird, Bob Cousy, Red Auerbach, and Other Legends Recall Great Moments In Celtics History.* New York, New York: Sports Publishing.

McClellan, M. & Carey, M. (2005). *Boston Celtics: Where Have You Gone?* Sports Publishing LLC.

Cousy, B. & Ryan, B. (1988). *Cousy On The Celtic Mystique.* McGraw-Hill.

Freedman, L. *Dynasty: Auerbach, Cousy, Havlicek, Russell and the Rise of the Boston Celtics.*

Bayne, B. *Elgin Baylor: The Man Who Changed Basketball.*

Shaughnessy, D. *Ever Green.*

Allen, R. & Arkush, M. *From The Outside: My Journey Through Life and The Game I Love.*

Carey, M. & Most, J. *High Above Courtside: The Lost Memoirs of Johnny Most.*

Havelicek, J. & Ryan, B. *Hondo: Celtic Man in Motion.*

Freedman, L. *Jump Shot, Kenny Sailors, Basketball Innovator and Alaskan Outfitter.*

MacMullen, J. *Larry Bird, Earvin "Magic" Johnson: When the Game Was Ours.*

Auerbach, R. & Feinstein, J. *Let Me Tell You a Story: A Lifetime in the Game.*

Jones, K.C.. & Warner, J. *Rebound: The Autobiography of K.C. Jones and An Inside Look at the Champion Boston Celtics.*

Auerbach, R. & Fitzgerald, J. *Red Auerbach, An Autobiography.*

Russell, B & Branch, T. *Second Wind: The Memoirs of an Opinionated Man.*

Shaughnessy, D. *Seeing Red: The Red Auerbach Story.*

Pearlman, J. *Showtime: Magic, Kareem, Riley, and The Los Angeles Lakers Dynasty Of The 1980s.*

May, P. *The Big Three.*

May, P. *The Last Banner: The Story of the 1985-86 Celtics, The NBA's Greatest Team of All Time.*

Pomerantz, G. *The Last Pass.*

Cousy, B. & Linn, E. *The Last Loud Roar.*

Taylor, J. *The Rivalry: Bill Russell, Wilt Chamberlain and the Golden Age of Basketball.*

Lovellette, C. & Freedman, L. *The Story of Basketball Great Clyde Lovellette.*

May, P. *Top of The World.*

West, J. & Coleman, J. *West By West: My Charmed, Tormented Life.*

Brunk, D. *Wildcat Memories: Inside Stories from Kentucky Basketball Greats.*

Auerbach, R. *Winning the Hard Way.*

MAGAZINES AND PUBLICATIONS

Basketball Times

Boston Celtics Game Program, April 21, 1995.

Boston Garden Banners Years 1928-1995. Commemorative Edition

Boston Sports Weekly.

NEWSPAPERS

Baltimore Sun
Boston Globe
Hartford Courant
Kansas City Star
Miami Herald
Los Angeles Times
New York Times
Philadelphia Bulletin
Philadelphia Inquirer
Providence Journal
St. Louis Post-Dispatch
Springfield (Massachusetts) Union
USA Today
Washington Post

PERSONAL INTERVIEWS

Larry Bird 1981
Gene Conley 2006
Mel Counts 2006
Bob Cousy 2006, 2013, 2019
Clarence Glover 1972
John Havlicek 2006, 2019
Gordon Hayward 2010, 2019
Tom Heinsohn 2006, 2019
Al Horford 2019
Bailey Howell 2006, 2019
Johnny "Red" Kerr 2006
Jim Loscutoff 1972, 2006
Frank Ramsey 2006
Bill Russell 2002
Kenny Sailors 1988, 2001, 2012, 2013,
   2014
Tom Sanders 2006
Bill Sharman 2006
Brad Stevens 2010, 2019
Jayson Tatum 2019

RADIO

kentuckysportsradio.com
sportshub.com/Boston

TELEVISION

ESPN Classic

WEBSITES

Bleacherreport.com
Boston.com
Bostonglobe.com
bostonlive.com
CBS.com
cnbc.com
cnn.com
celticsblog.com
Celticslife.com
Celtic-nation.com
celticswire.com
clutchpoints.com
Espn.com
hoopshype.com
interbasket.com
masslive.com
NBA.com
nba.com/celtics
NBCsports.com
Society for American Baseball Research
The Athletic
The Players Tribune
Thepost.com
Theundefeated.com
Twitter.com (Jaylen Brown)
Wbur.org
Yahoo.com

CHAPTER INDEX